Psychoanalysis and Revolution:
Critical Psychology for Liberation Movements

精神分析與革命

解放運動的批判心理學——
中英對照版

五南圖書出版公司 印行

實踐感知的相識與參看
——叢書作者們之間的關係發展

　　知識之間是怎麼發生關聯性的？知識工作者是如何探求與生產知識的？這篇序文對批判心理學叢書的介紹不由論述內涵來引介，而由叢書總編夏林清與作者們關係發生與發展的歷史性來給予讀者一個觀看參讀的視角。

　　心理學在臺灣已發展數十年，坊間對歐美心理學各種各類的理論與方法亦均多有傳播，唯獨尚未有對批判心理學有所介紹與探討的書籍。2021年春天我偶然與五南出版社王俐文交談了我這20年往來兩岸，感慨臺灣出版業在市場壓力下發展的不易，我自己多年與學生們積累的譯稿在大陸已陸續出版，王俐文當即邀約我選出幾本在臺灣出版。於是，我就快速選編了這一套批判心理學的叢書，這一突然增加的差事並不輕，但能在五南出版社的支援下，快馬加鞭地趕工卻是喜悅的！一來，在輔仁大學心理系任教時，曾卯力投入工作的《應用心理研究》期刊，一直也是蒙受著五南出版社的支援，此種只問耕耘不計收穫的心胸帶給我再次投入工作的力量。二來，由35年前知道批判心理學的這支路線迄今，我是在持續著的社會實踐的田野中與歐美批判心理學的思想與做法參照，沒想過要出書介紹他們，但我又確實與他們多次交流友情甚篤，能有機會幫他們的書出繁體中文版，十分高興。

　　我們將陸續出版下列六本書：《心理學的迷思》（已出版）、《精神分析與革命：解放運動的批判心理學》、《非科學的心理學：理解人類生活的後現代路徑》（已出版）、《心理的探尋考察：社會治療的實務指南》、《平民角落：自身處境的抵抗與轉化》、《一盞夠用的燈：兩岸參看的振動》（已出版）。前四本是英國與美國批判心理學的著作，後兩本則是臺灣在地的發展路徑、實踐經驗與論述討論。如序文題目所示，我想說明我自己與叢書作者們認識的小歷史，而我之所以會認識他們又是與臺灣的社會變化局勢中我的處境與作用的位置有什麼樣的關係；用這樣的角度來寫

篇序文是希望讀者能思辨一個主題：自己在心理學這一門幾乎完全移用來自歐美的知識方法中學習時，又是如何發展自身的？我的一個根本立場是：即便在現代性全球知識傾銷傳播的傾斜關係的政勢中，要能辨識出自身立足於在地的一方基石，始能有接地氣的創新力。

1. 張開的左眼與行走著的地

　　1970 年代，因保釣運動、《夏潮》雜誌與鄉土文學論戰而張開左翼眼睛的我，在後續 10 年分兩個時段在美國碩、博心理諮詢專業學習的機會裡，探尋著在歐美心理治療與諮詢發展光譜中的左翼思考與實踐。在美國心理諮詢這一行的研究所課程中缺失了世界的左翼思想似乎很正常，我是在課堂外的幾個巧遇拾讀中知道美國學院少有但歐陸有，而美國非學院的成人教育實踐中亦存在著。如星子般引導我行路的事件和人物依發生的時序是：1976 年初我初步了解了 1968 年歐洲學生運動對大學體制與 70 年代思潮的衝擊，但因保釣運動美國校園內臺灣學生右派左派鬥爭的攪動，只待在賓州州立大學十一個月就回臺工作，故根本不知道歐洲特別是德國，心理學發生了什麼爭論；這一對德國批判心理學的進一步閱讀則到了 1984-1987 年間才發生。會有感有知地搜尋式的閱讀推動力，則來自於實際生活中具體的經驗與實作。

　　1977-1982 年間，我自己下工廠也帶學生跑廣慈博愛院雛妓收容所，對工業勞動與階級處境開始有了體悟。1983-85 年在哈佛教育學院讀博時，兩件課堂外的事發生了。那兩年大陸改革開放後第一批到美國的留學生陸續到達哈佛教育學院，我因為當時已在臺灣實務界工作數年，稍具專業運作能力且比多數大陸同學早一年到校園，所以用課餘時間邀集了數位大陸同學進行了一段成長分享的友伴小團體，在日常學習生活中彼此也成了好朋友。我對大陸建國後的政經制度變革與兩代人日常社會生活方式的改變第一次有了直接的聽聞；我開始正視大陸社會在世界左翼的體制變革實驗的視野裡，有著重要且不容被簡化粗暴對待的位置，但這都只停留在校園同學生活的互動中，少數兩三筆被我轉代入課堂報告中，授課教師有欣賞亦有大表不解的否定訊息。另一意外的發現則是因為我已在臺灣啟動過工廠女工的工作方案，所以暑假期間跑到教育學院 Gutman 圖書館樓

上的成人教育中心翻讀美國成人教育歷史材料，意外讀到田納西高地學校（Highlander School）的建立與結束；高地學校是 1932 年 Myles Horton 為培養工人組織幹部而成立的學校，但被麥卡錫主義攻擊而關閉了；美國為排除勞動階級的力量無所不用其極是有具體事例的！也正在此時，保羅·弗萊雷（Paulo Freire）到哈佛演講，我沒趕上去現場但視野中有了巴西農民成人教育豐沛的樣態！

　　是這些具體的經歷，讓我接上對德國批判心理學的閱讀，這說明了我對缺了的知識的補讀動能來自生活的具體經驗。1985 年修完課程，徵得哈佛教育學院與臺北榮總醫院精神科的同意，我把 1 年的實習課放到榮總去完成了[1]。

　　1986、1988 年是我在臺灣實踐田野的重要拐點，我開始了與中小學老師的協作[2]與因鄭村棋的投入而跟進了《中國時報》的工會運動。原先我寫的博士資格小論文（相當於博士資格考試）的題目，是《臺灣社會的歷史變遷與成人學習》，1987 年秋天去交完後回到臺灣，1988 年轉入中時工會成立抗爭的現場，參與到工會成立與組織建立過程的複雜與動態中，我幾乎決定放棄論文工作了！某日在疲勞繁重工作中意識到拿到哈佛的博士會是把好用的劍，是腳踩在地上的鬥爭性讓我決定完成論文書寫工作。

2. 歷史中的社會活動與社會關係

　　中時工會成立的抗爭是臺灣解嚴歷史拐點上的一頁篇章，那兩三年我見證了各式社會活動是怎樣地提供了機會，促使著原本的社會關係的既定方式的被挑戰與變化，所謂成年人的學習與發展當然是要看他們在所參與的活動（任何活動都是社會活動）中與他人和環境的互動，互動中發生了什麼作用以及這些作用是如何發生的。1990 年，帶著一箱材料（那時還沒 USB，我在讀博過程中最貴的投資就是換了台電動打字機）到哈佛寫完論文，搜尋與閱讀到蘇聯與東歐的活動理論是在此時，初識 Fred Newman 也在這一年。

　　依憑能找到、有限的對蘇聯集體農場與東歐活動理論介紹的英文文章，我得以在心理學範疇中，放置了我們在臺灣自主工會運動脈絡中，對

個人、集體與社會體制變革的想像；那幾年當然同步知道一些大陸解放前後的實踐者的歷史材料，如王凡西與張聞天，但大陸的心理學界則尚剛剛走上另一條再出發，拚命與西方接軌的路上。「實踐者的行動理論」是我在哈佛師從 Donald A. Schön 與 Chris Argyris 的主軸，我開始運用這一實踐認識論的方法橫軸，在歷史時間的縱軸上下移動。必須看見的是，我會因在進出 Gutman 圖書館玻璃大門時注意到貼在門上的 Fred Newman 的社會治療活動傳單，是有其前述我這名實踐者的實踐與知識關聯發展的歷史緣由的[3]，美國內部竟然有一支馬克思主義者的哲學、心理與教育等專業工作者由 70 年代初走到現在，怎能不去一探究竟！應是 1991 年春天，我只遠遠於群聚的對話場中參與觀看了 Fred，並未深入。5 月論文一通過，沒等畢業典禮就回臺了。再見社會治療這群美國的實踐者們則是在 2002年了！當然這中間的 10 年亦是在臺灣全力拚搏工作著。2002 年，申請了到 Columbia Teacher's College 研修半年，大部分時間則在紐約東邊中心參與活動；見識到了 Fred 與 Lois Holzman 的知識解讀批判能力不是只在文章中，更落實在群體中的對話活動、非裔街區文化教育方案與政黨政治活動中，思維的意識型態形構方式、情緒產生的社會控制路徑、精神樣態被問題化病理化，無一不與美國資本主義的社會機制纏繞運作；他們所為和我在臺灣與日日春協會的協作[4]所實驗的做法，得到了參看的交流的機會，此一機緣翻轉了當時的疲憊身心。由 2003 年後到 2017 年，Lois 與其同志們不只來臺交流了三次，且與我共同參加了大陸的理論心理學與馬克思研究學會的兩次活動，社會關係是在例行化或有意識發動或無意但偶發促動的社會活動中或不變或變化著的。我與王波的關係[5]是在我為促進美國馬克思主義實踐者與大陸馬克思主義研究者認識的行動中發生的。

3. 心理學與馬克思思想

　　即便在過去 30 年，美國、大陸和臺灣在資本主義全球化發展過程中，各自在全然差異的政勢格局中，但行動者的作為仍可能讓不同社會歷史時空裡的體悟認識，得到相互衝擊的辨識學習。2009 年的某天，陳光興老師打電話給我說他的歐洲左翼學者朋友要他推薦一人能到南京師範大學即將舉辦的第十三屆國際理論心理學大會上發言，他推薦了我；我去

參加的同時便也邀了 Lois 一起參加。我想應要讓大陸同行也認識這位美國的馬克思主義者與發展心理學家。那時王波剛由南師大心理研究所畢業，且正在思索科學實驗室心理學的哲學與倫理的問題。稍後，王波選擇跟隨張異賓老師去南京大學讀博了。王波的此一選擇也牽引了我與 Lois 在 2011 年於杭州參加了馬克思的哲學學會所舉辦的「第三屆當代資本主義研究國際學術研討會」；我因此機緣認識了先前只知其文與名的 Ian Parker。Parker 給我的第一個印象是個怪怪的、不喜多言的獨行俠；研討會後主辦方請大家在西湖某處晚宴，大家都是坐車去的，唯不見 Parker，等到我們快吃完了，Parker 走來了，他自個走路找來餐廳！2015 年 4 月，我邀約他來參加輔仁大學社科院「2015 社會治療‧治療社會研討會」[6]，我知道他是不需主辦方太照顧他的！他只告訴我他兒子會與他相會並要去花東自駕旅遊；於是我們就幫忙買票、租車與保險，他與家人就自由行去了。Lois 與 Parker 都知道 2016 年發生在我身上的被不實臉書文誣陷的網路攻擊事件，兩人都傳遞了支援關切；2021 年年初，Parker 寄來了他最新的書稿《精神分析與革命：解放運動的批判心理學》，盼我們能翻譯並要我寫中文版的序文。Lois、Parker 與後起之秀的大陸年輕學者王波都讓我充滿讚歎地讀著他們對馬克思思想與心理學的解析與批判，相信讀者會在陸續出版的書中讀到；然而，前述互動何以發生在大陸呢？

　　要看見的一個脈絡背景是，2000 年後，大陸心理學界努力與國際接軌的快速發展，而大陸馬克思哲學與西方哲學的研究更是老幹新枝地對西方心理分析詳加探究；邀約 Lois 同去是我主觀企圖，在坐聽大陸馬哲學人與教育者的報告中，還遇見 Parker 以及大衛‧哈維則是意外收穫。這一點呼應了前段 1984 年於哈佛初遇大陸改革開放後留學生的感悟。除了對德國、英國和美國的批判心理學有所介紹外，這套叢書中有一本是夏林清與王波的文章合集，一本是廉兮、林香君與龔尤倩等人的文章集子，我與臺灣作者群的關係，可借用王波下面所陳述的分辨來放置：

　　「一般而言，英語世界區分了兩種批判心理學，大寫的批判心理學特指 K. Holzkamp 等學者於 1970 年代在柏林自由大學開創的德國心理學派；小寫的複數批判心理學指接續了馬克思批判議程預言的對傳統心理學不信

任的各種激進左派話語的鬆散結合……這裡要強調『批判心理學事業』和『批判心理學學科』的區分。德國批判心理學一度有試圖補充傳統心理學使之更完善的傾向，但小寫批判心理學基本都反對將自身作為心理學的二級學科。可以說，批判心理學家在從事『批判心理學』這項事業，但是反對有一個學術建制上的批判心理學。」（王波，〈德國批判心理學：歷史語境與核心問題〉，收於《一盞夠用的燈：兩岸參看的振動》，五南出版社）。

4. 平民角落的實踐者

「平民角落」一書的書名納入了廉兮與香君各自表達她們多年踐行的用語[7]。在臺灣，1947-1950 年代初期國民黨因恐共而埋葬地掃蕩島內左的力量，1997 年後政黨輪替更確立了統獨坐標為宗，左右的思想分類便以此坐標為準，服務於政治權力和資源的集中了。然而，我們一直走在自己認定的志業道路上，並不孤單！

2001 年與 1996 年與廉兮和香君相識，彼此對實踐落地的感通如同長途跋涉各自登山，行至半山處，三人於路邊茶寮喝著大碗茶、邊聊著天，通氣潤身是我們協作關係的質地。林香君可說是翻牆而出拓地實驗的臺灣師大心理人，她翻了牆但從未忘本且反哺有道，廉兮則是在與其父母1950 年赴臺生活的生命歷史由脫落（赴美深造）到接續，她是通過自己對美國批判教育學的反思，做下了踐行入花蓮的生命選擇，而後始與老年父母再相逢！這幾年她所逐漸地知曉了父母年輕時的某些生命碎片般的訊息，碎片已難整全，但是歷史碎片已俱足藉之返身的力道，廉兮正琢磨著呢。龔尤倩等其他諸位作者，則均於不同時期與我們三人是亦師亦友的同行者。我之所以決定要有「平民角落」的文集，就是要彰顯吾道不孤，山路縱崎嶇且會遇險境，但腳走在地上抬頭見明月，踏實的！

夏林清

2021 年 9 月 21 日中秋節於四川成都龍泉驛隔離旅館中完稿

註釋

1 見〈鑲嵌於地景中的花徑：與吳就君老師相識相熟的10年記事（1975-1986）〉，刊於《臺灣心理劇學刊》2021年8月專刊，頁97-101。

2 成立基層教師協會，見李文英《教師「群」像與主體生成：回顧基教社群發展與自身教育歷程交織成型》，2021.08.28，尚未出版。

3 見Fred Newman《心理學的迷思》一書中夏林清的中文版跋，頁250-251，五南出版社。

4 王芳萍《差異美學、關係跨界、底邊連線：妓權運動的文化實踐》，輔仁大學心理學研究所博士論文，2016。

5 見王波的〈知識返身解殖與去心理學化同行：來自臺灣心理學的經驗〉，收於《一盞夠用的燈：兩岸參看的振動》，五南出版社。

6 從3月18日到5月13日計八個場次的系列研討，Ian Parker參加的是4月30日第6場：社會思想論壇——在歷史中反思社會科學）

7 「平民」取自廉兮《庶民視角的教習踐行：邊界文本與抵殖民的家園政治》一文，見臺灣文學研究第6期，2014年6月；「角落」則取自香君於宜蘭創設的「中華角落關懷互助協會」。

致中文讀者序

　　將這本書翻譯成中文是一項艱鉅而費時的任務。無數的電子郵件來回討論特定單字和詞句的準確含義。由於這本書在兩種論述的交織處運作，並且最初由我和我的合著者戴維・帕馮-奎亞爾（David Pavón-Cuéllar）以英語和西班牙語書寫成，所以已經使得這項任務，以及在翻譯上採取謹慎措施的必要性，變得更加繁重和冗長。

　　這兩種論述——一種是關於精神分析的，另一種是關於我們對英國和墨西哥革命的理解——都由特殊用語組成。這種特殊用語的目的並不是要將我們侷限在一個與一般人群分離的學術中產階級世界中。這些用語的使用是為了讓我們作為精神分析的實踐者和政治運動者，以及作為讀者的您，能夠擺脫統治的意識形態、主流保守的世界觀並打破對個人和社會變革可能性的既定觀念。

　　更複雜的是，這兩種論述的交織——精神分析作為主體性和個人變革的理論和實踐，與革命作為社會和社會變革的理論與實踐——相當不易闡明。過往，無論是參與革命政治的精神分析學家，還是試圖理解無意識、重複、驅力和移情在他們自身活動中所扮演的角色的革命者，人們曾多次嘗試將兩者聯繫起來。我們肯認這些勇敢的嘗試，並試圖在本書中將其發揚光大。

　　精神分析和革命的兩種論述有一個共同點，那就是它們都是對「常識」的批判和顛覆。那在精神醫學、心理學和心理療法領域——「心理／精神相關學科」（'psy-displines'）[1]的三個核心——中通常被理解為主體性的，在精神分析中的概念是非常不同的。精神分析挑戰我們看待自己的方式，挑戰意識形態常識。革命也是一種與主流媒體通常所呈現的方式非常不同的事業，當人們參與革命行動時，他們也會在這個過程中打破常識。

　　這兩種論述的另一個共同點是他們對於獨特性與普遍性之間不尋常描述和處理方式。精神分析並沒有將每一個人類主體形成並體驗世界的性

---

[1]　請見本書「導讀暨譯序」以及正文「前言」該章頁下註1。

質，化約爲心理學科中被誤導地稱之爲「個別差異」的東西；精神分析也沒有將我們作爲人類的共同點，簡化爲同樣也被誤導地稱之爲「人性」的東西。革命還使我們能夠在集體變革的背景下成長爲個人，革命性的運動者知道，正如馬克思所說，我們每個人都是「社會關係的總合」。

我們對我們兩人寫這本書時所處的特定文化政治環境非常敏感，認識到世界其他地區的文化政治環境需要不同的語言來理解。這也意味著，我們歡迎這種「翻譯」的可能性，將其視爲一個機會，一個將我們的書的獨特之處，與在英語、西班牙語和中文世界中，爲使作爲人類的我們明白自己是誰而奮鬥的普遍性聯繫起來的機會，共同爲另一個世界一起工作。我們希望您享受與這本書的不同見解，並找到一種方法來自己撰寫另一個更好的論點版本。我們要對譯者表示深深的感謝，感謝她使您現在閱讀這本書時將承擔的這項任務成爲可能。

伊恩·帕克　于曼徹斯特

2022 年 12 月

Preface for our Chinese readers

Translation of this book into Chinese has been a momentous and time-consuming task. There have been many email messages backwards and forward discussing clarifications about the precise meaning of particular words and phrases. This task, and the necessity of care taken over the translation, has been made more burdensome and protracted because the book operates at the intersection of two discourses, and was initially written by myself and my co-author David Pavón-Cuéllar in English and Spanish.

Each of these two discourses – that pertaining to psychoanalysis and that pertaining to our understanding of revolution in Britain and Mexico – is composed of specialist terminology. That specialist terminology is not designed to enclose ourselves in an academic middle-class world separated from the general population. The terminology is designed to enable ourselves, as practitioners of psychoanalysis and as political activists, as well as you the readers, to break from the ruling ideology, from dominant reactionary way of understanding the world and conceptualising possibilities of personal and social change.

A further complication is that the intersection of the two discourses – psychoanalysis as a theory and practice of subjectivity and personal change, and revolution as a theory and practice of society and social change – is difficult to articulate. There have been many attempts to connect them in the past, both by psychoanalysts who have been involved in revolutionary politics and by revolutionaries who have sought to understand the role of the unconscious, repetition, drive and transference as phenomena in their own activity. We acknowledge those valiant attempts, and attempt to take them forward in this book.

One thing the two discourses of psychoanalysis and revolution have in common is that they are critical and subversive of 'commonsense'. What is usually understood as subjectivity in the domains of psychiatry, psychology and psychotherapy – the tripartite core of the 'psy-disciplines' – is very different from the way it is conceptualised in psychoanalysis. Psychoanalysis challenges the way we think about ourselves, and challenges ideological commonsense. Revolution is also a very different enterprise from the way it is usually presented in the mainstream media, and when people engage in revolutionary action they also, in the process, break from commonsense.

Another thing that the two discourses have in common is the unusual way they describe and work with the connection between singularity and universality. Psychoanalysis does not reduce the nature of each human subject as they have been formed and experience the world to what is misleadingly termed 'individual differences' in the psydisciplines. Neither does psychoanalysis reduce what we have in common as human beings to what is equally misleadingly termed 'human nature'. Revolution also enables us to grow as persons in the context of collective change, and revolutionary activists know that each of us is, as Marx put it, an 'ensemble of social relations'.

We are sensitive to the specific cultural-political context in which the two of us wrote the book, recognising that the cultural-political contexts in other parts of the world require different languages to make sense of them. It also means that we embrace the possibility of 'translation' of this kind as an opportunity to connect what is singular about our book with what is universal in the struggle to make sense of who we are as human beings in the English, Spanish and Chinese-speaking worlds working together for another world. We hope you enjoy disagreeing with this book, and find a way to compose another better version of the argument yourselves. And we want to express our profound gratitude to the translator for making this task that you will now undertake in reading the book possible.

Ian Parker, Manchester

December 2022

引言

對抗點──迂迴轉進的穿透性

　　Ian Parker 和 David Pavón-Cuéllar 為了「保護解放運動避免它們被心理學化」（見第 6 章）寫了本宣言書，林香君寫了篇萬言導讀文，這書與文合成一枝具穿透力量的入土飛箭。

　　此箭之箭身與箭頭是 Parker 製作，我甚至要說 Parker 的自身就如此箭！在精神分析與批判心理學領域的研究裡，他對 Freud 的精神分析與歐陸左翼歷史資糧的判讀理解，像是打造這支箭身的堅固材質，他一再指明與陳述分析當代資本主義心理學化所加深的異化問題，則如銳利的箭頭。這本書確立了一個對抗點，《精神分析與革命：解放運動的批判心理學》全書在清晰勾勒歐陸精神分析的歷史地景與衍生之困局時，還原確立了人們革命主體的存在。

　　2021 年春夏時節，Parker 來詢問能否翻譯此書，我心想要有這書的中譯本，這位譯者得要在撫觸箭身時，有身心的體感才行啊！在臺灣我以為只有林香君可擔此任務。Parker 的箭頭直中心理學化（心理熱）的濫商靶心，然而助它射中靶心且入土三分的一股勁風，是林香君的導讀文：〈歷史・語言・無意識──精神分析的辯證重構與未來世界〉。林香君是踩在臺灣（兩岸三地與亞洲的華文讀者亦定有同感）的精神分析與心理熱業已塊結化的社會性土壤上，細辨緩嚼此書，為做譯註查找資料，且來來回回地與作者討論檢核自己對書中語詞概念的理解是否有誤差；她的這篇導讀文為中文讀者構設了一個思索的空間，讓讀者能在迂迴轉進的過程中識得了、接得住 Parker 所傳來的穿透力道。譬如，Parker 的觀點「……個體性的意識自我（ego）不是每一個人的核心，但無意識也不是，我們在無意識中相互聯繫，在無意識中我們是社會關係的總合……」林香君在文中有很好的「歷史構成」的解說；導讀全文中多處的解說，不只是讓我們在閱讀時可以有多一層遊移想像的思維空間，同時也在臺灣心理學化的地層土塊內，曲徑延展了穿透臺灣歷史的對抗點。

　　翻譯這本書的心力一點也不輕鬆，香君深切期待著若讀者讀完全書「……可在當前中文世界一整片『心理熱』中拾得一片冰心醒腦」。或許，翻讀此書的閱讀過程可啟動讀者返身辨識自身之內與之外（社會內部）的異化土壤已塊結化的樣態，返身拆解與捏鬆土塊的工作則是我們自己可幹的活了！最後，爲了有助臺灣讀者對共產主義一詞能不再或遮蔽或阻抗的誤解，林香君還翻了《三民主義》的老底，引註了孫中山在《民生主義》中的金句「……故民生主義就是社會主義，又名共產主義，即是大同主義」；我們能如此地與國父重新相認，忍不住莞爾一笑！

夏林清 於四川
2023 春夏之交於四川綿陽文化藝術學院

歷史・語言・無意識
——精神分析的辯證重構與未來世界

進入之前

　　作者稱這本書是一份「宣言」，其目的不是要傳播某種精神分析理論或臨床實務，而是為建設切實可行的人類替代出路，站在解放運動的主體立場，對精神分析潛在的進步性與革命性政治效益可能作為一種「最基進的批判心理學」而展開辯證與重構。

　　作者這本「宣言」的主要對象是「和我們這個時代的壓迫、剝削和異化的現實作鬥爭的個人與群體」，因此，這篇中文版導讀也是基於這樣的對象設想，希望即使是對精神分析沒有接觸的讀者，也能經由導讀取得理解這份「宣言」的條件。同時也為此特別再請作者 Ian Parker 增寫《精神分析地景簡述》一文，為需要補充精神分析發展脈絡的讀者，提供精簡的歷史背景概述。

　　因此，如同作者刻意捨棄太過學術性的論述與引述方式，中文版及您現在正讀的這份導讀也是在這樣的意識下，盡力將艱深抽象的概念淺顯化、鋪陳理解脈絡及提供註解來處理，並盡可能在中文世界文化中尋找較可類喻的理解方式；不過，誠如作者也在書中提及的，有些關鍵概念確實不易使它們簡單通俗。由於本書同時交織於解放政治與精神分析兩個領域，作者對這些關鍵概念的意義都作了重新框定，大不同於現行主流的「*精神分析*」（特別加引號及斜體字以示區別），不太有接觸過的「素人」讀者，也許反而更易於把握作者的概念；相對地，越是熟諳「*精神分析*」的讀者，反倒需要小心，有必要先懸置既有的理解，特別是那些再典型不過的精神分析名詞諸如「無意識」、「重複」、「驅力」、「欲望」、「壓抑」、「移情」、「抗拒」……等概念，避免落入想當然爾的

錯解 [1]。

　　作爲一份「宣言」，這不是又一本某種精神分析流派的介紹書，事實上，作者全然無意擁護精神分析被以特定的形式被長久維持，而更關注它爲朝向未來世界的解放運動服務的潛力。基於此，作者在「宣言」中對現今盛行的「*精神分析*」連同心理學、心理治療等進行批判，對於興趣焦點在吸收精神分析知識的讀者，若仍願意帶著好奇與耐心，跟著作者的理路一覽全景的話，是可能在當前中文世界一整片「心理熱」（'psycho-boom'）中，拾得一片冰心醒腦。

　　作者將本書交給我們這一支「批判實踐取徑」團隊，作爲與中文世界對話的出發點，我們希望藉臺灣在國際地緣政治特殊位置與當前處境來創造條件，使本書中譯版的出版發揮最大的可能作用，這是本書以中英對照方式設計的脈絡，願使這份「宣言」能具備廣泛連結爲未來世界共同努力的最大潛力。

　　理解這本書最適合的方式，是如同作者將精神分析的發明放回佛洛伊德所面對的時代挑戰和任務、以及當時的歷史條件與限制的脈絡中重讀與對話，本書讀者也宜將作者的主張，放回他們所見當前時代的挑戰與需要的任務來作歷史辯證性的解讀。

　　作者來自英國與墨西哥，參與左翼解放運動，結合馬克思思想、語言學、拉岡精神分析、抵殖民政治、反種族主義與社會主義 - 多元交織政治女性主義的基進批判心理學是他們的共同的交集，也是本書涉及的知識背景 [2]；不過，實踐——他們在地方脈絡中的左翼解放運動的行動與反思，引

---

[1]　一個可能有幫助減少因想當然爾而作出錯誤解讀可能性的作法，是先讀第 6 章再回頭閱讀，作者對這些重要概念中的部分在該章有對其批判與重構作精要的收總。

[2]　作者於英文版最後列了背景閱讀整理來自精神分析政治、政治與批判心理學三個領域對作者有重要啟發（部分也同時有所批判）的著作，並附上不斷更新的閱讀資源網站，中文版在此補充作者彙集世界各地的譯本、序文與書評的網址與本書介紹及討論的英文視頻，謹供讀者參考如下：

https://psychoanalysisrevolution.com
https://www.facebook.com/watch/?v=869291420361168

領他們對任何背景知識的作脈絡性、歷史辯證性的參看與修正，並引領他們超越任何「*精神分析*」、心理學與心理治療（作者將其合稱爲 'psy professionals'，正文中譯爲「心理／精神相關專業」，在導讀中爲易於精簡表達暫且簡稱爲「psy 專業」）而有了作爲「最基進的批判心理學」、服務於解放運動的精神分析。

　　此書是兩位作者在當前的歷史節點上，基於他們在英、墨兩地社會與國際來往間親歷見聞人們的種種痛苦所進行的批判分析與政治運動，他們也看到所實踐的精神分析臨床對於這種痛苦的理解與承接具有轉化爲解放運動有效資源的革命性潛力；但同時，主流的「psy 專業」恰恰是維持與加劇這個世界痛苦的問題的一環。他們在書中不只一次謹慎地表明他們的觀點與主張並非放之四海皆準，作者對這份「宣言」以十多種語言在國際間翻譯出版的期待，就是邀請對話，邀請不同地域不同語言文化的讀者理解他們在此書想要說的話後，完全可以就自己所處的社會文化，提出不同的觀點，更進一步地，在自己的文化處境將思想觀點「轉譯」到在地處境的實踐之中。

　　以一本書而言，這份「宣言」本身文字並不算多，但也因此，它有相當濃縮的概念，爲鋪陳出讀者進入理解的條件，這份導讀構想讀者可能的提問，以此作爲書寫架構：1. 背景——作者究竟是看到什麼與痛苦的事？與我們何干？又與精神分析何干？2. 必要性——「*精神分析*」在心理市場上已經很多了，不也都在助人解決問題嗎？那些有什麼問題嗎？作者的精神分析有何不同？3. 關鍵概念——有哪些概念需要特別把握住以較易進入理解？4. 精神分析如真可以爲解放運動服務，它們所揭示的未來究竟是什麼樣？以上提問 1 以第一節回應，提問 2 以第二、三兩節說明，提問 3 安排於第四節，提問 4 則回應於第五節。在回答這些提問的布局中，實也依序作了各章菁要的介紹，希望這樣的安排，能有助於使作者的濃縮精華養分更易於被吸收。

---

https://www.youtube.com/watch?v=SHdSuf_A2KU&ab_channel=StudyGroupsonPsychoanalysisandPolitics

一、起點：「症狀」

（一）內外交相映——個人症狀是悲慘世界痛苦的表徵

　　這份「宣言」寫於 COVID-19 疫情嚴峻各國封關之際，致命病毒的到來更曝露世界經濟政治地理上的不均，全球「南方」國家[3]與資本發達國家中的窮人，以及與弱勢性／別、族群及因差異被社會所「障礙」的人們，往往遭受更多的苦難與死亡的威脅。在作者看來，人類的歷史環繞著階級、種族和性別向度而構建，今日世界已是一個被新自由主義資本主義（也被稱作「休克式資本主義」）、性別歧視、種族主義和新殖民主義等形式聯手異化、壓迫與剝削的「悲慘世界」[4]，不只人類自身，連同萬物生態同遭其害，地球生態危機深重。

　　這些看似在「外部」的「政治性」力道在各地以體制與文化意識形態運作著，層層穿透社會系統穿牆越戶交織作用於家內關係與個人身心，當衝突壓擠、痛苦承載極至，便濃縮凝結以「症狀」形式表現出來，看似「內部」的「症狀」實都有其「外部」的根源，所以「症狀」本質上是反映歷史的事物，也就是「歷史辯證」的、有故事、有脈絡的。所以作者說：「精神分析是辯證性的」、「精神分析治療的痛苦有其現代歷史脈絡性，『症狀』表徵了異化與資本主義權力關係的壓迫。」「精神分析把握了症狀作為社會痛苦跡象」。

　　作者說的這種「外部」政治力滲入「內部」表出為「症狀」的情形天天在發生，到處都存在這樣的事例文本，並不因疫情結束而消失，例如在美元霸權主導的現代國際秩序中，美國無限寬鬆引發通膨又急劇升息導致美國國債流動失靈，亞太地區包括大陸與臺灣在內在美元潮汐中總淪為被收割的對象，為生計勞動的龐大人口辛勤工作的成果一夕折損，個人與家庭生計脆弱如風中蠟燭，這些實質的經濟壓力轉成往內壓迫關係的張力與

---

[3]　「南方」概指地理上位處工業發達國家之南的亞、非、拉等低度開發或發展中國家，也就是所謂的「第三世界」。

[4]　十九世紀法國作家雨果名著《悲慘世界》（Les Misérables），作者引以顯喻今日世界。

身心痛苦，緊張、失眠、焦慮、各種「症狀」因人因條件而異，在今日往往被精神醫療、心理治療、心理諮商（連同「學校輔導」也忘了教育主體而錯置專業認同於這些「psy 專業」，一樣淪陷其中）以病名打包，力求「適應」，實是「維穩」新自由主義主導的國際秩序。作者告訴我們所謂「病」，是「被這個政治經濟體制、資本主義、父權制和殖民主義作用所致『病』的。」精神醫學的診斷將我們的痛苦的不同面向分出不同的成分加以特殊化成為不同類型的病，將我們一個個包裹在「病」中使我們分隔開來，使我們「忘記」了在社會中這些被標定為「病」的共同起源。

「症狀」的歷史脈絡性是佛洛伊德的寶貴洞察，他開創了精神分析──一種用「語言」來理解濃縮凝結於症狀中的痛苦的「談話治療」，在他之前，「前精神醫學」用的是幾近監禁與酷刑般的身體治療方法，這是他的歷史任務。不過，他的時代條件令他來不及把具體的「內」、「外」關係說清楚。

當受苦的人來到臨床中，藉由精神分析方法在獨特的臨床空間中藉由「語言」流淌其間，與濃縮於「症狀」之中的衝突相遇，轉成可被意識的矛盾，分析師的任務是「聆聽」（注意，不是代替「苦主」作分析及解釋，作者明白指出那是嚴重的錯誤），協助受苦的人洞察「內部」（看似個人心理的「症狀」）與「外部」之間的關連，藉由聽見自己的「語言」，面對攤在眼前的矛盾，作出自己的解釋。

所謂「外部」的，既是在我們之外也同時在我們之內，而所謂「內部」的，實際上反映著「外部」，這種內外交相滲透與反映的辯證，正是精神分析以語言在無意識領域工作所能夠把握並處理的；因此，精神分析臨床看似個人性的談話治療工作，實是作為一個轉化個人受苦經驗並連結到社會集體的場址，這就與解放運動的政治性關連起來。

（二）「無意識」的領地 ── 歷史、語言、象徵的世界

「症狀」是一種具有特定歷史意涵的衝突的標誌，個人的衝突來自所生成的社會中的結構，如制度、文化、價值、意識形態等，是歷史的濃縮表達，它們的具體涵義不易被日常的理性認知所理解，需要被放回歷史下的社會文化政治脈絡中來理解，這就是「歷史辯證」的理解方法。

　　然而，不只「症狀」是具歷史特性，社會文化是人類在歷史中建構的（所以也叫「歷史構成」），但一旦它們形成，就成了一種體制與意識形態，往往化為「常識」到多數人幾乎不知不覺、理所當然的地步，人類是透過符號象徵（也可說是廣義的「語言」，包括非口語及文字以外的任何形式）將這些體制與意識形態傳遞於歷史之中，對人們該成為什麼樣子、該怎麼做、該如何期盼與生活……都起著定義與主導的作用，這對人們往往是「無意識」的，生活在這個由符號、語言構成的象徵世界中，人們以「它我／他我」（德文 it 對譯到英文寫作 id，是無意識存在體[5]）的規則為規則，以「它我／他我」的欲望為欲望；所以，歷史與社會文化本身，以及語言符號作為人類傳遞社會文化與交流彼此的媒介本身，就是「無意識」。「無意識」並不玄，也不是深藏在腦袋內某處，是人類寓居其中，隨語言就穿梭於我們所有人之中、進出我們內與外（佛洛伊德發現「無意識」，可是沒把這部分說得夠清楚，把它這樣說清楚的人是拉岡）。衝突的「症狀」也根源於象徵世界，根源於這個「無意識」的領地。

　　每一個人的色、受、想、行、識之中都有他人的痕跡與回聲，我們與他人的關係將我們每個人聯繫在一起，透過歷史形塑我們成為現在的自己；因此，個人的構成是社會和文化的，也同時是歷史的。這種內外交相滲透與反映，實際上是人類存在的本質，人在歷史中，是「歷史構成」的，會不斷地變化，集體的社會與歷史也會。我們當前面對的剝削、壓迫和異化的情境也是歷史性的建構，不是本來就固有的，是可被變化的。在歷史中，人可以是象徵社會的「能動者」，也可以是它的「受害者」和「產物」；取決於人是否有條件歷史辯證地理解個別的與集體的「歷史構成」，進而選擇更想要的未來歷史，這是何以能夠透過精神分析辯證方法從受苦「症狀」帶來的洞察而轉變成為解放實踐的道理。當人們「忘記」自身與所有事物都是「歷史構成」的（即「去歷史脈絡」，不使用歷史辯證性方法作理解時，制度、儀式、常識、約定俗成……都會被看成是「本來固有」的，而詭異的「症狀」在現代精神病理成了流行文化的當前，快

---

[5]　id 坊間多譯作本我，但實際上更宜譯作「它我」或「他我」，本書並列以「它我（他我）」形式表達，更詳細說明請參考正文第 2 章註 5。

速地被以診斷標上病名且用藥打包起來。而這個「忘記」往往是來自被意識自我（ego）主導的「科學」理性所馴化，而使得脈絡性的歷史辯證性認識方法幾乎被遮蔽；當然，這種人類集體的「忘記」與意識自我的、「科學」理性的抬頭，本身也就是「歷史構成」的。果然，如作者所說：「無意識就是政治」，實現爲知識的政治、文化的政治、體制結構的政治。這部分拉岡沒說清楚，在他之後，把精神分析這樣說清楚的，是本書作者以及將拉岡精神分析再政治化的「拉岡左派」們。

二、精神分析的政治性

（一）分裂於歷史的精神分析

　　作者說：「精神分析本是一種基進的治療方法，它曾經明確地與左派理念結盟，但現已成了適應性的……」是的，本書談的精神分析和坊間市場盛行的「*精神分析*」從人是怎樣的存在觀（特別是關於人的「心理」是什麼的觀點）、問題觀（即痛苦如何形成）到改變觀（即關於如何改變，視不同的理路也被稱爲「治療觀」或「發展觀」），以及它們在對人與對當前世界的作用和通向怎樣的未來圖像，徹頭徹尾大相逕庭。在作者看來，這個極大的差異，始於佛洛伊德受制於他的「歷史構成」條件而形成的前後矛盾，以及精神分析本身遭逢的世界歷史變遷。扼要地說，這是一條從最初作爲劃時代革命性的「無意識」大發現的精神分析，轉變成現今主流當道的強調個體性與結合現代精神醫療病理診斷的個體心理以及所謂「自我心理學」（'ego psychology'）的「*精神分析*」，再轉到借助語言學與歷史辯證重返「無意識」而展開精神分析的革命性重構的三個迂迴轉折的歷史過程。導致這個演變的核心關鍵差異就在於──究竟人類主體的重心是「無意識它我／他我」（'the id of unconscious'）還是「意識自我」（'the ego of conscious'）？

　　首先，這牽涉到對於人和「心理」到底是什麼樣的一種存在的看法。

　　最初，佛洛伊德發現的「無意識」顛覆性地改變了十六、七世紀哥白尼、笛卡兒以降西方理性主義與近代科學主義的人類圖像，這反映佛

洛伊德一開始並沒接受把人及「心理」看作是那種既定的、想像中彷彿實體的、甚至是明顯可見、可量度的，也不把它視爲普遍的、統一的東西，這是精神分析革命性的根本基石，是佛洛伊德本人對他的時代的「對抗點」，也是拉岡借語言學呼籲「回歸佛洛伊德」「無意識」的「對抗點」，更是作者與基進的拉岡左派們對抗包藏個人主義意識形態的「psy專業」與資本主義合謀共構而加劇象徵世界異化與人們痛苦的堅實的「對抗點」。

但是，依作者的看法，兩個「歷史構成」的原因使得精神分析的革命性被模糊，第一個原因來自佛洛伊德本人在他的文本中留下某些易被解讀他標舉理性意識自我爲中心的陳述，開始了精神分析對「心理」的差異解讀，引發將人的主體重心放在「無意識」或「意識」的世紀爭議。尤其是他對尼采的《查拉圖斯特拉》的經典引用：「Wo Es war, soll Ich werden」，從德文轉譯到英、法語世界就有不同的意義解讀，其中一個英譯版本正是書中的「Where it was, there ego shall be.」作者對此話的解讀並非抽離脈絡，而是同時參看佛洛伊德其他文本中對意識自我與無意識它我／他我關係的比喻。貼著作者的解讀，這句話中譯是「凡它（指它我／他我）所在，吾（指意識自我）必取而代之」（見第 2 章），作者認爲這種看法反映佛洛伊德作爲資產階級男性的中心主義視角，階級、性別與族群的批判反思在他那個時代還方興未艾，另外，他的那個時代語言學尚未出現，雖然他已把無意識與語言關連起來，但他後期沒能再深化下去，而是使用當時發達的生物學隱喻作類比，使他的追隨者開始對無意識設想爲彷似實體的存在，而「正常」人格的「適應」社會，需要依賴理性意識自我的統御。

第二個原因與上個世紀二次大戰發生的許多猶太裔精神分析師流亡美國有關，他們當中許多人原本帶著革命性視野，去到資本主義社會爲生存適應而妥協，衍生了結合科技理性（包括結合了去除「歷史構成」脈絡的精神醫療診斷模式與客觀主義的「科學」）與個人主義意識形態的適應性「psy專業」。

（二）適應性的「psy 專業」們

　　抓住晚期佛洛伊德的三重心理結構說，以意識自我主導的《*精神分析*》把心理或人格簡化為「本我──自我（ego）──超我」仿如實體的人格調控裝置，意識自我擺脫了無意識，「驅力」與「欲望」同被視為出於動物性「本能」的「需要」，無意識彷彿深藏於內心晦暗深處不可測知、需被控制的威脅力量，需靠意識自我的理性調控才能「適應」現實世界。而人理當是理性意識自我的主體，是本質固有的內在統一的整體，是功能自主、自滿自足的獨立個體，治療的目的指向與社會規範和諧適應、「健康」、「強」的自我（ego）認同。意識自我成了世界的中心，萬物的準衡，不合乎這種圖像的人被分類為不良、有問題、次等、殘缺的，在資本主義與科技發達的時代中，衍生了對自然生態與地球資源的橫徵暴斂與對「異己他者」（'other'）的歧視、剝削與迫害。

　　在這種如實體存在的、理性自我的人觀與適應的治療觀之下，形成痛苦的根源（即問題觀）是發生於個人「內部」而導致因應「外部」世界時失功能──也就是「適應不良」，這種往個人「內部」歸因並訴求治療個人意識自我（或者視野看似較寬把問題仍然「去脈絡」地歸因於家庭「內部」的認識與治療方式），就是「心理學化」（'psychologization'）。「心理學化」，正是同為個人主義的資本主義（和它相屬關連的性別歧視、種族主義等）所需要的，它幫助遮蔽資本主義所製造的問題（這也就是「去政治化」（'depoliticized'）），它們是一對絕佳拍檔，「心理學化」粉飾資本主義的新式殖民，資本主義拓展「心理學化」的市場，而使我們生活在當中理所當然地甘於「自主」管理。所以作者說：「適應性精神分析的問題不僅在於它將事情的規則當然化……它更大的問題在於使我們將世界視為與我們每個人都分離開的外部『環境』，這使我們無法認識到我們是世界的一部分……。」

　　盛行的「psy 專業」潛藏著個人主義意識形態，與資本主義互為表裡，當人們忙著向內看，忙著管自己，就更看不見「外部」如何作用於「內部」，使我們無法認識到世界的和我們之間的關連，以為那是本來固有的，「忘記」了那是「歷史構成」的，只能任由「外部」被體制與意識形

態繼續掌控。而被視為「適應不良」的人們努力追求的「改變」的對象、目標及對治之道（治療觀），就基於聚焦於「內部」的各種盲人摸象的理論假定（例如把問題的原因假定是出在人格結構的自我調控、適應／不適應行為習慣養成、或不良認知、缺乏全然接納的關係、情感覺察、家內溝通模式、家內權力－界限模式……等）與對應的策略／方法，追求想像的目標──「改變」──其實是似變而實不變的「適應」。然而，在看不見內外關連之下，如果能經由「調適」「內部」而「適應」「外部」已是大幸，如果「調適」仍不能「適應」「外部」，那麼通向精神醫療的旋轉門早已打開，既已納入「自主」管理的下一環。

　　在當前新自由主義（跨國資本主義形式）及其衍生的新式殖民（就是表象看不見實體軍械武器的經濟與文化意識形態殖民）運作中，這種「心理學化」看待人我的認識方式，早已化作貼身眼鏡，已到達大多數人理所當然、渾然不覺地自動化「不思考」的地步，使人遵從隱形的「外部」「看不見的命令」去努力作一個「自主」的「主體」，全然不意識到已身陷弔詭之中，這個看似「自」以為「是」的結果，就是各種包藏著個人主義意識形態的身心靈套路（「心理熱」市場上「去脈絡」的情緒管理、正向／積極心理學自助手冊、壓力自我管理……以及個別的或團體的心理諮商、治療工作坊不勝枚舉的「商品」）──「心理學化／資本主義」世界與知識的再循環建構。所以，作者指出只要我們仍視彼此為分離孤立的個體，仍沒看到所有為生活勞動的人們彼此間的共同關連，那麼人類將會持續在現今「外部」的那些體制與意識形態下加劇痛苦，直到徹底失去這個世界。

三、我們是「社會關係的總合」

　　相對於立基於個人主義的適應性「psy 專業」，作者稱人為「主體」而不稱「個體」。

　　我們作為「心理」的主體，是存在於歷史、語言之中的、存在於「無意識」的關係網絡之中，我們是「社會生態性」的存在，不論多久遠的歷史都影響著我們的生成，不論多遙遠地方的「異己他者」都與我們有關，這就是「他者性」（'otherness'），是「無意識」的。我們也絕不是個體

性的意識自我，不是去脈絡虛構的統一、整合的存在；相反地，我們是不斷在關係網絡中與「異己他者」相遇、彼此衝擊而會「分裂」（'divided、split'）的。

因此，所謂的「心理」，從不是與外界孤立隔絕、只在「內部」、彷如實體的機制，而所謂「無意識」也從非深藏晦暗隱蔽的內核的想像，它就在我們的社會關係網絡之中展開，在我們集體的「歷史構成」之間，貫穿我們的「內部」與「外部」；所以，心理生活並不存在普遍不變的基本屬性，而是取決於文化、歷史時機與社會關係。所以，在「無意識」中，個別主體都反映集體，集體也投影在個別的主體，所以作者引述馬克思的話說：「我們是社會關係的總合」。

我們必須承認我們不可能全然自主，例如在父權的社會文化下，打娘胎起就已在性／別規範「天經地義」的「凝視」之中。又如與新自由主義資本主義、新殖民主義合謀的「心理學化」所形塑出「自主」主體性，其實是「聽令」於這些意識形態而無所知覺。我們總是不知不覺地受制於「無意識」，定義與形塑我們是誰的是「它我／他我」，從來不是渺小個體性的意識自我。但，另一方面，「無意識」與我們的關係也是持續變動的，「歷史構成」不是固定的，主體也不是全然受制就不再「離經叛道」的，如前述，一但從痛苦、從「症狀」展開辯證，經由語言使「無意識」的「症狀」濃縮的衝突痛苦顯化為矛盾，看見內外關連，取得洞察、覺醒，則「歷史構成」的改變就可能發生，所謂「哪裡有壓迫，哪裡就有反抗」。這就是革命性的基進精神分析的人觀、問題觀與改變觀（或治療觀）。

與歷史、語言、無意識關連的「分裂」與「他者性」這兩組概念，顛覆了視人為有完整統一個體性的理性意識自我的精神分析，由於這兩組概念都相當濃縮，也容易被望文生義地誤解，有必要再作些說明：

（一）我們是「分裂」的主體

在這裡，「分裂」的意義要被放在存在的層次來理解，是人存在於世的必然，我們是會「分裂的主體」（'split / divided subject'），因為會分裂，所以我們會經驗到痛苦，也會不斷生成、發展、擴充與變化。分

裂之必然，除了上面提到的因為「他者性」——我們與「異己他者」的關連與相遇使然外，這也是我們作為語言的存在的根本特性。因為任何人事物的「實在」（'the real'，這個哲學概念相當抽象，於下段再以類比作說明），在任何象徵符號（廣義的「語言」）的企圖描述下都只會是其中一部分，沒法說盡的，我們任何「語言」符號的描述，都只是對「實在」的暫時性和有限的表徵，「語言」描述一經給出，開顯某種「眞實」（'truth'）的當下也同時遮蔽了其他可能的「眞實」，設定的同時就是「分裂」。「實在」固然在象徵世界之中，卻又是永遠都逸出於任何象徵的捕捉、把握、界定。於是，看似弔詭地，「實在」如果穩定不變而可被說明完整就不是「實在」了，絕對意義的「實在」不存在這才是眞的「實在」。因此，它總是持續變動、不穩定、分裂、永遠有缺陷、裂隙，也是永遠開放、永遠存在可能性，沒法封閉的。

對中文世界的讀者而言，禪宗公案「以指指月，指非月」的隱喻應有助理解「語言」對「實在」的侷限。禪宗以「指」喻「言」，以「月」喻「道」，領會了就可忘「指」存「月」，但，這裡作為類比，還請讀者「指」、「月」皆忘，存「道」於心吧。至於「道」是什麼？則是「道」可道非常「道」，藉此隱喻以「道」類比「實在」，可被說盡就非「實在」了。（但也請小心，這裡只是借喻以利於理解高度抽象的「實在」，至於「實在」能不能眞拿來與中華文化中的「道」相提並論？還是請讀者保留給「分裂」、「裂隙」必然存在的開放空間，畢竟是不同文化脈絡的概念，可以對話但不宜簡化作等同對譯。）

從這樣看，「分裂」可能帶來解構、破裂、痛苦（甚至凝結為「症狀」），但另一面也可能帶來我們的開展與更新，歷史與文明正是在「分裂」中才有了不斷演化的機會，如此，「分裂」也可能是建設性的。因此，「分裂」不可避免，但重要的是「分裂」如何被人們理解？以及賦予「分裂」什麼樣的意義。

（二）「他者性」——人類主體的特徵

人類主體本身並不是獨立存在的個體，主體是由其自身與象徵符號所構成的「外部」世界的關係所特徵化的存在，這個「外部」世界也是「異

己他者」（'other'）共同存在的世界，作者表達為「Other」（譯作「大寫它／他者」，請注意，這意義不同於拉岡派詮釋者們常用的「大它者」，見下文說明），每個主體如何經驗並回應這個「大寫它／他者」就是他們主體性的一部分，就是在這個「大寫它／他者」中表現了人類是具有「他者性」（otherness）特徵的主體，個別主體與集體世界都是「社會關係的總合」。所以作者說：「一切屬於主體的事物都經由『大寫它／他者』，經由標誌著人類主體性的『他者性』的過程。」

作者在書中以及與譯者來回討論中提及他們批判性地沿用了一些拉岡學派的用語，作者表示對於拉岡學派來說，嬰兒透過學習言語的互動歷程進入社會關係世界，開始與照顧者建立關係，成為「大寫它／他者」領域的一部分，並在鏡映中與想像的自己相分裂，我們每個人都是與自己相分裂的、分離的、異於原初的「異己他者」，經由不斷分裂，逐漸區辨、分化與照顧者和其他人的不同，這是人皆有之的「原初異化」。但同時，我們也無意識地受制與「大寫它／他者」的關係方式。因此，構成和維持人類主體的所有內容都必須經由「大寫它／他者」，一切有關個別主體的都受制於他們與和外部世界間的關係，也就是「他者性」。

在「大寫它／他者」的象徵世界中，我們持續在體制、文化價值、意識形態的「象徵社會異化」中「分裂」，當它的壓迫性加劇，使主體客體化，主體經驗到壓抑、衝突，到展現為不滿、痛苦、甚至是「症狀」時，個人主義意識形態「心理學化」的「psy 專業」否認、忽視並掩蓋了這種來自象徵世界「大寫它／他者」對主體的異化，理性意識自我主導的「*精神分析*」是複製、鞏固「象徵社會的異化」，而非改善這種異化產生的處境，止於個人的「療癒」（實際上只是「撫慰」）然後把人再放回原來致使症狀發生的社會結構，這不是「改變」，而只是一種似變而實不變的「調適」、「適應」；而這正是基進精神分析的「欲望」有所不同之處，也是被異化的主體轉化為「革命性主體」尋求解放變革之處。

基進精神分析的治療目標並不放在「症狀」的消解（雖然不排除也可能連帶有這種「療效」），那是「psy 專業」的治療目標，但消解「症狀」只是似變而不變的「第一序改變」；基進精神分析的治療目標在於理解衝突、痛苦與壓抑之所以形成的「歷史構成」條件，以使改變支持問題存在

的條件成爲可能，進而改變條件以改變問題之所以發生的結構，這是「第二序改變」，是歷史質的改變。因爲辯證地理解，「症狀」被視爲「改變」的機會，革命性的基進精神分析的目標是使朝向不一樣的社會改變成爲可能，要與解放運動連結起來，所以作者說：「這是一項臨床任務，也是一項政治任務，所以說，臨床的本質是政治性的。」正是「個人即政治」、「臨床即政治」。

　　這裡有個重要必須說明的是，由於「Other」與「other」二字在字形上僅有大小寫的差異，爲使中文讀者易於區辨，特別爲「Other」的中譯冠上「大寫」一詞，雖然這是與作者討論後他所同意的，但不得不說這是個妥協的表達方式。事實上，作者並沒有在原文中加上「Big」，他並不像拉岡或齊澤克（Slavoj Žižek）那樣使用「Big Other」（中譯一般作「大它者」）來表達。作者在討論信件中說明他們基於兩個理由選擇不那樣表達：一是那會變成太過明顯拉岡式，他們並不希望這份宣言被誤解成一份「拉岡派精神分析的革命宣言」。二是作者認爲特別是在齊澤克使用「Big Other」（常見被譯作「大它者」）一詞上，固然這便於他將精神分析用於社會理論，但卻有使得「Other」太過於被想像爲是客觀既存在的歷史實體的危險。而這會使無意識其他面向的潛在意涵被單薄化，被看作只是對主體的壓迫，忽視「它我／他我」作爲是我們同體共生他者性的基質，也正承受意識自我的殖民、歧視與壓迫，同時也是我們集體團結奮鬥的資源。作者的觀點是：「無意識經由我們的言語而存在，在我們以言說主體的關係存在之前它並不存在。」這意味著，經由語言，我們固然一方面受制於象徵世界，但一方面我們也能藉由「語言」的改變，藉由無意識聯繫起來集體行動，改變被先前歷史中的「語言」形構的看似客觀實體存在的社會象徵，在歷史中建構一個不同於前的世界。所以作者說：「這對於精神分析的進步政治角色至關重要。如此，它可以幫助我們自身的復元，使我們從壓迫、抑制和鎮壓我們的集體存在與自由聯想的事物中解放出來。」

　　上面這個看似微細而實爲重大的差異，反映作著並非如同早期的「批判理論」將「歷史實在」想像爲一種「固定既存實體的『實在』」，而是一種主體與象徵世界參與互動的、變動性的「實踐觀」的「實在」。作者

並不是重複以「固定實體般的歷史文本」異化主體經驗的老套路，這一點，也反映在他們書中再三強調臨床實踐中，對其經驗作分析、解釋的人是「分析主體」（即當事人，請見「前言第 1 章」及註 3）而不是分析師。

正是「革命的主體性」使作者在這一系列「異己他者」（'other'）、「大寫它／他者」（'Other'）與「他者性」（'otherness'）的意義範疇超越了心理領域，涉及日常生活中處於脆弱邊緣位置上的人們；也指涉那些被認同政治、生命政治以及衍生管理與分配政策中被歧視、或者被削足適履地忽略而歸類納編於某種主流化中的主體；還指涉承認我們不是孤立獨存個體，生態中遙未相識的眾生容顏（face），是與我們集體休戚與共的倫理實踐對象。

四、關鍵概念的辯證重構

為了能在臨床實踐中連結「內部」與「外部」，除了將「無意識」從語言、分裂主體、他者性等進行一系列重構，使基進的精神分析有堅實的基石，從理性中心意識自我那兒將心理主體帶回「無意識」的領地之外，作者認為還需要對精神分析的重要概念：「重複」、「驅力」和「移情」進行辯證重構，因為它們的意義，已經在理性意識自我主導的「*精神分析*」那裡被去脈絡地化約，並且被意識形態地普適化「應用」，這樣被扭曲、破壞的「*精神分析*」本身成為解放運動的阻礙。

對於「無意識」部分的閱讀理解條件，在上述已作了相當的鋪陳。很重要的就是作者訴求的：堅持不再將我們同體共生的「無意識」視為深藏於個體內部的黑洞，「它我／他我」是我們主體存在和行動的關係網絡，是我們集體團結奮鬥的資源；同時，停止以任何階級、性／別、種族、意識形態繼續對「無意識」殖民。

對於「重複」、「驅力」和「移情」等關鍵概念，作者一一指出它們的辯證性，都存在看似矛盾的兩個面向，為讀者易於把握精髓，下面，就它們有別於主流既定概念之處以及作者的訴求，作簡要導引。

（一）「重複」

　　除了「強迫性重複」，我們也有「自由性的重複」。「自由性的重複」是我們在象徵世界有限的自由中，根據情境脈絡設計行動與反思，不輟地學習、修正、再創造的能力，是對「不同」的重複，而不是同樣老路的重複。「強迫性的重複」則是加劇的異化，只要我們沒能洞識這些結構，衝突的張力往往就以強迫的行為「症狀」形式被表達；或者，在政治領域，我們以為找到的解方總是令我們一再繞回原地，我們以為破框而出了，實質上前提的邏輯層次沒被覺察，只不過是一個似變而實不變的重複。

　　從政治權力的視角看，去政治是一種政治，精神分析的臨床實踐要面對自身的政治性，它可以是製造適應於新自由主義資本主義、父權與種族主義的空間、可以做許多似變而實不變的「治療」，但是如果那樣，就是選擇了將人類主體置於「強迫性的重複」之中的政治立場，作者訴求將臨床與解放運動連結起來，將臨床成為一個構建「不同」的世界的機會，一個轉向「自由性的重複」與社會變革的節點。

（二）「驅力」

　　因我們的「他者性」，有一種渴望與他人言說交流和行動的創造性、生產性的、集體關係的、以及性的「生之驅力」面向，以及另一種機械性的、惰性的、致命的、破壞性的和自我毀滅的「死之驅力」面向。但是，這兩種面向卻不是簡單二元對立的，而是辯證性地變動其性質，每個「生之驅力」都潛在地可能是「死之驅力」，相反地每個「死之驅力」也可能潛在地是另一個「生之驅力」。例如，資本既是激發勞動者創造性的活力——「生之驅力」，也在它追求利潤剝削勞動者的同時成了「死之驅力」。又如作者提及的：「在資本主義的腹地產生了推翻它的力量」，則使資本主義被推翻的「死之驅力」，相對地是世界秩序得以更新的「生之驅力」，使我們反抗的那股自發的力量就是「驅力」。

　　「驅力」並不是單獨生物性地存在，它在身體中但同時座落於語言文化之中，即使是確實有食、性生物面的需要，也是在語言文化下生成的，但它的意義沒法被任何語言符號表徵道盡，因為它來自「實在」自身。「驅力」表現的衝動看似出於「內部」但實際是與「外部」互動的，因

此，我們存在有異化下的驅力，例如資本主義下強迫性重複於商品消費的驅力，也存在有起而反抗的驅力。「驅力」可能被「壓抑」與「踰越」，性在精神分析之所以如此被關切的原因之一就是禁令規範與踰越、壓抑與煽惑、享樂與痛苦在性上如此緊密被連結。

　　然而，「驅力」在「壓抑」下也不僅只是被「壓迫」，它也可能組建出「欲望」。「欲望」是「驅力」轉向他者連結與被他者認可的渴望，是在「社會關係的總合」中與集體連結共同渴望創造想像的未來的力量。性在精神分析之被關切另一個原因是，性成為對權力傳遞與反叛的社會節點，它一則是體現了階級社會症狀的核心與宰制關係，一則是體現了從「壓抑」轉成反抗父權與資本主義的「欲望」。對於「驅力」，作者訴求我們不要再把它想像成個體內在的動物本能，而是在我們的語言裡體現為反抗異化與霸權的政治性「欲望」，對世界發聲，不再假裝客觀中立地「去政治」、不再沉默假裝沒問題而落入「無結構暴力」。

（三）「移情」

　　作者精準地重新定義「移情」為「欲望和權力的結構性現象從一個領域轉移到另一個領域」，「移情」既發生在臨床之內也在外部世界。因為「移情」會精確地反映主體涉及欲望與權力結構中的關係模式，它被精神分析臨床用作一種召喚權力關係的投影而現身，「分析主體」得以對權力採取重複或不同的回應，且進行自己的分析進而取得可能的洞察與解放的能動性；因為「移情」作為一種結構性複製的性質，這種欲望和權力的「結構」一直在我們的關係網絡與象徵世界之間轉移、複製，不論是意識形態的常識、科技理性、個人主義、資本主義的剩餘分配模式及各種文化慣例等，任何結構都是透過在整個社會領域中複製並傳遞到家庭與組織。而權力與欲望間的關係更是辯證而雙重矛盾的：欲望既被權力壓制也被它激發，權力既被欲望維持也被它顛覆。在社會生活與臨床中發生的移情內容平行反映著性的欲望受制於父權家庭內的禁令壓抑與激發，以及對父權規範的順應、維持或踰越、顛覆。

　　作者再三強調，為了「分析主體」能消解令其異化痛苦的壓迫性權力，分析師要保持大量的沉默，不作解釋，必須是由分析主體作分析、解

釋，反抗的欲望才有機會轉爲行動的力量，這只能由自己取得而不能被傳授。分析師一但站上「專家」、「知者」的位置進行分析，就立即複製了「分析主體」與權力結構間的關係模式。

　　假設問題只是在家庭或個人「內部」，把「移情」看作是早年關係在與分析師關係中的轉移，依樣畫葫蘆的去脈絡「應用」，對「分析主體」（及其家庭）施予實際上是父權意識形態的「伊底帕斯化」，以臨床指導實際上是「內」「外」交相映的政治性關係，還試圖能使臨床所得的成果再轉移、複製到「外部」複雜的政治領域互動中，這既是簡化、誤用了「移情」，從政治領域視角看，這種「應用」，這種意識形態的普適化，也正是分析師自身的父權化關係模式無意識地「移情」到臨床中對「分析主體」的強加，同時這導致對「分析主體」本是具有鮮明的政治性的「抗拒／抵抗」作狹猥的曲解和誤認，「症狀」或是「病」也只被視爲「不適應」，臨床就落得成爲爲既存意識形態壓迫性結構維穩的「好公民」製造暨維修廠。

　　「移情」需要被歷史辯證地重構，任何臨床的「專業知識」有其脈絡性，不可「應用」於「分析主體」甚至指導政治領域及解放運動，跳脫中立、客觀、「科學」與「去政治」的假裝，重新認識「症狀」與「病」作爲「抗拒／抵抗」權力結構的政治性武器與「藥」，讓分析主體自陳其分析，這是作者對「移情」的訴求。

五、辯證揚棄

　　這節，定位精神分析作爲解放運動的一個歷史過程，並回應作爲與解放運動結合的基進精神分析對人類未來世界圖像的勾畫。

（一）當前精神分析之「不可能」

　　作者指出，當前我們生活在一個「需要」精神分析但卻「不可能」取得的世界，這一則是因爲它已成私有化且昂貴的收費只服務於少數付得起的人；再則是因爲精神分析連同它的關鍵概念都已遭扭曲破壞，「無意識」被異化成對意識自我的威脅，欲殖之、制之甚至除之而後快；「重

複」只剩牢籠般的「重複性強迫」；「驅力」如一台致死的機器；而「移情」被變質成早年依賴關係的複製而不是政治抵抗的節點，臨床因而實際上成了製造並維持這個世界的問題於不變，甚至是問題加劇的結構性「溫床」。

歸結起來，現今主流個人主義理性意識自我的「*精神分析*」已去除了革命性並與資本主義及其連結的父權與種族主義合謀共構，它本身是大有問題的，它本身就是問題的共同建構者，它的問題即是反映這個世界的問題。我們需要的精神分析是能與解放運動連結起來的精神分析，在這個精神分析有需要但不可能的世界，我們要改變世界，就同時要改變主流的「*精神分析*」以及它所屬的「psy 專業複合體」（'psy complex'）。

這本「宣言」就是作者使用革命基進的精神分析來實現對保守適應的「*精神分析*」的「辯證揚棄」，也就是藉由改造並超越當前的「*精神分析*」，使精神分析之「不可能」被克服，然後使精神分析被需要的處境條件被取消，使世界不再需要精神分析。

（二）朝向精神分析「可能」但「不需要」的未來

如同解放運動一路充滿陷阱，精神分析也是；不只是前述的意識形態普適化「應用」或在臨床中落入權力與欲望糾結複製了壓制性的結構，作者還提示了一些發生在臨床空間之外以及可能的未來的重大陷阱。

作者提醒我們，基進的精神分析臨床確實能為主體打開解放的潛在空間，但它的真正潛力仍是要被落實在臨床之外的政治領域，只有實現將私領域化作公共的、集體的、具變革性的解放行動，才可能有真正的改變；如果只停留在臨床內所謂的「療癒」，對原本壓制性的「結構」「知」而不「行」，這種「療癒」本身是對同受結構之苦的「異己他者」的一種「無結構暴力」，或者，即使採取解放行動，但幻想一勞永逸地擺脫壓迫我們的結構，徹底釋放出來，從此走上康莊大道，這種個人「療癒」的「欲望」只是一時假裝超越權力，其實仍是對權力的維持，權力就一再使欲望被壓制又激起，可以一直玩著「第一序」似變而實不變的重複套路的遊戲。這是精神分析的陷阱之一。作者提醒我們歷史／過去永遠不會完全離我們而去，歷史構成的重複不會停止，並且與人類文化不可分離，精神分析治療

的終止意味著繼續的不停息的奮鬥的開始，革命也是一樣，當一個簡單的政治勝利作爲結束時，革命會失敗，我們必須不停地克服陷阱，才能繼續前進。

　　另一個陷阱與這有關，那就是幻想存在一個完全自由、不再有衝突的烏托邦，作者直言對精神分析或革命宣稱或承諾「有完全的自由」是騙人的。我們只能透過覺察到阻礙我們自由的原因來進行解放，另一個更好的世界是可能的，但不是那種虛假的未來。

　　還有一個陷阱是，錯把精神分析當永世的福音，對它擁抱、傳播、熱切執迷，以爲只有它能有作用，以弘揚它爲畢生志業。不論是作爲分析主體的或是作爲分析師的，不論任何人，當我們把錯「工具／方法」本身當作是「目的／結果」時，我們永遠到不了眞正想去的地方，這讓我們又落入「第一序改變」的遊戲中。這特別是這個「心理熱」的時代需要反思的。

　　精神分析作爲一種被發明出來的「工具／方法」，是現代歷史特有的產物，它出現在資產階級興起的歐陸，被用來處理這種特定社會脈絡中反映於個人的身心「症狀」，在晚期現代性的當前歷史處境中正切合我們的需要，但也因爲這種歷史特性，它也會在未來歷史質轉變歷程中，在解放運動完成階段性任務時，歷史條件不同，需要不同時，成爲過往歷史；這就是「辯證揚棄」。

　　一個關於「辯證揚棄」較易懂（但不見得足夠適切）的比喻是「馬上得天下，不能馬上治天下」，我們使用精神分析是爲了當前結構世界的痛苦和「症狀」得到理解，進而改變使結構得以有效運作的條件，追求的是歷史質的「第二序」改變，當前需要精神分析表示歷史質的「典範轉移」還沒成形，痛苦和「症狀」仍待轉化爲集體解放政治的資糧，我們不應本末倒置，爲了「工具／方法」而荒謬地刻意用力維持痛苦問題滋長的結構，也不應在需要其它「工具／方法」開拓未來歷史時還緊抓不放。沒有任何方法能被普適地「應用」於不同的歷史條件與需要中，作爲歷史產物的精神分析也一樣。

　　所以作者表明，解放運動「不需要被精神分析的概念所註解、辯護、證明，更不需要它來指揮……解放運動必須在前進的過程中保持道路暢通，確定方向……」解放運動不只是可以使用精神分析，也絕不能只用

精神分析；對於主體而言，也是一樣，主體轉化也並不只有精神分析方法，參與到政治性變革的轉化實踐中，也能直接帶來主體的解放。

（三）未來世界的圖像

那麼，一個精神分析欲望朝向的未來世界、一個使它實現對其自身辯證揚棄成為可能的世界究竟是怎樣的圖像呢？作者這樣勾畫：

「另一個世界是可能的，這是一個我們自由相互聯繫的世界，在這個世界中，每個人的自由發展是所有人的自由發展的條件。」

「每個人的自由發展是所有人的自由發展的條件」來自馬克思為建立一個替代舊階級社會的新世界願景所描述的一段話。是的，作者說得直接了當、精簡有力：「這另一個世界就是我們所稱的 'communism'」。請容譯者先保留英文原文來討論這個世界的關鍵「能指」，目的是希望爭取像譯者一樣生長在臺灣的讀者對這個「能指」給出重新認識的空間。

'communism' 一詞在中文世界譯作「共產主義」概無爭議，但它究竟是什麼意思？它的字首 commun-（也作 common-）意思是公共、共同體，因此，'communism' 原意是「以社區、社群和社會作為共同體的思想主張」，讀者大概不難與禮運大同篇天下為公、世界大同的理想相連結起來，這確實也是作者貫穿這份宣言的政治立場。不過，這個 'communism'「能指」跨洲越洋從西方來到亞細亞，它的真正意義因二十世紀迄今的國際地緣政治分斷格局，在非社會主義地區（特別是臺灣）遭到意識形態的扭曲、貶抑、化約、毀損與毒化，多數人民普遍沒有條件真實地知道它是什麼，得到的片面印象往往被與獨裁、反人性、反民主、反自由，甚至貪腐的印象以及體制失敗、普遍貧窮相連結。但，我們必須面對這樣的認知及印象是在壓制、禁令與不足的社會歷史條件下，不斷地被生產與封閉地再生產。

譯者為正確把握作者使用 'communism' 的完整意義，又為盡可能爭取讀者開放的閱讀理解空間，避免太快落入既定意識形態的解讀，曾一度考慮以「社群主義」或「共產／社群主義」作表達，但仔細研究後發現一則「社群主義」已被另一個符號（能指）'Communitarianism' 的中譯給占用了，與作者 Ian Parker 討論 'Communitarianism' 的內涵與實踐，既與

'communism' 似是而非，又與中文「社群主義」望文生義所傳達的意象相差甚遠，Parker 指出「'Communitarianism' 的問題在於它假裝在一個社群中跨階級運作，卻掩蓋了勞動者的階級鬥爭（而這正是 'communism' 關注的問題）；此外，在英國兩個標榜 'Communitarianism' 的政黨中，實際上都帶有仇外心理的危險性，例如，社會民主黨是一個不批評資本主義的小型自由黨，而愛爾蘭北部的民主統一黨是一個忠於英國王室（主要是新教徒）的政黨，捍衛其「自由主義」卻反對融入愛爾蘭（並反對天主教徒）。」（20230209 Parker 電郵）復又探跡索隱，問學於賢達，意外得知孫中山先生對共產主義的討論，原來三民主義中的民生主義就是共產主義，就是社會主義，就是大同主義。摘錄孫先生在民生主義第一及二講中的幾句金言（取自國父紀念館中山學術資料庫）：

「……故民生主義就是社會主義，又名共產主義，即是大同主義。」

「共產主義是民生的理想，民生主義是共產的實行；所以兩種主義沒有什麼分別，要分別的還是在方法。」

「民生主義就是共產主義，就是社會主義。所以我們對於共產主義，不但不能說是和民生主義相衝突，並且是一個好朋友，主張民生主義的人應該要細心去研究的。」

「殊不知民生主義就是共產主義。」

「民生主義，目的就是要把社會上的財源弄到平均。所以民生主義就是社會主義，也就是共產主義，不過辦法各有不同。我們的頭一個辦法，是解決土地問題。」

「這種民生主義就是共產主義。所以國民黨員既是贊成了三民主義，便不應該反對共產主義。因為三民主義之中的民生主義，大目的就是要眾人能夠共產。」

「我們要拿外國已成的資本，來造成中國將來的共產世界，能夠這樣做去，才是事半功倍。」

「我們要解決中國的社會問題，和外國是有相同的目標。這個目標，就是要全國人民都可以得安樂，都不致受財產分配不均的痛苦。要不受這種痛苦的意思，就是要共產。所以我們不能說共產主義與民生主義不同。我們三民主義的意思，就是民有、民治、民享。這個民有、民治、民享的

意思，就是國家是人民所共有，政治是人民所共管，利益是人民所共用。照這樣的說法，人民對於國家不只是共產，一切事權都是要共的。這才是真正的民生主義，就是孔子所希望之大同世界。」

　　這些孫中山先生關於「共產主義」的說明從不在學校的三民主義教本中，對長成於臺灣熟背三民主義教本應試得力的譯者而言，在被政治歷史隔絕大半生後，這是個石破天驚的發現，感謝這個意外的過程，譯者得以接續起被地緣政治意識形態與戰爭撕裂的歷史，也為這一個 'communism'「能指」在這本「宣言」中譯版，創造了這樣的表達方式，譯作「共產主義／大同主義」。但願這個蘊涵歷史政治脈絡的中文新「能指」，能為中文世界，特別是臺灣地區的讀者撐開對本書作歷史辯證性閱讀的空間。

致謝

　　穿越疫情三年，本書中文版譯注暨導讀迄今始告尾聲，整個工作的完成，要感謝很多人，夏林清教授與五南圖書王俐文女士開關批判心理學系列，臺灣行動研究學會高旭寬、王卓脩、陳文賢與李憶微四位老師們參與到協同討論與費心的潤稿工作中、廉兮老師對中英對照出版的建議，擴展了這本書的可能性。以及，淡江大學王蔚婷老師在譯者時間擠壓中協助作者中文版序的初譯，佛光大學林明昌教授在偶然交談中知無不言地貢獻孫文留下的金聲玉振，在此致上深深的感謝。兩位作者為世界寫作這本宣言，並把版權無償獻給全人類；特別是 Ian Parker 教授對譯者無比耐心的等待與來回討論提問的立即回應和提供支持，為此謹代表臺灣批判實踐社群，也是台灣行動研究學會，致上最深的敬意。當前，國際政勢風雲詭譎，捲起千堆雪，在此覺醒時刻，此書的出版意義重大，而中文世界作為人類百年一遇之大變局的振動核心地域，譯者有幸擔綱中譯暨導讀任務，機遇畢生難逢，謹以此書中譯版的完成，與作者及各地的同志們共同參與到推進世界歷史變革的行列之中。

林香君

（2023）癸卯年四月於臺灣宜蘭佛光大學

精神分析地景簡述

　　精神分析作爲一種情緒困擾的理論與治療實務，是在十九世紀末的維也納爲佛洛伊德所發明，用以作爲主流醫療精神醫學治療的一種替代方案。佛洛伊德認爲，我們「壓抑」或將無法忍受的想法包括對創傷事件的記憶逐出意識，而這些無法忍受的想法仍繼續在我們當下的覺知之外無意識地運作。精神分析使病人（我們現在稱其爲分析主體（analysand）[1]）參與到試圖將被壓抑的想法轉變爲言語的嘗試之中。

　　遵循著「自由聯想」的基本技術規則，分析主體對著某個受過傾聽訓練的分析師談論幻想和夢境，如此，當分析主體聽到自己所說的話時，他們便能注意到那些他們所重複的，和那些驅使他們以自我毀滅的方式去思考和行爲的東西。儘管佛洛伊德和早期的精神分析學家經常做出解釋，但我們現在認識到若能由分析主體自己來做解釋才是最好的。第一批病人或者分析主體之中有一位名爲「安娜 O」，她將這個過程描述爲「談話治療」（'talking cure'）。

　　二十世紀初，佛洛伊德聚集了一群追隨者，這些人以多種不同的方式發展新的精神分析思想。同時，佛洛伊德與世界各地想要建立自己的精神分析學會的合作者們交往聯絡，這包括了亞洲。一個國際精神分析協會於1910 年在歐洲成立（卡爾・榮格（Carl Jung）擔任第一任主席）。

　　早期的精神分析辯論涉及不同形式的情緒困擾或「精神官能症」（'neurosis'）；這些困擾的形式包括：「強迫性精神官能症」（'obsessional neurosis'）──受苦者會不斷地思考或試圖不去思考，已經發生或可能發生的事；以及，「歇斯底里」（'hysteria'）──被壓抑的想法轉化爲身體的不適。早期的精神分析學家專注於童年的創傷、壓抑並在後來的生活中無意識地重複的經驗。佛洛伊德將焦點從實際的兒童性虐待轉移到幻想，他主張，這些幻想無意識地運作著，然後繼續驅動行爲。

　　維也納和歐洲大陸其他地區的許多精神分析學家都是猶太人，當納粹

---

[1] 「分析主體」（'analysand'）一詞的說明，請見本書正文「前言」該章註 3。

掌權時，精神分析被譴責爲「猶太科學」。佛洛伊德和許多其他精神分析學家逃往其他國家，這增進了辯論和實踐的國際化。佛洛伊德於 1939 年在倫敦流亡中去世。第二次世界大戰後，精神分析組織分裂，一些精神分析學家特別是在美國，將「談話治療」變成了精神醫學的一部分，與生理和藥物治療並用。在其他地方，有強調早期關係是後來情緒困擾的原因，或強調個體與語言的關係。一個核心問題是，精神分析應該促使人們適應社會（在美國經常就是這樣的情形），或是鼓勵人們對現有社會規範作出挑戰。

那些把重點關注於幫助人們適應社會的心理學教科書，聚焦於佛洛伊德和早期的精神分析學家，通常對精神分析提供有限且具有誤導性的說明。這些教科書中描述的早期另立門戶運動導致了有別於精神分析的處理困擾方法取向。阿爾弗雷德·阿德勒（Alfred Adler）發展了自己的「個體心理學」（'individual psychology'），淡化了性的重要性，強調了個人的自我力量。這種運動勢力現在非常小，在大多數國家已不存在。卡爾·榮格（曾在德國納粹心理治療組織工作）相信一個不可能的目標 —— 經驗的意識和無意識面向可以完全整合[2]，他並認爲一個專精的「分析心理學家」（'analytical psychologist'），應解釋普遍性的和種族特殊性的象徵，也就是解釋所謂的「集體無意識」（'collective unconscious'），這種導致治療師指導患者的方法取向並不是精神分析的。

許多形式的「保守性」（'conservative'）精神分析關注於適應 —— 促使人們成爲適合社會的好公民 —— 在世界各地發展起來。二戰後，精神分析學家在製定主要精神醫學手冊中的診斷分類方面發揮了重要作用，儘管他們的影響力現在已經減弱。在戰前和戰後，也有許多不同形式的「進步性」（'progressive'）精神分析與基進政治聯繫在一起，並採取不同的發

---

[2] 這裡依作者原文直接的譯法是：「卡爾·榮格（曾在德國納粹心理治療組織工作）認爲經驗的意識和無意識面向可以完全整合，一個不可能的目標，他並認爲……」，由於此順序在中文上易將「一個不可能的目標」誤讀爲也是榮格的意思，但，這與作者確認，這是作者表達他對於榮格相信意識與無意識可能完全整合的直接評論，故在中譯上，爲避免產生誤讀，以倒裝手法表達。

展路徑。

持左翼立場的精神分析學家，包括視西方核心家庭爲法西斯主義溫床的威廉‧賴希（Wilhelm Reich），以及專注於對自由的存在需求以及人們用來逃避這種自由的策略的埃里希‧弗洛姆（Erich Fromm）。還有其他非臨床實踐的理論家，例如赫伯特‧馬爾庫塞（Herbert Marcuse）和流亡德國的「法蘭克福學派」（'Frankfurt School'）的作者們，他們也運用精神分析的觀點來解釋爲什麼人們會被威權運動所吸引。

在世界不同地區執業的精神分析師，傾聽來自不同文化背景的人，必須考慮到不同的育兒模式。因此，基進的工作就包括了對種族主義的反殖民分析，當中最重要的是阿爾及利亞精神醫學家弗朗茨‧法農（Frantz Fanon）。女性經常被主流精神醫學和保守的精神分析學家視爲低劣、病態的，對此進行了反抗。傾聽著這些女性的聲音，基進精神分析家們受到女性主義政治的影響，這就是凱倫‧霍尼（Karen Horney）等分析家早期工作的影響力所在。國際精神分析協會（IPA）也分裂了，現在有許多不同的國際組織。

二次世界大戰期間 IPA 內部出現了三個主要的競爭支系，西格蒙德‧佛洛伊德的女兒安娜‧佛洛伊德（Anna Freud），強調人們用以避免思考他們的童年和關係方面的「防衛機制」（'defense mechanisms'）的作用，而這一系列工作和那些把注意力從無意識轉成以強化自我和適應性自我防衛機制爲目標的美國「自我心理學家」（'ego psychologists'）[3] 非常接近。對比於此，梅蘭妮‧克萊恩（Melanie Klein）的追隨者，則主張無可逃避的無意識本能力量導致人們對他人進行侵略性的、破壞的和偏執妄想的攻擊，或者可能在治療指導下，會進入對自己內在衝突的一種「憂鬱的」接受（'depressive' acceptance）狀態。另外，包括約翰‧鮑爾比（John Bowlby）和唐納德‧溫尼科特（Donald Winnicott）等第三支系則著重於「獨立」或「客體-關係」（'independent' or 'object-relations'），強調母

---

[3]　這裡的「自我」指的是 'ego'，在進入本書正文之後，爲避免與 'self' 在中譯上混淆（一般也譯作「自我」或「自體」，後者主要是客體關係論脈絡使用）相混淆，遂將 'ego' 譯作「意識自我」。

嬰關係的影響以及兩者之間的「依附」（'attachment'）形式。

　　在 IPA 之外，還有許多不同的路線，其中最突出的是由法國精神分析學家雅克‧拉岡（Jacques Lacan）的工作發展而來的取向，他試圖「回歸佛洛伊德」（'return to Freud'），包括返回佛洛伊德作品重新探究「創傷」是溯及既往的這個概念，也就是說，生命中後期的事件會觸發並製造早期的創傷經歷。拉岡認爲，精神分析的「談話治療」意味著視無意識即是一種如語言的結構，而且也不僅僅存在於個人的內部。此一從固定本質化的「本能」和固定的發展階段，轉變到文化型塑的「驅力」以及主體與語言的關係，激發了學術論壇（包括斯拉沃伊‧齊澤克（Slavoj Žižek）的著作）以及臨床實務（包括拉岡的追隨者雅各 - 阿蘭‧米勒（Jacques-Alain Miller）、派翠西亞‧格羅維奇（Patricia Gherovici）和內斯特‧布朗斯坦（Nestor Braunstein）的激烈論辯。

　　如今，雖然有一些以海因茨‧科哈特（Heinz Kohut）的工作爲基礎的不同的「自體心理學」（'self psychology'）取向，以及以斯蒂芬‧米切爾（Stephen Mitchell）的工作爲基礎的「關係精神分析」（'relational psychoanalysis'）支派，大多美國的精神分析仍然聲稱是一種「醫療的」（'medical'）治療。這與歐洲和拉丁美洲非常不同，許多精神分析學家視他們的工作爲外於醫學的替代選擇，就是一種「談話治療」，儘管仍有一些人與精神醫學和心理學密切相關。精神分析在一些國家很普遍，特別是阿根廷，以及猶太精神分析學家逃離納粹後所抵達的以色列。

　　許多對精神分析一無所知的人，受到電影及小說中流行的佛洛伊德概念影響，而以那樣的方式談論自己。關於創傷、被壓抑的記憶、無意識的作用、夢的意義以及在安全保密的環境中與他人交談的治療價值等想法，已經進入其他非精神分析的治療和日常生活中。某些治療非常反對這些概念，特別是精神醫學和認知行爲心理治療，這些治療避免談論過去。著名的心理治療傳統如「認知行爲療法（CBT）」（'Cognitive Behavioural Therapy'）和「理性情緒行爲療法（REBT）」（'Rational Emotive Behaviour Therapy'）分別由亞倫‧貝克（Aaron Beck）和亞爾伯特‧艾利斯（Albert Ellis）等人所開展，他們曾接受過精神分析師培訓，但爲順應對個別問題提供快速適應性解決的要求，都脫離了精神分析。

在當今的實際實務和理論中，「佛洛伊德」這個名字有很多不同的含義。它並不總是基進的，但對於精神分析曾經的基進，存在著一股隱隱「被壓抑的」記憶，一些精神分析學家仍然致力於使其與基進政治結盟。精神分析的基進歷史，以及它作為有別於主流「心理／精神相關專業」（'psy professions'）[4] 替代選擇的可能性，正是本宣言所要討論的。

伊恩・帕克

A brief sketch of the landscape of psychoanalysis

Psychoanalysis was invented as a theory of emotional distress and a practical treatment, as an alternative to mainstream medical psychiatry by Sigmund Freud in Vienna at the end of the nineteenth century. Freud argued that we 'repress' or push away out of consciousness unbearable thoughts, including memories of traumatic events, and that these unbearable ideas continue to operate unconsciously, out of our immediate awareness. Psychoanalysis involves the patient, whom we now refer to as the 'analysand', attempting to put repressed ideas into words.

The analysand speaks about fantasies and dreams, following the basic technical rule of 'free association', to someone, the analyst who is trained to listen, thus, and as the analysand hears themselves speak they are able to notice what they repeat and what drives them to think and behave in self-destructive ways. Although Freud and the early psychoanalysts often made interpretations, we now recognise that it is best if the analysand themselves does this. One of the first patients or analysands, known as 'Anna O', described the process as a 'talking cure'.

In the early years of the twentieth century, Freud gathered around him a group of followers who developed the new psychoanalytic ideas in many different ways, and he corresponded with colleagues around the world who wanted to set up their own psychoanalytic societies, including in Asia. An International Psychoanalytical Association was founded in Europe in 1910 (with Carl Jung as the first President).

The early psychoanalytic debates concerned different forms of emotional distress or 'neurosis'; these forms of distress included 'obsessional neurosis' in which the sufferer keeps thinking, or trying not to think, about what has happened or what may happen, and 'hysteria' in which the repressed ideas are converted into physical complaints. The early psychoanalysts focused on childhood experiences which become traumatic, and repressed, and repeated unconsciously later in life. Freud shifted focus from actual child sexual abuse to fantasies that, he argued, operated unconsciously, and that then continue to drive behaviour.

Many of the psychoanalysts in Vienna and other parts of continental Europe were Jews, and psychoanalysis was condemned as a 'Jewish science' when the Nazis came to power. Freud, and many other psychoanalysts, fled to other countries, and this increased the internationalisation of debate and practice. Freud died in exile in London in 1939. After the Second World War, psychoanalytic organisations divided, with some psychoanalysts, especially in the United States turning the 'talking cure' into part of psychiatry, operating alongside physical and drug treatments. In other places there was an emphasis on early relationships as the cause of later emotional distress or on the relation of the individual to language. A key question was whether psychoanalysis should adapt people to society, which was often the case in the United States, or whether psychoanalysis should encourage a challenge to existing social norms.

Psychology textbooks, which are mainly concerned with helping people adapt to society, usually provide a limited and misleading account of psychoanalysis, focusing on Freud and early psychoanalysts. The early breakaway movements described in these textbooks led to approaches to distress that departed from psychoanalysis. Alfred Adler developed his own 'individual psychology' which downplayed the importance of sexuality and emphasised individual ego strength; this movement is now very small, non-existent in most countries. Carl Jung (who worked with the Nazi psychotherapy organisation in Germany) believed that the conscious and unconscious aspects of experience could be fully integrated, an impossible goal, and that an expert 'analytical psychologist' should interpret universal and racially-specific symbols in the so-called 'collective unconscious' of the patient. This approach, which leads to the therapist guiding the patient, is not psychoanalytic.

Many forms of 'conservative' psychoanalysis concerned with adaptation, making people fit into society as good citizens, developed around the world. Psychoanalysts played an important role in formulating the diagnostic categories in the main psychiatric handbooks after the Second World War, though their influence has now waned. There were also, before and after the War, many different forms of 'progressive' psychoanalysis that made links with radical politics, and these have taken different paths.

Psychoanalysts who remained on the left included Wilhelm Reich, who saw the Western nuclear family as a seed-bed for fascism, and Erich Fromm who focused on existential needs for freedom and on the strategies that people use for avoiding that freedom. There were other theorists who did not practice clinically, such as Herbert Marcuse and writers in the 'Frankfurt School' in exile from Germany, who also drew on psychoanalytic ideas to explain why people were attracted to authoritarian movements.

Psychoanalysts practising in different parts of the world, listening to people from different cultures, had to take into account different patterns of child-rearing. The radical strand of work thus included anti-colonial analyses of racism, most importantly by the Algerian psychiatrist Frantz Fanon. Women who had often been treated as inferior, pathological, by mainstream psychiatry and then also by conservative psychoanalysts, rebelled. Radical psychoanalysts listening to these women were influenced by feminist politics and this is where the earlier work of analysts like Karen Horney were influential. The International Psychoanalytic Association, IPA, also split, and there are now many different international organisations.

Inside the IPA, three main competing strands of work emerged during the Second World War. Sigmund Freud's daughter, Anna Freud, emphasised the role of 'defence mechanisms' that people use to avoid thinking about aspects of their childhood and relationships, and this strand of work was very close to that of the US-American 'ego psychologists' who shifted attention to from the unconscious to the goal of strengthening the ego and adaptive ego defence mechanisms. Followers of Melanie Klein, in contrast, argued that there were unavoidable unconscious instinctual forces that led people into aggressive destructive and paranoid attacks on others or, with therapeutic guidance, into a 'depressive' acceptance of their internal conflicts. A third 'independent' or 'object-relations' strand, which included John Bowlby and Donald Winnicott, emphasised the impact of the relationship between mother and baby, and the forms of 'attachment' between the two.

Outside the IPA, there have been many varied approaches, including most prominently, those developed from the work of the French psychoanalyst Jacques Lacan. His attempt to 'return to Freud' included retrieving from Freud's work the idea that 'trauma' is retroactive; that is, that events later in life will trigger and make traumatic early experiences. Lacan argued that the psychoanalytic 'talking cure' entails a view of the unconscious

as being structured like a language and so also as not only being inside the inside the individual. That shift from wired-in 'instincts' and fixed developmental stages to culturally-
shaped 'drives' and the relation of the subject to language provoked psychoanalytic debate
in academic forums (including the work of Slavoj Žižek) as well as in clinical practice
(including followers Jacques-Alain Miller, Patricia Gherovici and Nestor Braunstein).

Today, much psychoanalysis in the United States still claims to be a 'medical' treatment, though there are alternative 'self psychology' approaches following the work of
Heinz Kohut and 'relational psychoanalysis' strands of work that follow the work of
Stephen Mitchell. This is very different from Europe and Latin America where there are
many psychoanalysts who see their work as an alternative to medicine, as a 'talking cure',
though there are still some who are closely connected with psychiatry and psychology.
Psychoanalysis is popular in some countries, particularly in Argentina, and in Israel where
Jewish psychoanalysts arrived after fleeing from the Nazis.

Many people who know nothing about psychoanalysis as such talk about themselves
in ways that are influenced by Freud's ideas, which became popularised through film and
novels. Ideas about trauma, repressed memories, the role of the unconscious, the meaning
of dreams and the therapeutic value of speaking to another person in a safe confidential
setting have found their way into other non-psychoanalytic treatments and into everyday
life. Some treatments are very hostile to these ideas, particularly psychiatric and cog-
nitivebehavioural psychological treatments. These treatments avoid speaking about the
past. Well-known traditions of psychological treatment, such as 'Cognitive Behavioural
Therapy' (CBT) and 'Rational Emotive Behaviour Therapy (REBT) were developed by
figures, such as Aaron Beck and Albert Ellis, who were trained as psychoanalyst but who
broke from psychoanalysis in order to conform to the demand for quick adaptive solutions
to individual problems.

In its actual present-day practice and theory, the name 'Freud' means many different
things. It has not always been radical, but there is a hidden 'repressed' memory of what
psychoanalysis has been, and some psychoanalysts are still committed to make it work in
alliance with radical politics. The radical history of psychoanalysis and its possibilities as
an alternative to mainstream 'psy professions' is what this manifesto is about.

Jan Parker

目 錄

CONTENTS

前言

　　這份宣言是為解放運動、為了更美好的世界而寫的。它是針對那些對抗我們這個時代的壓迫、剝削和異化的現實的個人和群體所寫的。它關注當今悲慘的外部現實與我們的「內在」（'internal'）生活之間的相互關係，這個「內在」生活，即我們所謂的「心理」（'psychology'），感覺上好像深藏「於我們之內」（'within us'），似乎不是頻頻向現實低頭屈從，就必得是——我們希望是——起而反抗現實。為了他人和我們自己的理由，我們必須反抗。

　　有時我們感到自己的反抗力不從心、無以抒解、沒法化作行動，那彷彿是某種啃噬著我們的內心的東西，它可能嚴重影響到我們的生活，然後我們可能就被告知我們有某種心理障礙。

　　許多問題被社會、被大眾文化以及受過專業訓練的人士如心理學家、精神科醫生和其他各種「心理／精神相關」專業人士（'psy' professionals）[1] 化約為個人心理層次的問題，這些問題感覺起來真的很像是「心理的」，但其實不是。我們應該如何政治化這些問題呢？如何能夠對那些感覺上像是「裡面的」（'inside'）但實際上是根源自「外面的」（'outside'）問題進行對抗呢？

　　個人「內在的」（'inner'）世界與社會「外在的」（'outer'）世界之

---

[1] 'psy' 是心、靈、精神和心理的共同字根，作者用 'psy' profession 表達涉及這些內涵的相關專業領域，亦於第 6 章中使用 'psy-complex' 表達綜合此一相關專業的網絡，在《致中文者序》中也以 'psy disciplines' 指涉精神醫學、心理學和心理療法等「心理／精神相關學科」。故 'psy professionals' 即指這些相關領域的專業人士，包括心理學家、使用心理治療理論從事心理治療、諮商／諮詢、輔導的工作者、精神分析師、精神分析出現之前以物理性治療精神症狀的醫生、精神病理學家、精神科醫師，以及涉及靈性（spiritual）的工作者。由於中文語境中沒能找到可把這諸多概念包含於一個對應 'psy' 的詞彙，與作者討論，直譯為「心理／精神相關」專業（'psy' profession）、「心理／精神相關專業複合體」（'psy-complex'）、「心理／精神相關」專業人士（或人員）（'psy' professionals）。

間的關係對解放運動而言至關重要，這也就是爲什麼這些運動可以受益於
這種最初作爲一種臨床取徑而被發展的精神分析，該方法花了一個多世紀
的時間來了解現實和我們每個人內心深處之間的密切關聯；我們必須藉助
各種包括精神分析在內的不同途徑來了解這種相互關聯的性質。我們這樣
做是爲了與壓迫、剝削和異化我們的事物作鬥爭，同時也是爲了不同於資
本主義、性別歧視、種族主義和新殖民主義的形式，建設一條切實可行的
替代出路。

精神分析

　　什麼是精神分析？精神分析是西格蒙德・佛洛伊德（Sigmund
Freud）於十九世紀末在歐洲發明的一種治療實踐，作爲一種有別於主流
醫學精神病學（medical psychiatric approaches）[2] 治療痛苦的替代方法，精
神分析師不再讓處於困境中的人接受監禁、可怖的身體處遇和藥物，而
是在他們的診療所會見他們的個案或病人 —— 我們稱其爲「分析主體」
（'analysand'）[3]，他們的任務是去**聆聽**（listen to）這個說話的主體，爲這
個分析主體提供一個特殊而隱蔽的空間，讓他們談他們的痛苦，並在他們
自己的言語（speech）中聽見過去與現在之間的關聯，聽見那些他們前所
未聞的關聯。

---

[2] Psychiatry（形容詞 psychiatric）可譯爲精神病學或精神醫學（的），本文視脈
　　絡及閱讀的流暢性交替使用。在此，「主流醫學精神病學」指的主要是相對於
　　精神分析「談話治療」而以對身體施以水浸、電療等幾近酷刑爲特徵（當然也
　　有用藥）的舊醫學精神醫療。當今新的醫學精神醫療則是奠基於生化藥物的發
　　展。

[3] 'analysand' 指的是帶著痛苦或症狀來見精神分析師的當事人，作者強烈主張他
　　們才是作出分析與解釋的人。作者強調經由創造一個可讓當事人說出任何話
　　的特殊空間，當事人是治療中爲自己作出解釋的主體，解釋不能出於精神分析
　　師，那是對精神分析的錯誤使用，一旦由精神分析師給出解釋，就複製了權力
　　關係。作者於本書第 5 章中有更詳細的論述。由於在中文語境中，考量如果
　　將此一字詞照一般慣用直譯作「受分析者」時，恰恰與作者意圖表達的意義相
　　違，與作者討論後，在中文語境中創造「分析主體」一詞。

　　流行電影中分析主體躺在長沙發上的經典印象是眞的，但分析師作筆記然後下診斷且給予明智解釋這部分則是一種誤導。精神分析爲作爲言語主體的分析主體打開一個空間，使他們最終給出令他們感到眞實的解釋，然後以此作爲「洞察」（'insight'）和改變的動力。精神分析可以僅僅針對分析主體帶著來見分析師的「症狀」（'symptom'）作處理，它也可以爲分析主體帶來生命的改變。在本宣言中我們虛心地提出我們的精神分析主張，但我們確信這是有別於精神醫學和心理學的一個進步的治療性替代方案，我們將會解釋原因。

　　在以下各章中，我們將描述精神分析的關鍵要素，我們會聚焦在**無意識**（unconscious）的觀念，展示我們的生活如何無意識地重複著模式然後又複製於臨床之中；我們指出這種時而自我挫敗和痛苦的**重複**（repetition）模式是如何表達一種可能爲生或爲死而運作的**驅力**（drive），以及這種重複如何在臨床中被精神分析師以**移情**（transference）來進行處理。我們之所以堅持臨床要扎根在這四個要素上是因爲精神分析已經出現並發展爲一種臨床方法，並不是因爲我們試圖鼓吹精神分析治療或將其推薦給我們的讀者。相反地，我們的目的是爲了要突顯我們認爲在精神分析中潛藏的革命性內涵，以及它如何在當前的鬥爭中爲解放運動服務。

　　我們在此的旨趣乃著眼於精神分析具進步性與革命性的政治效益，而不是要來傳播精神分析理論或臨床實務，儘管我們的討論確實包含了將「臨床」（'clinic'）接合爲政治性實踐的潛在進步空間。這份宣言並不是要介紹精神分析，這不是諸多精神分析導論書籍的又一本，而是論證精神分析與革命的聯繫。如果我們的讀者願意，可以在其他介紹精神分析的文本中閱讀更多關於該方法和理論的內容，但請記得我們關於精神分析被改編和扭曲的形式的諸多提醒。

　　另一個世界是可能的，而精神分析是我們現在需要實現這個目的的一種寶貴的工具，使用精神分析作爲這樣的工具並不意味著導入精神分析意識形態到我們的鬥爭形式中，或是去想像它將永遠與我們同在，精神分析以一種可爲我們所用的特定形式出現，當它的工作完成時它也將會消失。

　　在本宣言，我們的任務是將精神分析重構成一個眞正的「**批判心理學**」（'critical psychology'）並將它作爲解放運動的一個有效資源。你會

看到我們對心理學以及所有的心理／精神相關專業（psy profession）非常嚴厲的批判。精神分析被辯證性地理解、承認其錯誤並強調其優勢，這引領我們逸出其他路數。

我們堅信，爲了有用於解放運動，精神分析必須批判和改造自身。考慮這些運動的特殊需要，在此我們要檢驗無意識、重複、驅力和移情在臨床與政治分析及實踐中的角色與作用，以解決主體的改變與現實轉化的問題。雖然我們不迴避理論問題，但**實踐**（*practice*）才是關鍵所在，而我們能從精神分析臨床實踐所學到的東西乃與解放實踐相聯繫。

革命

爲反資本主義、反父權制、反種族主義和反殖民運動所構想的解放目的將始終出現在這份宣言的視野中；以下篇章便是胸懷此志爲解放運動而寫成。這些運動反對剝削和壓迫，我們堅定地與它們站在一起。我們的精神分析也與「反對的」（'negative'）、「對抗的」（'anti'）、以及我們內在使我們能夠反抗的力量同聲相應。並且，和這些政治性運動相同，我們的精神分析也爲人類主體的本性打開了積極的面向——包括評估、反思和有能力去改變，使世界更利於創造和變革。

這份宣言寫成於政治經濟危機深重之時，作爲我們人類共同居住的象徵世界[4]（the symbolic world）正在受到攪亂和動盪，而我們能夠爲自己想

---

[4]　象徵，也有譯作符號（但學術上也有將兩者區分的討論），象徵世界是指人們共同構建的一個符號系統，它包括了人們的語言、文化、價值觀、信仰等等，這些形成於歷史之中，就是無意識，人類的思想、行爲和情感等方面在不知不覺中受著深刻的牽引，當然當它被人們所覺知時，它也能被改變，作者也以 Other（譯作「大寫它／他者」）表達（此用法與拉岡派的其他詮釋者之間存在著微細卻重要的差異，請見導讀），是貫穿全書的重點。

讀者於本節將會看到作者將「象徵」（'symbolic'）、「想像」（'imagine'）與「實在」（'real, the real'）嵌於文句中，接觸過拉岡精神分析的讀者不難看出作者拉岡主義的背景，固然作者於本書《背景閱讀》中表明拉岡對他們有重要的影響（當然，他們也對其有所批判），由於這份旨在解放運動的「宣言」有其主體位置與目的，作者並不希望這份宣言太過拉岡式表現，作者選擇將其語

像創造的未來世界受到了難以捉摸的實在的物質力量的衝擊和威脅，這些力量完全超出了我們的控制。我們人類存在的深不可測的生物基質——我們那無法知曉的本性，在這樣的時刻湧入我們的象徵宇宙，當此之時，它加劇了我們所遭受的社會矛盾，如果我們要抵抗並存活下來，我們就必須理解和克服這些矛盾。面對這樣的危險，我們越是分隔割裂就越加脆弱。

例如，致命的病毒對我們世界上所有人都是威脅，但是它的到來非常清楚地表明並非我們所有人都一起受到同等的衝擊，那些所謂「低度開發」國家（'less developed' countries）的人們遭受更多的苦難，那些已受苦於種族主義的人們大量地死去，而婦女如果有被限制在家中的情形，會更容易遭受到暴力攻擊。每一個受到壓迫的群體——那些被社會致使其障礙的人們、那些已被它弱化了的人們、已病了的人們，會更加可能致死。

這份宣言寫於封城[5]之際，於作者之間來回往復並諮詢世界各地的同志們，這裡面包含了一些常被認為是「困難」（'difficult'）的概念，也因這個理由往往避而不談，這些概念不易變成簡單敘事形式的通俗讀本。您將會看到我們一再圍繞著主要的概念，我們在文本的不同重點處以略微不同的方式重複關鍵的主張，以使它們更加清晰。每種被書寫下的語言都是一種翻譯（translation）形式，現在我們希望您將其翻譯到實踐中。

大多數人類都處在新自由主義資本家所青睞的那種「休克資本主義」（'shock capitalism'）[6]的危險中，因為它有利於資本家們。這種形式的資

　彙嵌入文句之中並使用小寫表達，在攜帶源自拉岡式符號中，撐開再賦新義的可能空間，也使讀者不必受限於拉岡術語的門檻。基於此，在中譯上也避免直接的拉岡式專有術語，謹於本節貼合著作者在文句中使用到的拉岡語彙包括現實（reality）與「象徵」、「想像」及「實在」引出三個界域與現實世界之間的關係時，為想更多知道這些語彙在拉岡的原義的讀者作簡要說明（請見本節註8）。

[5]　這份宣言英文原版寫成於 COVID-19 世界疫情嚴峻各國關境封城之際，英文版於 2021 年 9 月由倫敦 1968 出版社（1968 Press）發行；在此前，已展開全球十六種語言地區的譯本工作，最先發行的是 2021 年 8 月俄文譯版（Horizontal Publishers 出版），接著是義大利文版，較英文原版更早出版。

[6]　這裡採直接音譯，也可譯作「震撼資本主義」，與中文世界常聽到的「休克療法」、「休克主義」、「災難資本主義」等詞意相通。

本主義與以前的資本主義形式一樣但規模更大，沒有它滋生出來的危機就無法運作。對於得到利益的人來說，任何理由都是進入危機模式的好藉口。

　　從實在[7]（the real）爆發出來的危機確實令人震驚，它震撼了我們的核心，而精神分析最能把握這個實在（real）、對發生在我們身上的事情我們所嘗試的想像（imagine）、以及我們所共享的象徵宇宙（the symbolic universe）三者之間的緊密關聯[8]。把握這種關聯需要一種意識形態批判，

---

[7]　在此上下文脈絡中，'the real' 可譯作「實在」或「真實」，並非指現實世界（reality），是個較為抽象的概念，可理解為「存在」發生的本身（因此，它不是任何可被說明的「存在」形式或「現實」，它可被理解為所有如果任何「存在」形式或「現實」看不見的背景，是彷彿虛無又是真空妙「有」或妙「無」的，對中文世界讀者也或可以「道」來作想像。）考量本書另一個概念 'truth' 在特定上下文脈絡中也譯作「真實」，為中文讀者不被混淆，選擇將此脈絡中的 real 譯作「實在」，但是，這個「實在」不可想像為「實存」（這是對彷彿是實體有固定形態甚至可量測事物的存在的描述，作者表示這是佛洛伊德開始的革命性精神分析所拒絕的「心理」想像）。

[8]　作者在句中嵌入的「實在」、「想像」及「象徵」，源自拉岡語彙，對應於「實在界」（或常被譯作「真實界」）、「想像界」、與「象徵界」，為想更多了解這三個者詞所攜帶的原本意涵及它們與「現實」（'reality'）的關係的讀者，簡要說明於下：
- 「現實」是指日常生活中的種種，需經由「象徵」與「想像」的組織，否則無法理解。
- 「象徵界」指的是將現實世界中的種種現象加以篩選、組織並賦予符號特定意義概念或架構所形成的世界，這不僅運作於心理與思維層面，更是在語言運作的文化與社會中，包括法律、體制、習俗、倫理及道德規範，以及文化與社會中的種種事物。
- 「想像界」是指我們想像他人眼中照見的我們以及我們理想的鏡像。
- 「實在界」，在「象徵界」之內，但它是「象徵界」所沒法表徵、整合、消化、理解和把握住的，是象徵界永遠的缺陷、匱乏、黑洞、裂隙。「實在」近似中文語境的「太初有道」，剛出生的嬰兒是最接近「實在」的，一切混沌、無分別、不可知，沒有「存在」的概念，一經任何符號象徵就與「實在」永遠分離。

「實在界」會以某種對「想像界」與「象徵界」具有創傷性的方式爆發、湧入「現

它必須與我們的經驗、與我們作爲主體所遭受的痛苦聯繫起來，這樣我們才能更好地採取行動來改變現實。這是精神分析的一項任務，但它必須是一項集體的政治任務，而不是個體的心理任務。

我們的個體性以及它的心理學，是這整個問題的一部分，我們必須質疑它們，我們需要一種特別的心理學批判──一個精神分析的「批判心理學」，現在我們需要精神分析。

實」之中，對原先的「想像」與「象徵」可能產生內在的破裂與「創傷」，使我們「分裂」，可能帶來緊張與必須面對變化，所以「象徵界」往往對「實在界」加以壓抑與排除，但是，人類作爲主體也可能透過某些覺醒的歷程，能動地選擇打破幻象，眞切地承接與「實在界」的「創傷」交融。故「創傷」、「分裂」的意義並非如字眼想當然爾地固定在單面與負向，它也富含改變歷史的潛力的積極面向，能使我們重構新的「想像」與「象徵」，創造不同於前的「現實」世界。（亦可參考本書《導讀暨譯序》中有關語言與「分裂」的討論）。

PREFACE

This manifesto is for movements of liberation, for a better world. It is written for and addressed to individuals and groups that fight against the oppressive, exploitative and alienating reality of our time. It is about the interrelationship between this miserable external reality of life today and our 'internal' lives, what can be called our 'psychology', that which feels to be deep down 'within us', that seems to be either too-often resigning itself to reality or, we hope, rebelling against it. We need to rebel, for the sake of others and for ourselves.

Sometimes we feel that our own rebellion cannot come out from within us, find release, and turn into action. It is as if it were something that eats away inside us which may seriously affect our lives. We may then be told that we have a psychological disorder.

Many problems are reduced to the level of individual psychology by society, by mass culture and by professionals trained to do exactly that; psychologists, psychiatrists and other 'psy' professionals. The problems do feel to be 'psychological', but they are not. How should we politicise them? How can we fight 'outside' against the roots of what we feel 'inside'?

The relationship between the personal 'inner' and the social 'outer' world is crucial for liberation movements. That is why these movements can benefit from psychoanalysis developed first as a clinical approach that has spent more than a century grasping the intimate interconnection between reality and what feels deep within each of us. We must understand the nature of that interconnection, with the help of different approaches, including those from psychoanalysis. We do this in order to fight against what oppresses us, exploits and alienates us, but also to build a practical alternative to capitalism, sexism, racism and new forms of colonialism.

Psychoanalysis

What is psychoanalysis? Psychoanalysis is a therapeutic practice that was invented by Sigmund Freud in Europe at the end of the nineteenth century as an alternative to mainstream medical psychiatric approaches to distress. Instead of subjecting people in distress to incarceration, terrible physical treatments and drugs, the psychoanalyst meets their client or patient, the one that we term 'analysand', in their clinic. Their task is to *listen* to this speaking subject, providing a strange confidential space for this analysand to speak of their distress and to hear connections made between past and present in their own speech, connections that they have never heard before.

The classic images in popular film of the analysand lying on a couch in the clinic are true, but there is something misleading in the images of the psychoanalyst taking notes and issuing a diagnosis and giving wise interpretations. Psychoanalysis opens a space for the analysand as speaking subject to eventually give interpretations that strike them as true, and that then operate as the motor of 'insight' and change. Psychoanalysis can enable an analysand to simply address the 'symptom' that brings them to see the psychoanalyst, or it can be life-changing. We are modest in our claims for psychoanalysis in this manifesto, but we do believe that it is a progressive therapeutic alternative to psychiatry and psychology, and we will explain why.

We will describe crucial elements of psychoanalysis in the following chapters, focusing on the notion of the *unconscious*, showing how our lives unconsciously repeat patterns that are then repeated in the clinic; we show how this *repetition* of sometimes selfdefeating and painful patterns is an expression of a *drive* that can operate for life or for death, and how this repetition is handled by the psychoanalyst in the clinic as *transference*. We insist on the clinical grounding of these four elements because psychoanalysis has emerged and developed as a clinical method, not because we seek to promote psychoanalytic treatment or recommend it to our readers. Rather, our purpose is to highlight what we consider potentially revolutionary in psychoanalysis and how it serve the liberation movements in their current struggles.

Our interest here is in the progressive and revolutionary political effectiveness of psychoanalysis, and not in the dissemination of psychoanalytic theory or clinical practice, though we do include discussion about the articulation of the 'clinic' as a potentially progressive space with political practice. This manifesto is not another introduction to psychoanalysis, another among many others, but it is an argument for the link between psychoanalysis and revolution. Our readers can read more about the method and the theory in other introductory texts if they wish, but bearing in mind our warnings about the way that psychoanalysis has been adapted and distorted.

Another world is possible, and psychoanalysis is one valuable tool we need now to make that happen. Using psychoanalysis as such a tool does not mean importing psychoanalytic ideology into our forms of struggle or imagining it will always be with us. Psychoanalysis came into a being in a particular form that we can make work for us, and it will disappear when its work is done.

Our task in this manifesto is to reconstruct psychoanalysis as an authentic 'critical psychology' and as an effective resource for liberation movements. You will see that we are very critical of psychology as such, as we are of all of the psy professions. Psychoanalysis understood dialectically, acknowledging its faults and emphasising its strengths, takes us way beyond those other approaches.

Our conviction is that psychoanalysis must criticize and transform itself in order to be useful to the liberation movements. Thinking about the specific needs of these movements, we examine here the role of the unconscious, repetition, drive and transference in clinical and political analysis and practice in order to address questions of subjective change and transformations of reality. Although we will not avoid theoretical questions, it is *practice* that is the key, and what we can learn from psychoanalytic clinical practice connects with the practice of liberation.

Revolution

The goal of liberation, as conceived by the anti-capitalist, anti-patriarchal, anti-racist and anti-colonial movements, will always be present at the horizon of this manifesto. The following pages are for the liberation movements and were written with them in mind. These movements are against exploitation and oppression, and we stand in solidarity with them. Our psychoanalysis is also attuned to the 'negative', to what is 'anti', to what it is in us that enables us to rebel. And, like these political movements, our psychoanalysis opens up something positive about the nature of the human subject; a capacity to take stock and reflect and change the world, to make it better suited to creativity and transformation.

This manifesto is written at a time of deep political-economic crisis in which the symbolic world we all inhabit as human beings is being perturbed and shaken, and the future worlds we can imagine creating for ourselves are impacted and threatened by enigmatic real material forces that are operating completely out of our control. The fathomless biological substrate of our being, our unknowable nature, erupts into our symbolic universe at times like this, and when it does so, it exacerbates the societal contradictions we are subjected to, contradictions we must understand and overcome if we are to resist and survive. We are weaker when we are more divided in the face of such danger.

A deadly virus, for example, is a threat to all of us in this world, but its arrival shows very clearly that we are not all in this together, not impacted equally. Those in the so-called 'less developed' countries will suffer more, those already suffering from racism will die in greater numbers, and women confined to their homes, if they have them, will be more prone to violent attack. Every oppressed group, those disabled by this society, and those already weakened by it, already sick, will be more likely to die.

This manifesto was written under lockdown, sent backwards and forwards between the authors, and with consultation with comrades around the world. It contains some ideas often considered 'difficult', often avoided for that reason. The ideas are not easily turned into the easy narrative form of popular texts, and you will experience us circling around key ideas to make them clearer. We repeat key claims in a slightly different way at different points in the text to make them clearer still. Every language is written as a form of translation, and now we want you to translate it back into practice.

Most of humanity is in danger under 'shock capitalism' of the sort favoured by neoliberal capitalists because it favours them. This form of capitalism, like the previous ones but to a greater extent, cannot function without the crises that it fosters. Any reason is good excuse to go into crisis mode for those who benefit.

A crisis that erupts from the real is indeed shocking, it shocks us to our core, and it is psychoanalysis that can best grasp the intimate connection between this real, our attempts to imagine what is happening to us and the symbolic universe we share with us. Grasping this connection requires an ideology critique that must be linked with what we experience, with what we suffer as subjects, so we can better act to change reality. It is a task for psychoanalysis, but it must be a collective political task, not an individual psychological one.

Our individuality and its psychology are part of the problem. We must question them. We need a particular kind of critique of psychology, a 'critical psychology' that is psychoanalytic. Now we need psychoanalysis.

第一章

導論：苦痛[1]、辯證與解放

　　症狀（*symptoms*）告訴我們關於這個令它們被激化（甚至在某些情形中是被創造）出來的病態社會什麼樣的訊息呢？每一個承受壓力的人——無論是在工廠、辦公室、商店、農田、街道還是家庭的工作者，在生命中的某些時刻都會需要有實際的與情感的支持，致力於改變世界的社會運動者們更是如此，在解放運動中積極採取社會變革行動，這對於社會運動者們往往是非常艱辛的考驗，他們必須與過去決裂、離開既定的角色、對抗環境、質疑自己、捨下先前的身分、放下牽絆、放棄緊抓既有特權的誘惑。

　　有時候，對於超級富豪、那 1% 的人來說，我們的特權是巨大的，但那些分隔我們彼此的特權卻往往出奇地微小；令人驚訝的是，它們對我們來說如此微不足道卻又是如此重要，它們的掌控是實質的，但同時也是「心理的」（'psychological'）——這是精神分析所理解並能改變的。

　　我們必須放鬆心理上的枷鎖，才能意識到我們作為不同種類的勞動者[2]我們究竟是什麼。儘管我們之間差異巨大，但為生計而勞動工作這一點將我們團結在一起，我們必須認知到這點才能夠結合力量以贏得這個世界，只要我們依然困在我們被迫成為的個體裡，或是陷在被設定的身分類別中，我們就會持續失去這個世界，直到徹徹底底地失去它為止。

　　每一個人不僅要解放自己也要從單一個別的自我中解放出來，個別的

1　本章將 misery 譯作苦痛，試圖傳達作者所指包括歷史的、集體的苦難與辯證地濃縮在個人身心痛苦症狀的意涵。

2　workers，如同作者於接下來的段落中說明的，並不只是指一般印象中藍領勞工，而是現今為生計而勞動工作的每一個人，故譯「勞動者」或「工作者」。

自我是逃離悲傷世界的避難所，但也將我們禁錮在其中。這個歷程導致內在破裂（internal ruptures），甚至是創傷的形式[3]，這些可以被加以思考、研究與治療，它們無法被完全解決，但可以透過維也納醫生西格蒙德・佛洛伊德在十九世紀末開展的精神分析理論和實踐來理解、理解和轉化。這一理論和實踐在過去一百年中由他的門徒和追隨者們不斷完善和發展。

這段佛洛伊德開宗立範留給後世傳承的歷史，是對治現代主體性（modern subjectivity）內在破裂的一個獨特、無可比擬的治療的歷史，也是與解放的終極目標有著極為複雜、曖昧和矛盾的關係的歷史，這個歷史包含了進步、分歧、迂迴和挫敗。一開始佛洛伊德受到他那個時代的影響，浸淫在性別歧視和種族主義意識形態以及他自己的精神醫學訓練中，但他打破了關於心理學和人性的主流思想，為更具潛在進步性的「批判心理學」開闢了道路。

佛洛伊德對心理範疇的理解是批判的、懷疑的，他不接受它被當作某種既定的、實在的和全然顯明的、可被客觀得知的東西；他也不把它視為某種統一的、在每個人身上總是相同的東西。所有這一切使他對於人類苦痛的本質乃是歷史性的事物、透過辯證的歷程我們能理解被濃縮凝結於*症狀*（symptoms）之中的苦痛、以及理解和解放之間的關係，都有著寶貴的洞察。

苦痛症狀即歷史現象

佛洛伊德所做的事是去理解那些緊緊封鎖人的心理的「症狀」，這些「症狀」看似是醫學上的症狀但實則大不相同，這些「症狀」沒法用醫學來解釋或治療，需要完全不同的理論和方法的實踐。佛洛伊德發展精神分析，即使他過去接受傳統「精神醫生」（'mind doctor'）訓練，他的方式既是完全跳脫醫學精神病學，同時也擺脫了仍然在相當機械的醫學模式中

---

[3] 破裂與創傷，是不可避免的內在鬥爭，治療不是也不可能使它完全解決消失，而是去理解它的意涵而能有所不同地往前轉化，所以它可能被症狀表徵也可能朝向重構而發展，請參考「前言」該章註7。

處理痛苦的那種心理學。如我們即將看到的，不同於醫學症狀，精神分析的「症狀」並非簡單可見的跡象，它們更像是要求被聆聽的話、需要*言說*（*speak*）的話；這些症狀訴說著痛苦和抵抗的存在，並打開了改變的可能性。

透過像精神分析那樣看待症狀、傾聽症狀、認真對待並據以採取行動，這個世界可以被轉化。變革的、顛覆的和潛在的革命性政治行動可能來自我們對痛苦的症狀的訴說、來自無法再像過去那樣做、來自那些必須改變的事，這就是為什麼這些症狀是我們在這本書中的起點。

在此，我們特別關注以精神分析連結言語與行動——試圖解決和克服造成我們痛苦的最根本社會原因的政治性行動。我們所承受的擠壓與內在破裂訴說著這個不幸的社會裡痛苦的特性，我們是如此渴望改變這個社會，而精神分析是這個歷程中一個潛在的強大盟友。

我們的任務是將社會鬥爭與精神分析理論所描述的那種不可避免的內在鬥爭聯繫起來，實際目的並不是自我撫慰、往內與自己與社會和解的那種一般常見的治療目標，而是前進到我們內在鬥爭的社會根源的基進（radical）[4] 政治目標，這使得我們這裡的精神分析旨趣大不同於任何受到精神分析啟發的適應性個體治療。

精神分析——這一種關於我們掙扎拉扯、分裂的「內心生活」（'internal mental lives'）的理論和實踐經常是與權力聯繫在一起，而它實際上提供了一個關於苦痛的臨床和政治性的批判。它不是什麼令人畏懼的事，它不是為征服我們而設計的，不是要讓我們的存在適應既定秩序、讓我們不相信我們的變革理想、讓我們背離集體鬥爭、將自己封鎖在我們個人的思想中、抑或阻止我們對統治最直接的抵抗。

弗洛依德留給我們的不是一種孤立、順從及征服的工具；的確，精神

4　radical 譯作「基進」，其字根為「root」，意為「根本」，雖然在中文世界亦常見到有譯為「激進」，但細究其意義，「基進」——徹底根本地改造或者將事理回到根本，可說是一種具有「激進」的成分，但是，相反地，「激進」未必真能返回根本，恐怕不足表達 radical 的原意，為符合作者行文脈絡，故取「基進」。

分析有時就是這樣運作的，就像對待我們心理生活的每一種專業方法一樣，這在階級社會中並不奇怪，這個階級社會將專業治療者與其他人劃分開，指定他們與權力有關的精確職能。

精神分析也教我們認識到每一種專業人員──無論是醫生、精神科醫生或非醫學的心理學家或心理治療師，也都是被他們衝突的生活所分裂、掙扎拉扯的；他們可能為成功的生涯而努力，但有時他們也會記起最初是什麼讓他們開始接受這個關懷他人的訓練，我們所有人都生活在這些張力中與之應對，而通常是將其掩蓋起來，關鍵問題是我們將這些衝突和矛盾處理成什麼樣──我們是否能使它們為我們服務，而不是對我們不利？

儘管它已經被以保守主義的方式使用著，但精神分析本質上並非保守主義的；它不必被當作統治工具用，相反地，它可以是一種對抗權力的武器；它可以使用來展示我們的心理學如何被現實（這種活在資本主義下不幸的現實）所殖民，也可以用來展現我們在進行自我解放時如何發聲與行動以反對這種個體主義化的心理學。

我們的可能性遠超過我們從各種心理／精神相關專業人員那兒聽聞到的「心理學」，我們並非註定要被封閉在個體性之內、或是被禁錮在忍受現實或苦痛之中、或是被困囿於資本主義體制裡面，我們被告知我們沒法改變事情，但我們可以，並且我們需要一個立基於改變可能性的方法。

適應

精神分析，這個發明於二十世紀初針對痛苦的重要心理學取向和基進的治療方法，它曾經明確地與左派理念結盟，而今卻經常被操作成一種*適應性*（*adaptation*）的工具。在被歐陸法西斯主義者摧毀他們的機構而逃往世界各地之前，大多數精神分析學家是共產主義或社會主義的成員或支持者，這些精神分析學家致力於改變世界，因為他們可以從病患看見與聽見這個世界有著怎樣的苦痛。

「症狀」在早期第一批精神分析師們聽來並不是醫學上的器質性（organic）問題的簡單跡象而已，它們是衝突的標誌──不僅是個人衝突，也是意識形態、政治和歷史的衝突，「症狀」本身是衝突的濃縮並以語言表達於其言語之中，精神分析懂得如何去聆聽這種症狀。

許多精神分析家失去聆聽的藝術，他們的聆聽有時被客觀化與分類化的凝視（gaze）所取代，精神分析逐漸變成一個醫學的或心理學的專長，它的實踐只變成一種據稱是科學的並且被刻意去政治化（depoliticized）的「技術」（'technique'）。

即使是早期第一批精神分析師，在他們逃到新的居住國家之後，在敵意環境下也不得不放棄政治戰鬥力，並保護自己免受第二次世界大戰及後來的冷戰期間西方國家對共產主義者的迫害；他們假裝不關注政治以適應他們的新現實，同時他們使精神分析去政治化和被修改，將精神分析轉變成為一種適應性的治療，這種適應性對於精神分析作為一種臨床治療模式的故事，以及它在大眾文化中所占據的地位，有著非常重大的影響。

那種由症狀所表徵的衝突現在被看作是個人層次要解決的問題，而政治被排除於臨床之外；然而，當精神分析的思想觀念被錯誤地「應用」於社會時，正是這種化約的適應性精神分析被拿來用作一個社會該如何運作以及任何社會都會是什麼樣子的模型。

在那些艱難險峻的年代（對精神分析師和他們所治療的人們來說都是很嚴峻的時期），佛洛伊德創新的理論和實踐的基進歷史彷彿已幾近消逝，一些實務工作者掙扎堅持下去，而一些社會理論家使用它來把握使它忘記自己過去背後潛在的歷史條件。幾乎他們所有人都以某種方式了解得很清楚──精神分析已經投降了，它已經允許自己被吸收和馴服、調整並成為適應性的。現在，我們必須從其適應的歷史關連中將精神分析釋放出來，認真對待其基進的、真實的、歷史的核心，並使它重燃生機。

如果我們必須拒絕適應性的精神分析，那是因為這種主導性的保守版精神分析放棄了變革的潛力，它使我們無法改變自己而只能去適應，從而接受並延續現實，無論它是多麼壓迫、剝削和異化；那麼，儘管資本主義不公平也沒法容忍，但我們似乎把它當作我們的天然環境去適應，彷彿它不是歷史性的、可被克服的。

適應性精神分析的問題不僅在於它將事情的規則當然化（使得事情看來似乎是天然固有而非出於歷史的），它更大的問題在於使我們將世界視為與我們每個人都分離開的外部「環境」，這使我們無法認識到我們是世界的一部分、我們在世界之內也屬於世界、我們既能透過改造自己來改造

世界、也可以透過改造世界來改造自己。我們是這個生態相聯繫的世界的一部分，彼此連結，作爲被剝削和被壓迫的人、作爲鬥爭中的同志，我們對彼此相互承擔、負責。這個世界，及在其中的他人，從不只是「環境」，遠超於此，更是一個我們自身的（of our selves）親密的部分。

每一個解放運動都會在某個點上認識到「環境」和「生態」之間的重大差異，當他們將他們的鬥爭與對我們世界的生態社會主義理解聯繫起來時，這種差異就會變得明顯。說是「環境」意味著視這世界爲某種與我們分開的東西，因而我們就學著去適應或試著去主宰；而說是「生態」則指涉我們與世界之間密切的聯繫，我們的生活在休戚與共且具政治性的意識網絡中以一種生態方式聯繫在一起，以至於我們感受到他人在掙扎鬥爭中所遭受的痛苦，並且知道如果我們試圖統治和剝削他人時，無論他們是否是人類同胞或者其他眾生，我們都只會使這個世界變得更糟。這種我們與他人相聯繫的生態意識是精神分析的核心。

正如精神分析所設想的那樣，個體並不是眞的單獨、孤立和彼此相隔，我們是他人生命的一部分，我們的行動和言語可能對他們造成致命的後果，不知何故，我們知道如同我們對自己負責，我們也對他們負有責任，我們的連結不只是「外在的」（'external'），他人並非只是在「外面的」（'outside'），圍繞著我們；而同時也是在我們「裡面的」（'inside'），在我們每一個人之內、在我們所思、所言和所作爲之內。我們的姿態中有他人的痕跡，我們的言語和思想中也有他人聲音的迴響；過往與他人的關係不僅是重現在現在的關係中，而更是將我們每個人聯繫在一起且形塑我們成爲現在的自己；個人的構成是社會和文化的，也同時是歷史的，這使它具有不斷變化的傾向。

正如我們面對的剝削、壓迫和異化的情境是被建構的（被歷史性地建構）所以我們可以結束它一樣，我們特有的異化形式的心理學也是歷史的產物，是可被改變的。儘管大多數精神醫生，心理學家和心理治療師聲稱他們致力於探討心理生活普遍不變的基本屬性，事實上他們所探討的是取決於文化、歷史時機與既有社會關係極爲可變異的因素。

保守的適應性精神分析師與大多數心理／精神相關專業人員將不斷變化的人類生存的歷史本質變成了固定之物，在萬事變化快速到彷彿所有固

體都要氣化般的當前社會中，這眞是更加奇怪又反進步的。我們自己被迫得更有彈性並學習在每時每刻以不同的方式存在著，但心理／精神相關專業人員在他們研究與嘗試治療時，固定化了我們的存在，從而背離了我們人性中最爲基進和最具變革的傾向。

他們對於人性的圖像差不多就是一台複雜的機械，是那種只存在人類的想像中僅具本能機制的野獸，人類與動物相比自感優越高等，但誰想得到同樣的人類最終竟會因爲對動物的貶低而貶低了自己的形象呢？就像舊有的將動物貶低以強調人類的高貴，當前心理學和其他心理／精神相關專業也包括保守的精神分析，已經爲將我們所有人類貶低作好了準備。

相反地，基進的精神分析告訴我們，反思人們的社會處境是人類的天性，我們所有人都需要不斷嘗試改變這些處境和我們自身。當我們試圖改變而失敗時，基進的精神分析和相伴隨的基進政治實踐，會向我們顯現我們失敗的原因，以及我們是如何被鎖定於社會的宰制性觀念和每個人獨特的歷史過程之中。我們不能希望使我們成爲這樣的自己的歷史處境消失，我們也不能指望將我們捆綁進壓迫之中的內在障礙停止，這些障礙在我們憎恨壓迫並試圖逃開的同時也激發我們渴望壓迫，我們可能永遠無法完全擺脫對壓迫的渴望，但我們可以知道它，在它干擾、爆發、阻礙我們時辨別它，而這種知識可以成爲我們解放的第一步。

渴望壓迫是一件最奇特的事情，是主體性的痛苦矛盾之一。假裝沒有矛盾是最簡單的，但遲早我們會因此被絆倒而損害我們的解放鬥爭，也許到頭來，我們創造新形式的壓迫取代了那些我們解放出自己的壓迫；爲免於此，我們必須認眞面對是什麼讓我們回到原點、是什麼阻礙了我們或把我們往回拖，我們必須嚴肅認眞地處理這一切，不是要把這些只當作彷彿是心理的和不可避免的事來怪罪在過程中的受害者，而是爲了理解在這個悲慘世界中人皆有之的矛盾特性。

歷史

精神分析──如同馬克思主義（Marxism）和其他權力以及解放理論一樣──在特定的歷史時期出現，乃是爲了概念化、理解和解決歷史上產生的一系列問題。我們必須於歷史自身中把握精神分析的**歷史**（*his-*

tory），並使其成為我們的；精神分析若離開上兩個世紀的脈絡，它對我們的意義就不會同它所做的這樣；如果我們把馬克思主義移植到另一個時代去，同樣也會意義闕失。

舉例來說，很難想像古羅馬想要逃離統治者的奴隸會如何看待馬克思主義對「剩餘價值」（'surplus value'）[5]的分析，例如資本家從工人那裡獲得的隱藏份額，或者試圖建立革命政黨和國際協會。在斯巴達時期，作為工業僱傭勞動者的無產階級並不存在，擺脫奴隸制與擺脫僱傭勞動的剝削不同，這就是為什麼馬克思主義只有在資本主義本身作為一種主要的生產方式出現時才開始變得有用的原因。同樣地，殖民國家和帝國主義的發展對於反殖民和反帝國主義解放運動而言也是必要的；每一個政治運動的興起都是為了與特定的剝削或壓迫條件作鬥爭。

以精神分析來說，它被發明來理解和治療的痛苦「症狀」是現代社會特有的，這些症狀與奇特的佛洛伊德式心理表徵一樣具有歷史意義，「無意識」與我們在資本主義現代性中遭受的特殊異化形式有密切相關。

資本主義異化製造了「內在」衝突，這種衝突本身是無形的，但它在人們身上引起的或激發的作用便是眾所週知的了，像是無以名之的痛苦、紊亂的生活或荒唐的決定與怪異的行動，這些有時是具有破壞性或自我毀滅性的。在目前的工作經驗中所有這一切都是顯而易見的，人們被鎖定在他們作為勞動者的生活中，他們重複相同類型的任務，然後他們的生活體驗被以一種他們無法控制的特定重複方式結構起來。

勞動者，現今工作的每一個人，都受到經濟迫切的驅使，所以受制於工作和生存的「驅力」（'drive'）是與資本主義息息相關的。資本主義的統治塑造了將我們彼此聯繫在一起的權力關係，但這些關係也重複了早期的權力關係，因此重複被無意識地驅動，然後在臨床內以精神分析師所稱的「移情」形式重新出現。我們將在本書的章節中討論所有這些議題，並透過它們表明精神分析把握了症狀作為社會痛苦跡象的特性。

5　工人在生產過程中所創造的價值稱為勞動價值，勞動價值和勞動報酬（即工資）之間的差額即是剩餘價值，在剝削體制下，這些勞動者生產的剩餘價值全都被資本家無償占有，成為資本家的利潤。

　　症狀被以這種方式創造出來，使得精神分析這個歷史性的發明適合用來解讀它們，它幫助我們去探看它們作為個人生活中的衝突和表達社會衝突的樣貌。一個特定的社會和這個社會中的單一個人是以症狀方式顯現問題的載體，症狀是某些事出錯了的跡象，它們是關於痛苦如何出現在每一個單獨的主體的訊息。

主體

　　在這個宣言中，我們將人類稱為「**主體**」（‘*subjects*’），因為「個體」（‘individual’）一詞過於化約，它意味著我們的主體性是不分裂的（undivided[6]）而且是分隔、孤立、對立於社會並被鎖在其個體性之內的。「主體」並不僅僅是個體，它包括其他人，它被社會世界打開和穿越、為外界所寓居和分裂，此即其存在的生態空間。無論是在個人層面還是在集體政治進程的層面，主體會與其自身相矛盾，也因此它可成為能動性和變化的源泉。

---

[6] 讀者將在本書中看到「分裂的」（‘divided’）、「不分裂的」（‘undivided’）以及相關聯的名詞「分裂」（‘division’）、「分裂的主體」（‘divided subject’）等一組字彙，這指涉了對於主體與主體性是受無意識而非意識自我主導的存在的觀點，在此觀點下主體因為會與外部互動而「分裂」，而不是以意識自我主導的「自我心理學」（‘ego psychology’）所認為的，主體是完整統一的、功能獨立自主的「不分裂的」存在。作者在與譯者往返討論中表示，就拉岡學說而言，在英語中 divided 與 split 意義等同，故兩者交互使用，例如本書中會見到 divided subject 與 split subject，是同一個意義，即「分裂的主體」。在此要特別提醒中文讀者的是，由於在中文語境中，「分裂」一詞常在主流心理學結合精神醫療的視野下被使用而普遍傳播，它往往指涉精神病理（如人格分裂、精神分裂症等），故接觸大眾心理學的讀者可能想當然爾地將「分裂」與病理醫療作聯結，但這對作者或拉岡學說而言，是很大的錯解；作者在下一節正討論到主流的意識自我心理學的精神分析欲否認「分裂」會造成對異化的遮蔽，「分裂」是基進精神分析所認可的。為了避免中文讀者落入錯解，譯者曾考慮避開「分裂」而試過用「分離」、「裂隙」、「斷裂」等接近原本意義的中文字詞來替代，但都發現不易以一詞適用於本書中作者他處相關行文而能作到完足的表達，仍是譯作「分裂」較能涵蓋其意義，並於本書〈導讀暨譯序〉作必要的脈絡補充與闡述。

主體可以是歷史的能動者，也可以是受害者和歷史的產物，以不同的方式影響我們並決定我們的事件，現在可以透過精神分析來處理。精神分析的思維是我們了解和改變現代經驗的最強大資源之一。那些發生在作為晚期現代性主體的我們的事，在十九到二十世紀間，隨著佛洛伊德理論的發展，突然具有了基進的新意義。針對我們的痛苦的醫學命名被發明出來，同時精神分析被發明來處理它們，對抗它們所指涉的意涵並轉變這種痛苦。

精神分析仍然是了解我們當今在先進的新自由主義資本主義及其連帶的性別歧視、種族主義和殖民主義形式下生活中苦痛症狀的本質[7]的最佳方法之一。這些精神分析症狀無意識地運作，然後在醫生和心理學家觀察的可見症狀上發現扭曲的表達，與我們個人生平以及當前的生活狀況有著更深層的聯繫，症狀是具有雙重意義的歷史現象，它們產生於每個人的個人歷史中，它們整體的樣貌是由我們生活其中並試著了解的社會類型構成的。

我們的過去和我們的世界困擾著我們，使我們生病且令我們受苦，這就要面對我們是否要全然被意識形態所蠱惑而相信這是所有可能世界中最好的、沒理由要擔心的？或者我們是否要作一個知道事情很糟並且必須改變的社會運動者？衝突和矛盾困擾著我們所有人，而這些衝突和矛盾會深入我們的內心，滲透到我們體內，將我們撕裂，然後以可能令人痛苦且似乎無法解釋的症狀形式出現。

精神分析是辯證的，既非心理學亦非精神醫學

精神分析取向通往主體性的歷史迂迴曲折，並與被理解為科學或偽科學而被視為一門專業和學術學科的心理學並行發展。這種心理學不應與精

7　nature 譯作「本質」或「性質」時，指的是事物內在的特性、內涵，但這是辯證性的，是某事物在特定脈絡中的內在特性，意義上大不同於「本質主義（或本質論、本質化）」（‘Essentialism’）所指的那種固有、不變、普遍、實在的「本質」。

神分析相混淆，雖然心理學時常設法吸收精神分析，但它在前提、思想、方法和目標上都與精神分析不一致；事實上，構成心理學的許多內容正是我們試圖透過精神分析想要解決的問題，從精神分析的角度來看，心理領域是有問題的。

　　心理學為我們型塑一種虛幻假象、欺騙的、甚至是妄想的經驗，這是一種把我們每一個人都當作是完整不分裂且獨自分開的個體，可以像一個物體一樣完全了解和控制自己的經驗；這種單一整體的自我恰恰是問題的一部分，因為它使每個人都想像自己應該為自己不想要的不愉快感覺負責，如果他們感到「被分裂」（'divided'）、如果他們覺得自己的生活存在無意識的面向，就會讓他們感覺更糟。這種分裂（division），影響著我們所有人，被精神分析辨認出來，卻被心理學所否認，心理學的否認掩蓋了我們的異化，使我們無法抵抗異化我們的東西，如此，它便使宰制我們的東西看來像是「來自內在」，操縱我們，並在意識形態上管理我們。

　　我們現在面臨的一個關鍵問題是個人孤立經驗的歷史建構，這種孤立經驗與我們的社會存在不相符，無法在我們的感受和思想中辨識自身，本身沒有力量或意義，因此容易受制於宰制的、操縱的和意識形態的管理。這就是與我們人類生活集體共享的特性相背離的心理學的問題；根本上，這是資本主義社會中的個人主義及它的心理學的表現的問題。

心理學

　　心理學（*Psychology*）學科致力於維護將每個個別的自我當作單一個體的心理範疇、當作他們自己個人的心理經驗，就像每個被看作是與他人相孤立的勞動者的心理經驗那樣。心理學，這門學術性的專業學科，以及該學科所依據的我們個體非分裂的心理學意識，與資本主義本身同時形成，並與資本主義一起傳播到世界各地。資本在世界範圍內的擴張，也正是它的心理工具的全球傳播，這不僅是在大學和衛生機構，也在所有生活層面；一切都傾向於帶有心理色彩。這一心理學化過程涉及原子化、去社會化、去政治化、去歷史化、病態化、歸咎於個人和適應資本主義社會的機制。

　　是的，今日我們生活在全球資本主義之下，在殘酷的新自由主義的資

本主義之下，但要了解資本主義如何運作，我們需要的不僅僅是這個問題的名字。精神分析（也不只有精神分析）告訴我們：在資本主義下，不可能談到生活、談到階級而不提到性別歧視、種族主義與對障礙者許多其他形式的壓迫。基進的精神分析已是「多元交織政治的」（'intersectional'），處理不同形式壓迫之間主體的深層連結，不同的解放運動為打擊和結束這些壓迫而興起。

要從階級、種族和性的壓迫性經歷中把我們自己釋放出來，也需要在我們自己「之內」（'within'）與它們抗爭。在這裡，在主體的範疇中，被壓迫者不只是顯現受到衝擊影響，也會表現對壓迫的順從或適應，這種適應使壓迫我們的事物得以維持和延續，通常被心理學家與精神醫師看作是「心理健康」（'mental health'）。

心理學與處理痛苦的醫療模式緊密聯繫，已在世界範圍內發展成為一種心理治療工具，使人們適應現實，而不是使他們能夠改變現實。心理學拾起醫學精神醫學大部分的歷史意識形態包袱，並聲稱將其人性化，專注於個案可觀察、可測量的行為症狀而不是不可見的心理疾病症狀。從疾病轉向行為這並沒有進步多少，精神分析顯示了這種微乎其微的焦點轉移的侷限性。

精神分析不是精神醫學。雖然心理學家將自己表現得更為友善、進步和「心理治療性的」（'psychotherapeutic'），但精神醫學的醫學遺緒仍然存在於心理學裡。精神醫師（受過醫學培訓）、心理學家（化約個體行為和思維模式）與心理治療師（混搭任何最能緩解痛苦使人們重新適合這世界的取向）之間，存在著重要的理論差異和專業位置上的爭議，我們應當對此有所明辨。

目前，心理學家以其聲稱擁有科學專業知識而居中心地位，他們認為較之精神醫學、心理治療和精神分析實踐，他們自己是最有效能的。如果心理學沒作用，我們對精神分析價值論證的任務會容易些；但問題正是它真的起作用，心理學與剝削和壓迫的社會關係配合得非常好，它在使人適應以維持這樣的世界順暢運作上發揮了很好的作用，它順暢地運行直到出現症狀，然後心理學就用其所謂的心理治療性的技巧來緩解症狀。

心理學在全世界傳播並進入我們的日常生活，這對我們的經驗、對我

們感受的方式、對我們關於自身的思考與言語帶來化約、矛盾與簡化，我們的行為越來越像心理的諷刺漫畫（caricatures），這些諷刺漫畫圖像四處包圍著我們並簡化人類的存在，它們透過電影和電視、雜誌和報紙、暢銷書和自助手冊、情感再教育、商業指導、諮詢、專家意見、社交網絡、甚至五句節派教會（Pentecostal churches）[8] 等方式傳播。

　　整個文化領域都充斥著簡化平庸的心理表徵，這對資本主義制度非常有用，我們當然就會以這些心理表徵來認識自己，我們那樣認識自己並不是因為它們如此忠實地反映我們的真實樣貌，而是因為它們如此強大以至於使我們去符合它們，以現在我們在如此悲慘的生活條件下的狀態去實現它們。

　　心理學之所以如此成功是因為它藉由我們的存在而實現了它的開展並確立了它現在的樣貌；有時這種存在似乎體現了偉大的心理學傳統的概念，包括行為主義者、人本主義者和認知學科的大師們的思想；例如，消費者已經學會了對廣告刺激作出反應，認同出售給他們的人性形象，處理購買所需的訊息，並臣服於將他們推向消費主義作為一種意識形態與物質實踐的隱形驅力。

　　就如同有精神醫學的精神分析版本一樣，甚至也有成功的心理學的精神分析版本了，我們需要謹慎提防這些冒充者——這些對本應是基進解放取向的意識形態扭曲並向「常態」（'normality'）投降的版本。精神分析不可能變成精神醫學或心理學，除非它不再是它本來的樣子，也就是在過程中失去了它對解放運動的作用，甚至還有害於它們，不僅藉由心理學化（psychologizing）或精神醫療化（psychiatrizing）而令它們被去政治化，

8　對非基督教的華人讀者可能對「五句節派教會」感到陌生，這是二十世紀初基督新教中一支強調方言、治病與靈恩的教派，中文也有譯者直接稱之為「靈恩派」，但基督教會中存在有對「五句節派教會」與「靈恩派」有別的論述。它最初是從美國傳到加、英國與歐陸，繼而傳播到其他地方，連帶使基督新教價值的影響力遍及世界；傳入中國後在各地方又再產生了許多分支，如在臺灣常見的真耶穌教會、靈糧堂、錫安堂，也被認為屬於此宗。就行文脈絡，作者在此的舉例指涉了心理學、廣為傳播的基督新教教會價值與資本主義三者在的意識形態上的緊密連繫。

甚至還致力於適應與征服而不是解放。

　　把精神分析弄得像心理學那樣去幫助主體變成他們應該的樣子，以利於最有效地將自己融入資本主義，這樣做可能使精神分析被摻假且降低了價值。然而，如果我們想要保存精神分析真正的面貌和可能性，我們就必須將它從這樣的過程分離出來，並展示精神分析如何使我們能夠抵抗此一過程。由於精神分析所經歷的適應性歷史，它已經與意識形態牽連在一起，但精神分析本身就是反叛的，彷彿精神分析本身就是一個被壓迫的症狀而現在可以說話了，在好好地訴說精神分析的過程中，我們可以解放它同時解放我們自己。

　　精神分析充滿衝突，同時它在處理我們歷史建構的人性時也涉及衝突。它在一個確切的歷史時刻浮現，反映了內心深處承載著這個世界的矛盾的人類主體矛盾的需要、傾向、渴望和抱負，這也是為什麼我們也可以將精神分析本身視為一種症狀。

　　精神分析方法不只是處理主體痛苦的症狀表現，它本身就是一種症狀，它和它所要解決的對象一樣矛盾。在我們要求精神分析關注資本主義下生活的矛盾本質之此一時刻，我們注意到這個社會今日出現的症狀，所以我們也要求精神分析必須是一個能檢驗自身而具反身性的「批判心理學」（reflexive 'critical psychology'），我們必須分析什麼使得精神分析適應社會，又是什麼使得它抵制並成為顛覆性和解放性的方法。

衝突

　　正如精神分析一樣，每一個內心有著症狀的人也是如此，他們都受**衝突**（*conflict*）所困擾。個人常常被特定的生命經歷模式（biographically-distinct pattern）受困在有害的壓迫關係中，這種模式定義了他們是誰，這就是人們使自身在自己、家人和朋友眼中是可辨識的同一個人的道理。

　　我們每個人獨特之處就在於我們受困於某些無意識（某些抗拒和重複、矛盾和衝突）之中。在我們每個人特有的症狀中，都有一種內在的衝突。這種症狀會使我們癱瘓，阻止我們改變自己，改變壓迫和傷害我們的關係。當一些戲劇性的或創傷性的事情發生在我們身上時，變化往往就會發生，讓我們擺脫那些無意識驅動的模式，而社會變革是刺激個人變革的

一個重要因素。

　　症狀的變化過程和衝突的結晶化（crystallisation）可以被辯證地理解。衝突使我們陷於困境，使我們無法動彈，但同時也是促使我們努力解決它並擺脫它。我們的前進移動同時受到衝突的驅動和阻礙，這使我們一點一點地移動，舉步蹣跚，改變著那些似乎什麼都沒被改變的東西，當一系列微小變化導致轉變時，量增爲質變鋪好道路，改變就突然明朗起來。這在政治層面上發生——當透過持續多年努力的集體奮鬥，最終使新的可能性和新形式的主體性出現；而這在臨床中發生——當症狀表現爲公開的衝突，並要求就如何繼續生活做出決定。症狀不但是一種障礙，辯證性地理解，它也是一種機會。

　　症狀是改變的機會，而不僅僅是認識我們自己而已。這就是爲什麼症狀不應該被消除的道理，消除症狀是心理學家和精神醫生通常企圖去做的事；然而，那樣只是確保什麼都沒有發現而一切維持不變，爲了發現和改變自己，就必須像精神分析這樣，以最大的注意力傾聽症狀。

　　由於這個病態社會中的每個人都被症狀困擾著，人們來接受精神分析並不是因爲他們有症狀，而是這些症狀變得難以忍受，苦痛的量大到某種質變即將發生；臨床精神分析的任務之一是以這種方式指引治療，使這種質變的發生作爲反思和決定如何生活的機會形式，而不是在精神崩潰和絕望的邊緣搖搖欲墜。精神分析幫助主體不被症狀所表現的事給壓倒或打敗，進而克服它，這唯有透過聆聽症狀並採取相應的行動才有可能。症狀本質上是辯證的，而精神分析是一種辯證的方法，它幫助個別主體面對新的課題——朝向適應或解放？

　　要進行解放，精神分析就必須被解放，它必須從非其所是與不應成爲的樣子被釋放出來，它必須對神祕化、偏見、惡毒的道德價值觀、教條、刻板印象和幻想的沉渣加以淨化，這些東西已將它從一種進步的方法轉變爲一種對資本主義和殖民主義以及壓迫性的性別關係有用的工具。

　　精神分析已經在令其自身試圖去適應的連續脈絡中被工具化了；這些脈絡使精神分析充滿了它們的規範、信仰、偏見和價值觀，要求它減低其基進的目標並做出妥協。在它的歷史過程中，各種保守的意識形態內容都被注入到它的基進形式裡。那種意識形態的內容——包括男人和女人之間

本質[9]的根本差異、以及他們對於彼此之間在性取向和性別關係上的有毒觀念——被掩蔽於精神分析體內作為一種實踐形式，一種言語實踐。這很嚴重，因為精神分析本身是一種向我們展示我們所說的與我們所做的之間如何相互聯繫的「談話治療」（'talking cure'）。

我們階級社會的衝突與矛盾離不開我們的言語，也離不開我們的性生活——這也是精神分析的核心，我們將試著在這個宣言中解釋為何會這樣，以及精神分析何以因為看待性作為我們生活親密的核心而精確地對準性。

我們談論到性，這是精神分析經常為人所知的，但為什麼呢？如果說在資本主義發展時核心家庭的地位是這個無情世界的核心，那麼性的地位就是我們自身最私密和最隱祕的部分。而它不僅被「壓抑」（'repressed'）、被視為可恥的事情而予以掩蓋、被視為壞事而將其推開，同時它也煽惑挑逗、對我們索求。因此，它變成了一種無法擺脫的念頭（obsession），也是我們最大的弱點，一個開放的傷口，不斷受到刺激，以「異性戀父權的」（'heteropatriarchal'）邏輯宰制著我們。

父權制總是「異性戀的父權制」（'heteropatriarchy'），它總是「異性戀霸權的」（'heteronormative'），因為它強制男性對女性的權力、老年男性對年輕男性的權力，並且對不同形式的性傾向予以排除或勉強容忍，它使異性戀強制成為我們全球化世界的核心親密社會的契約基礎。即使父權資本主義使用扭曲版的女權主義話語來反對左派，或將各種性偏好轉變為有利基的市場，情況也是如此。

正如父權的資本主義能將女性主義以及性的多樣性予以工具化，吸收和扭曲這些基進的觀念並將它們轉為反對我們——以此，它也能使精神分析轉變成正常化和剝削我們的性生活的工具。所以，不僅是在文化領域中我們的性冒著被父權話語制約的危險，在精神分析臨床環境中也是一樣。我們現在可以清除這種意識形態毒藥的精神分析，讓它為我們說話，而不是取代我們或反對我們。

9　此處「本質」原文是 essential，指的是固有的、不變的、普遍的、實在的性質，
　　不同於本章譯註 7 原文 nature 所指的具辯證性、脈絡性的「本質、性質」。

　　所以，對比心理學和精神醫學以及大多數形式的心理治療，精神分析是這些心理／精神相關專業中與眾不同的一個，它知道如何聆聽我們而不是取代我們說話。因此，不假裝事情能被固定看待，它將我們的困擾症狀視爲一種來自主體關乎其痛苦情境的訊息，同時，很重要地，也是關於需要改變的訊息。在這樣的方式下，它可能成爲解放運動的寶貴盟友，它的本質就是解放的辯證理論與實踐。

在臨床與文化中解放

　　精神分析已被有權力的人冒用，這是事實，但這並不意味著我們應該放手，讓它落入他們的手中；相反地，我們必須重申精神分析。爲此，我們需要掌握它的臨床工作與持續變化的歷史脈絡之間的辯證關係。看到精神分析的誕生、資本主義下的異化以及西歐核心家庭生活的剝削與壓迫本質的歷史處境，正是精神分析要去了解與對抗的處境；正是在這些處境下，性被經驗爲創傷性的，因爲性被壓抑但同時又不停地被談論、被挑動。

　　精神分析出現的條件和起作用的意識形態力量進入了精神分析，扭曲了它。不存在「純粹的」（'pure'）非意識形態的精神分析，但可以對其理論闡述持續淘洗，對其關鍵概念進行永不停息的淨化；其臨床形式和理論意識形態面向之間的複雜辯證關係可以在實踐中不斷地闡明和超越。這是與權力鬥爭、對意識形態批判和抵抗心理學化（psychologization）的一個連續、永不終止的歷程。

　　精神分析的四個關鍵概念——**無意識、重複、驅力和移情**——是該理論基進形式的要素，這些要素使我們能夠抵制深層意識形態的心理學化歷程，這些術語在精神分析中具有特殊的含義，但我們的目標是使它們在這裡對那些不僅尋求改變自己而且尋求改變世界的基進改革者們具有意義。

　　無意識、重複、驅力和移情在世界範圍內運作，而不僅僅是在精神分析師的沙發上；我們必須在臨床作爲轉化工作的私空間和我們的歷史脈絡之間的辯證張力空間中考量這四個概念，這四個關鍵概念需要重構，以使它們具有完整的歷史意義；這是爲了避免落入把它們「應用」（'applying'）到解放運動中而使它們從導引革命實踐變爲意識形態工具的陷阱。

我們必須理解，我們的鬥爭不需要被精神分析的概念所註解、辯護、證明，更不需要它來指揮；我們也無意將這些概念運作成一種放諸四海皆準的普適性意義從而限制和封閉了我們奮鬥的自由視野。我們的解放運動必須在前進的過程中保持道路暢通，確定方向和範圍，擴大它們所能設想和完成的工作。它們不應該讓精神分析像個固定的參照點一般來指導，但他們可以使用它作爲一種方法，並且改造精神分析，一如他們在對抗我們的生活處境而改造所有一切那樣。

我們面對著特殊的現代文化處境，資本主義混合著殖民主義與其必需的種族主義和性別歧視形式，以及病理化那些不願或無法像健康的、表現良好的、有生產力的公民那樣適應這個世界的人們的其他方式。精神分析爲這種全球文化下主體性的潛在本質以及使世上的人們彼此分裂的差異提供了寶貴的洞察。然而，它的眞正貢獻在於臨床，而我們在本宣言的以下章節中更詳細討論的四個關鍵概念——無意識、重複、驅力和移情，皆以其臨床工作爲基礎。

正是在臨床之中，我們發現了我們難以理解的事——我們如何重複自我毀滅的關係、如何被驅使而這樣做、以及移情現象如何在與精神分析師的殊異關係中運作。精神分析臨床的這些發現並不外於這個主流文化世界，不管好的壞的，它們都以其邏輯反饋到文化中；因此，我們也要說一些關於在臨床之外「應用」精神分析的危險，那是對它的實踐不可避免的學術性扭曲。

超越這種有問題的、可被質疑的應用，精神分析必須被我們重新改造爲主體性的基進工作的工具，如果要成功推翻既存的處境，這種主體性的基進工作工具的重新改造是必要的。這個工具是佛洛伊德及其追隨者理論闡述的結果，辯證性地理解他們，使我們能夠將它用於臨床的基進工作和解放運動。它所生產的是使我們能去創造更多的創造性過程的一部分。對於這使其成爲可能的，我們名之爲「革命的主體性」（'revolutionary sub-jectivity'），一種「革命的主體」（'revolutionary subject'）。

臨床如此，政治亦然，革命主體顯現與消失——在鬥爭中形成，在任務完成後再次消失。所有這些都不會將我們變成英雄般的革命者、有魅力

的社會運動者或者戰果輝煌的領導者。我們關心的不是領導力或性格的形成，而是創造一個集體變革過程，預見我們想要建立的世界，僅此而已。

這不會把我們變成精神分析師，遠非如此，精神分析的最終目標是使人類主體能夠踢掉他們用來到達新地方的梯子。精神分析的觀點不應該關閉我們的視野。這是機會，不是陷阱。當我們結束造成如此多苦痛的世界時，我們也期待精神分析的結束；精神分析作為一種革命性的方法，是作為該歷史過程的工具和結果而發揮作用。下一章，我們就從**無意識**（*unconscious*）開始。

INTRODUCTION: MISERY, DIALECTICS AND LIBERATION

What do *symptoms* tell us about the kind of sick society that intensifies them, in some cases creating them? Everyone under pressure, whether they are workers in the factory, the office, the store, the fields, the streets or the home, needs practical and emotional support at some point in their lives, and all the more so activists struggling to change the world. Activism in liberation movements is often a hard test for people who must break with their past, leave their assigned roles, confront their environment, question themselves, detach themselves from their previous identities and shake themselves from what holds them in their place, give up the privileges that tempt them to cling onto what they already have.

Sometimes our privileges, in the case of the super-rich, the 1%, are massive, but often those privileges that divide us from each other are surprisingly little. It is surprising that being so insignificant they can be so important to us. Their grip is material but also 'psychological', something psychoanalysis understands and can transform.

We must loosen our psychological chains if we are to realise what we are as workers of different kinds. As great as the differences between us are, there is the work we do to live that unites us, and we must recognize that in order to join forces and win the world. We will continue to lose the world, until losing it completely, as long as we remain trapped inside of what we have been forced to be as individuals or trapped inside identity categories handed down to us.

Each one must liberate not only oneself but be liberated from oneself, the individual self which is a refuge from a sad world but in which we are also imprisoned. This process causes internal ruptures, even forms of trauma that can be considered, studied and treated. They cannot be completely resolved, but understood, understood and transformed by the psychoanalytic theory and practice of the Viennese medical doctor Sigmund Freud beginning his work at the end of nineteenth century, theory and practice refined and developed by his disciples and followers over the last hundred years.

The history of the Freudian heritage is that of a unique, unparalleled treatment of internal ruptures of modern subjectivity. It is also the history of a complex, ambivalent and contradictory relationship with the ultimate goal of liberation. This history comprises advances, deviations, detours and setbacks. From the beginning, Freud was a child of his time, steeped in sexist and racist ideology and in his own psychiatric training, but he broke from dominant ideas about psychology and human nature to open the way to a more potentially progressive 'critical psychology'.

Freud related critically, sceptically to the psychological sphere. He did not accept it as something given, real and entirely manifest, as something that could be known objectively. Nor did he see it as something unitary that would always be the self-same and the same in every person. All this allowed him to have valuable insights into the human nature of misery as something historical, into the dialectical process through which we can understand that misery as something condensed in *symptoms*, and into the relationship between understanding and liberation.

Symptoms of misery as historical phenomena

What Freud did was to understand what looked like medical symptoms that locked people in place psychologically as 'symptoms' of a very different kind. These 'symptoms' could no longer be explained or treated by medicine, but required other quite different theoretical and practical means. Psychoanalysis was developed by Freud, even though he was trained as a traditional 'mind doctor', in such a way as to break completely from medical psychiatry and from the kinds of psychology that still treat distress within a rather mechanistic medical model. As we will see, unlike the symptoms of medicine, psychoanalytic 'symptoms' are not simply visible signs. They are more like words that demand to be listened to, that *speak*; these symptoms speak of distress and resistance, and they open up possibilities of change.

The world can be transformed by treating symptoms as psychoanalysis does, by listening to them, taking them seriously, and acting accordingly. Transformative, subversive and potentially revolutionary political action may arise from the symptomatic speech of our suffering, from what cannot continue as is has done, from what must change. That is why such symptoms are our starting point in this manifesto.

We are particularly concerned here with the psychoanalytic link between speech and action, political action that tries to address and overcome the most fundamental social causes of our suffering. The pressure and internal ruptures that we suffer from speak of the particular nature of distress in this wretched society that we want so much to change, and psychoanalysis is a potentially powerful ally in that process.

Our task is to connect social struggle with the kind of unavoidable internal struggle described by psychoanalytic theory. The practical purpose is not the usual therapeutic aim of pacifying ourselves, internally reconciling ourselves with ourselves and with society, but the radical political aim of going to the root of our internal struggle. This makes the psychoanalysis that interests us here differ significantly from any psychoanalytically-inspired adaptive individual therapy.

Psychoanalysis, a theory and practice of our torn, divided, 'internal mental lives', has often been allied with power, but it actually provides a clinical and political critique of misery. It is not something to be afraid of. It was not designed to subjugate us by adapting our existence to the established order, by making us distrust our transformative ideals, by turning us away from our collective struggles, by locking ourselves inside our individual minds or by blocking our most intimate resistance against domination.

What Freud has left us is not an instrument of isolation, resignation and subjection. It is true that psychoanalysis sometimes functions like that, as every professional approach to our mental lives has. This is not surprising in class society, which divides professional healers from the rest of the people, assigning them a precise function linked to power.

Psychoanalysis also teaches us that every professional, whether a medical doctor, a psychiatrist or non-medical psychologist or psychotherapist, is also divided, torn by their conflicted lives. They may strive for a successful career but they also sometimes remember what brought them into training to care for others in the first place. We all live those tensions in some way or another, manage them, and usually cover them over. The key question is what we do with those conflicts and contradictions, whether we will make them work for us instead of against us.

Although it has been used in reactionary ways, psychoanalysis is not itself reactionary. It is not necessarily an instrument of domination. On the contrary, it can be a weapon against power. It is possible for it to be used, to show how our own psychology is colonised by reality, this miserable reality of life under capitalism, and how we can speak and act against that individualised psychology as we engage in own liberation.

We are more than what we are told is our 'psychology' by the psy professionals. We are not condemned to shut ourselves up within our individuality or to endure reality or its misery or the capitalist system. We are told that we cannot change things, but we can, and we need an approach that is grounded in the possibility of change.

Adaptation

Psychoanalysis – which is a critical psychological approach to distress and a radical treatment invented at the beginning of the twentieth century – was once explicitly allied to the left. Now it often operates as a tool of *adaptation*. Most psychoanalysts were members or supporters of the communist or socialist movements before their own organisations were destroyed by fascism in Europe and before they fled to different parts of the world. These psychoanalysts had a commitment to changing the world because they could see, and hear from their patients, what misery there was in the world.

The 'symptoms' listened to by the first psychoanalysts were not simple indications of medical organic problems. They were signs of conflict, of conflicts that were not only personal, but ideological, political and historical. The symptoms were themselves conflicts condensed and expressed in language addressed to others, speech. This is the kind of symptom psychoanalysis knows how to listen to.

Many psychoanalysts lost the art of listening. Their listening sometimes gave way to an objectifying and classifying gaze. Psychoanalysis gradually became a medical or psychological speciality. Its practice turned into a simple 'technique' that was purportedly scientific and deliberately depoliticized.

Even the first psychoanalysts, under the hostile conditions in their new host countries to which they had fled, had to renounce political militancy and protect themselves against the anti-communist persecution characteristic of Western countries during the Second World War and then the Cold War. They pretended to be apolitical and thus adapted to their new reality, and they depoliticised and adapted psychoanalysis, turning psychoanalysis itself into an adaptive treatment. This adaptation is crucial to the story of psychoanalysis as a mode of treatment in the clinic and in the place it occupies in popular culture.

The kinds of conflicts that symptoms spoke of were now seen as things to be resolved at a personal level, and politics was kept out of the clinic. Then, when psychoanalytic ideas were mistakenly 'applied' to society, it was this reduced adaptive kind of psychoanalysis that was used as a model for how society functioned and for what any and every society could look like.

During those grim times, and they were grim times for the psychoanalysts as well as for those they treated, it was almost as if the radical history of Freud's innovative theory and practice had died. Some practitioners struggled to keep going, and some social theorists tried to use it in order to grasp the underlying historical conditions that had led it to forget its own past. Almost all of them understood very well, in one way or another, that psychoanalysis had given in, that it had allowed itself to be absorbed and tamed, adapting and becoming adaptive. Now we need to free psychoanalysis from this historical link with adaptation, take its radical authentic historical core seriously, and bring it to life again.

If we must reject adaptive psychoanalysis, it is because this dominant conservative version of psychoanalysis renounces its transformative potential. It does not make it possible for us to transform ourselves, but only to adapt and thus accept and perpetuate reality as it is, however oppressive, exploitative and alienating it may be. Then, although capitalism is unfair and intolerable, we adapt to it as if it were our natural environment, as if it were not historical and therefore surmountable.

The problem of adaptive psychoanalysis is not only that it naturalizes the order of things, making this order seem natural rather than historical, but that it makes us see the world as an external 'environment' separate from each one of us. This prevents us from recognising that we are part of the world, that we are in it and of it and that we can transform it by transforming ourselves, but also transform ourselves by transforming it. We are part of the ecologically-interconnected nature of this world, and connected to each other, responsible for each other as the exploited and oppressed and as comrades in struggle. The world, and other people in it, is not simply an 'environment'; it is more than that, and a more intimate part of our selves.

Every liberation movement learns at some point that there is a crucial difference between an 'environment' and 'ecology', and this difference becomes explicit when they connect their struggle with an ecosocialist understanding of our world. To speak of 'environment' is to speak of the world as something separate from us that we then learn to adjust to or try to dominate, while 'ecology' refers to the intimate interconnection between us and the world. Our lives are linked together in networks of solidarity and political consciousness in such an ecological way that we feel the pain of others in struggle, and know that we will only make this world worse if we try to dominate and exploit others, whether they are fellow human beings or other sentient beings. This ecological consciousness of our link with others is at the heart of psychoanalysis.

As conceived of by psychoanalysis, individuals are not truly alone, isolated and separated from one another. We are part of the lives of others and our actions and words can have fatal consequences for them. Somehow we know that we are as responsible for them as we are for ourselves. Our links are not only 'external'. The others are not only 'outside', around us, but also 'inside', inside each one of us, in what we think, say and do. In our gestures there are traces of others as well as in our words and ideas, and there are also echoes of other voices. Past relationships with others not only reappear in present relationships, but are tied into each of us and make us who we are. The constitution of the individual is social and cultural, but also historical, which makes it incessantly transformative.

Just as the conditions of exploitation, oppression and alienation we face are constructed, historically constructed, and so can be put to an end by us, so our peculiar alienated forms of psychology are products of history and can be changed. This is despite the claims of most psychiatrists, psychologists and psychotherapists to be working on universal unchanging essential properties of mental life. Their work is actually on extremely variable factors determined by culture, by the historical moment, by existing social relations.

Conservative adaptive psychoanalysts, along with most psy professionals, turn the continually changing historical nature of human existence into something fixed. This is all the more curious and reactionary in present-day society in which everything is changing so fast, where it is indeed as if all that is solid melts into air. We ourselves are forced to be flexible and we learn to exist at each moment in a different way, but the psy professionals fix our existence in place as if it were an object as they study and attempt to treat it, thus betraying what is most radical and transformative about our human nature as such.

Their image of human nature is of it as being not much more than a complicated machine. This is the brute animal as a mere instinctual mechanism which only existed in the imagination of human beings who felt superior when comparing themselves to it. Who would have thought that these same human beings would be finally confused with their degrading representation of the animal? It is as if the old degradation of the animal in contrast to the human being has served to prepare us all for the current degradation of the human being in psychology and in other psy professions, including conservative psychoanalysis.

Radical psychoanalysis, in contrast, teaches us that it is in the nature of human beings to reflect on their social conditions and for us all to continually attempt to transform these conditions and ourselves. We attempt to change and we fail, and it is radical psychoanalysis alongside radical political practice that shows us why we fail, and how we are locked in place by the dominant ideals of society and by the unique biography of each person. We cannot wish away the historical conditions that make us who we are, and neither can we wish away the internal obstacles that bind us to our oppression, that incite us to desire oppression at the same time as we resent it and try to escape it. We may not ever be able to free ourselves entirely from our desire for oppression, but we can know it, discern it when it intervenes, erupts, blocks us, and this knowledge can be the first step towards our liberation.

To desire oppression is a most peculiar thing, one of the painful paradoxes of subjectivity. The easiest thing is to pretend that there is no such paradox, but sooner or later we will stumble upon it and this may compromise our struggle for liberation. Perhaps in the end, responding to our desire, we will create new forms of oppression to replace those from which we liberate ourselves. To avoid this, we must take seriously what brings us back to where we started, what stops us or drags us back. We must take all this seriously not in order to blame the victim of this process as if it were simply psychological and inevitable but in order to understand the contradictory nature of each us as human beings in this wretched world.

History

Psychoanalysis, like Marxism and other theories of power and liberation, came into being at a specific historical period in order to conceptualise, understand and solve a historicallycreated series of problems. We need to grasp the *history* of psychoanalysis in history itself, and make it ours. Outside the historical context of the last two centuries, psychoanalysis would not make all the sense that it does for us. The same lack of sense would also beset Marxism if we transplanted it to another era.

It is difficult to imagine what slaves wanting to escape their rulers in ancient Rome would have made of Marxist analyses of 'surplus value', the hidden share the capitalist takes from a worker, for example, or of attempts to build revolutionary parties and international associations. The proletariat as industrial wage-labourer did not exist at the time of Spartacus. Freeing oneself from slavery was not the same as freeing oneself from the exploitation of wage labour. That is why Marxism only started to become useful when capitalism itself came into the world as a dominant mode of production. Likewise, the development of the colonial states and imperialism was necessary for there to be a need for anti-colonial and anti-imperialist liberation movements. Each political movement arose to combat particular exploitative or oppressive conditions.

In the case of psychoanalysis, the 'symptoms' of distress it was invented to understand and treat are quite specific to modern society. These symptoms are as historical as is the specific strange Freudian representation of the psyche. What is 'unconscious' is very much tied up with the peculiar form of alienation we suffer from in capitalist modernity.

Alienation in capitalism produces 'inner' conflicts that can be invisible as such, but which are known for their effects, for what they cause or motivate in people, such as their inexplicable suffering, the derangement of their lives, their absurd decisions or their erratic actions, sometimes destructive or self-destructive. All this is evident in current work experience. People are locked into their lives as workers in such a way that they repeat the same kinds of tasks, and their life-experience is then structured in a particular repetitive way that is outside their control.

Workers, everyone who works today, are driven to do so by economic imperatives, and so what it is to be subject to a 'drive' to work and to survive is bound up with capitalism. Capitalist domination shapes the power relations that bind us to each other, but these relations also repeat earlier power relations so that repetition is unconsciously driven and then reappears as what psychoanalysts call 'transference' inside the clinic. We will address each of these issues in the course of this book, and through them show that psychoanalysis grasps the nature of symptoms as indications of distress in this society.

Symptoms have been created in such a way that psychoanalysis, a historical invention, is geared to read them, and it helps us to see them for what they are, as conflicts in personal life and as expressing social conflicts. A particular society and a singular person in this society are what make manifest problems in a symptomatic way. Symptoms are indicators that something is wrong, they are messages about how distress is appearing in each separate subject.

Subjects

We refer to human beings as '*subjects*' here in this manifesto because the term 'individual' is too reduced a term, and it implies that our subjectivity is undivided and separate, isolated, opposed to society and as locked in its individuality. A 'subject' is more than the individual, it includes other people, it is open and crossed by the social world, inhabited and divided by the outside as its ecological space of being. The subject is in contradiction with itself and for this reason it can be the source of agency and change, whether that is at the level of an individual person or at the level of a collective political process.

The subject can be a historical agent, but also a victim and a product of history. Events affect us and determine us in different ways that can now be approached through psychoanalysis. Psychoanalytic thinking is one of the most powerful resources available to us to understand and change our experience in modern times. What was happening to us as subjects in late modernity, between the nineteenth and twentieth centuries, suddenly took on, with the development of Freudian theory, a radically new sense. Medical names for our distress were invented, and at the same time psychoanalysis was invented to deal with them, to rebel against what they meant, to transform that distress.

Psychoanalysis is still one of the best means to grasp the nature of our present-day symptoms of misery in life under advanced, neoliberal capitalism, with its associated forms of sexism, racism and colonialism. These psychoanalytic symptoms which operate unconsciously and then find distorted expression in the visible symptoms that the medical doctors and psychologists observe have a deeper connection with our individual biographies and with current conditions of life. Symptoms are historical phenomena in this double sense; they are produced in the personal history of each individual and their overall shape is structured by the kind of society we live in and try to make sense of.

Our past and our world haunt us, make us sick and make us suffer. This is whether we are completely bewitched by ideology and believe that this is the best of all possible worlds, no reason to worry, or whether we are an activist who knows that things are bad and have got to change. Conflict and contradiction bedevil us all, and those conflicts and contradictions reach down inside us, worm their way into us, tear us apart and then take the form of symptoms that can be painful and apparently inexplicable.

Psychoanalysis is dialectical, neither psychology nor psychiatry

The tortuous path of the history of the psychoanalytic approach to subjectivity went alongside the development of psychology understood as a scientific or pseudoscientific specialty and as a professional and academic discipline. This psychology should not be confused with psychoanalysis. Although it has frequently managed to absorb it, it disagrees with it in its premises, ideas, methods and objectives. Psychology, in fact, is constituted by much of what we try to solve through psychoanalysis. From the psychoanalytic point of view, the psychological sphere is problematic.

Psychology takes shape for us as an illusory, deceptive and even delusional experience, namely, the experience of each of us as an undivided and separate individual who can fully know and control themself as if an object. This unitary self is exactly part of the problem because it leads each person to imagine that they should take responsibility for their unwanted unpleasant feelings and makes them feel all the worse if they feel 'divided', if they sense that there is an unconscious dimension to their lives. Such a division, which affects us all, is recognized by psychoanalysis and denied by psychology. Its denial conceals our alienation and prevents us from resisting what alienates us. It thus contributes to what dominates us as if 'from the inside', to manipulate us and to manage us ideologically.

One key problem we face now is the historical construction of an individual isolated experience that does not correspond to our social existence, cannot recognize itself in our feelings and thoughts, has no power or sense in itself and is therefore vulnerable to domination, manipulation and ideological management. Here is the problem of psychology separated from the collective shared nature of our lives as human beings. It is, at root, a problem of individualism in capitalist society and its psychological manifestations.

Psychology

The discipline of *psychology* is devoted to the maintenance of each individual self as a separate psychological sphere, as the experience of their own personal psychology, like that of each worker isolated from the others. Psychology, the academic professional discipline and the sense of our own individual undivided psychology that the discipline works upon, was formed at the same time as capitalism itself, and it has spread, with capitalism, around the world. The expansion of capital around the world has also been a global dissemination of its psychological devices not only in university and health institutions, but in all spheres of life. Everything tends to be coloured with a psychological tone. This process of psychologization involves mechanisms of atomization, desocialization, depoliticization, dehistorization, pathologization, incrimination of individuals and adaptation to capitalist society.

Yes, we live under global capitalism, under brutal neoliberal capitalism today, but to understand how that capitalism functions we need something more than simply one name for the problem. Psychoanalysis, and not only psychoanalysis, teaches us that it is impossible to speak of life under capitalism, to speak of class, without also speaking of sexism and racism and the manifold other forms of oppression that disable people. Radical psychoanalysis is already 'intersectional', addressing the deep subjective link between different forms of oppression that the different liberation movements have arisen to combat and put an end to it.

Freeing ourselves from the oppressive experiences of class, race and sex requires us to combat them 'within' ourselves as well. Here, in the subjective sphere, what is oppressed appears not only as affected, but also as resigned or adapted to oppression. This adaptation, which sustains and perpetuates what oppresses us, is often viewed as 'mental health' by psychologists and psychiatrists.

Closely linked with a psychiatric medical model of distress, psychology has developed worldwide as a psychotherapeutic tool to adapt people to reality instead of enabling them to change it. Psychology picks up most of the historical ideological baggage of medical psychiatry and claims to humanise it, focusing on observable measurable symptoms in the behaviour of its clients instead of symptoms of invisible mental diseases. This shift to behaviour from disease is not much of a step forward, and psychoanalysis shows the limitations of this minimal shift of focus.

Psychoanalysis is not psychiatry. But the medical legacy of psychiatry is still present inside psychology even when psychologists present themselves as more friendly and progressive and 'psychotherapeutic'. We should be clear here that there are important theoretical differences, as well as professional status disputes, between psychiatrists who are medically-trained, psychologists who have their own reduced models of individual behaviour and thinking, and psychotherapists who mix and match whichever approach seems to work best in soothing distress and fitting people back into the world.

At the moment, it is psychologists who are centre-stage with their claims to scientific expertise. They consider themselves to be the most effective and compare their effectiveness with that attributed to psychiatry, psychotherapy and psychoanalytic practice. It would be easier for our task, to argue for the value of psychoanalysis, if psychology did not work. The problem is precisely that it does work; psychology fits very well with exploitative and oppressive social relationships, and it functions very well in adapting people so they keep that kind of world running fairly smoothly. It runs smoothly until there are symptoms, which psychology then uses its supposedly psychotherapeutic skills to sooth.

The spread of psychology around the world and into our everyday lives is bringing about a reduction, contraction and simplification of experience, of the way we feel, think and speak about ourselves. Our behaviour is more and more similar to that of the simplistic psychological caricatures of human existence that surround us everywhere. These caricatures are disseminated by means such as film and television, magazines and newspapers, bestsellers and self-help manuals, emotional re-education, business coaching, counselling, expert opinions, social networks and even Pentecostal churches.

The entire cultural realm is saturated with simplified banal psychological representations, highly functional for the capitalist system, in which we certainly recognize ourselves. We recognise ourselves in them, not because they are so faithful that they reflect us as we really could be, but because they are so powerful that they make us correspond to them, live them out in what we are at the moment in these miserable conditions of life.

Psychology is so successful because it manages to unfold through our existence, confirming it as it is now. Sometimes this existence seems to materialize concepts of the great psychological traditions, including those of the behaviourist, the humanist, and the cognitive disciplinary masters. Consumers have learned, for instance, to respond to advertising stimuli, to identify with the image of human nature that is sold to them, to process the information required to buy and to surrender to the hidden drives that push them into consumerism as an ideology and material practice.

There are even successful psychoanalytic versions of psychology, just as there are psychoanalytic versions of psychiatry. We need to beware of these imposters, these ideological distortions and capitulations to 'normality' of what should be a radical liberatory approach. Psychoanalysis cannot become psychiatry or psychology without ceasing to be what it is, losing its usefulness for liberation movements in the process and even becoming harmful to them, not only depoliticizing them by psychologizing or psychiatrizing, but contributing to adapt and subjugate rather than liberate.

It is possible to adulterate and degrade psychoanalysis by making it work like psychology and to help subjects to be what they should be in order to insert themselves most efficiently into capitalism. However, if we want to preserve psychoanalysis for what it really is and can be, we need to separate it from this process, and show how psychoanalysis can enable us to resist it. Psychoanalysis itself, because of the history of adaptation it has been subject to, has become implicated with ideology, but it rebels. It is as if psychoanalysis is itself a symptom of oppression that now can be made to speak, and in the process of speaking well of psychoanalysis we may liberate it and liberate ourselves.

Psychoanalysis is riven by conflict, and it speaks of conflict in its approach to our historically-constructed human nature. It has emerged at a precise historical moment, reflecting the contradictory needs, inclinations, desires and aspirations of the kind of human subject who carries the contradictions of this world deep inside them, and that is why we can also speak of psychoanalysis itself as a symptom.

The psychoanalytic approach not only deals with symptomatic manifestations of the suffering of the subject, but itself is a symptom. It is as contradictory as what it addresses. At the very same moment as we demand of psychoanalysis that it attend to the contradictory nature of life under capitalism, attend to the symptoms that arise today in this society, so we also demand that it must be a reflexive 'critical psychology' able to examine itself; we must analyse what makes psychoanalysis adapt to society and what makes it resist and become something subversive and liberating.

Conflict

As it is with psychoanalysis, so it is with each individual who carries a symptom within themselves. They are beset by *conflict*. Individuals are routinely trapped in harmful oppressive relationships by a particular biographically-distinct pattern of experience, and that is what comes to define who they are. This is what makes them recognisable as the same person to themselves, their family and friends.

What is distinctive about each of us is something unconscious in which we are trapped, something resistant and repetitive, as well as contradictory, conflictive. There is internal conflict which is given shape in the symptom peculiar to each one of us. This symptom can paralyse us and prevent us from transforming ourselves and modifying the relationships that oppress and harm us. Change often happens when something dramatic or traumatic happens to us, breaks us from those unconsciously driven patterns, and social change is one big factor in the spur to individual change.

The process of change and the crystallisation of conflict in the symptom can be understood dialectically. Conflict is what traps us, what immobilizes us, but is at the same time what makes us move to solve it and free ourselves from it. Our movement forward is both driven and hampered by conflict. This makes us move little by little, advance and stumble, changing without changing almost anything, something that is particularly apparent when there is a series of little changes that suddenly lead to a transformation, quantitative incremental changes that prepare the way for a qualitative shift. This happens at the political level when sustained collective struggle leads finally, after years of effort, to new possibilities and new forms of subjectivity appearing. And it happens in the clinic when the symptom manifests itself as an open conflict and calls for a decision about how to go on with life. The symptom is an obstacle but also, dialectically understood, it is an opportunity.

The symptom is an opportunity to change and not just to know ourselves. This is why the symptom should not be eliminated, as psychologists and psychiatrists usually try to do, thus ensuring that nothing is discovered and everything remains the same. In order to discover and transform oneself, one must listen to the symptom with the greatest attention, as is done in psychoanalysis.

People come to a psychoanalyst not because they have symptoms, for everyone in this sick society is beset by symptoms, but when those symptoms become unbearable, when there is an impending shift from quantitative misery to qualitative change of some kind. One of tasks of clinical psychoanalysis is to direct the treatment in such a way that this qualitative change takes place in the form of opportunity for reflection and decided choice about how to live one's life instead of teetering on the edge of breakdown and despair. Psychoanalysis helps the subject not to be overwhelmed or defeated by what is manifested in the symptom, to overcome it, which is only possible by listening to the symptom and acting accordingly. The symptom is dialectical in nature, and psychoanalysis is a dialectical approach which helps the individual subject take a new course, towards adaptation or liberation.

To be liberating, psychoanalysis must be liberated. It has to be released from what it is not and is not meant to be. It must be purified of the sediment of mystifications, prejudices, malign moral values, dogmas, stereotypes and illusions that have turned it from being a progressive approach into one that is instrumentally useful to capitalism and colonialism and to oppressive gender relations.

Psychoanalysis has been instrumentalised in the successive contexts it has attempted to adapt itself to. These contexts have imbued psychoanalysis with their norms, beliefs, prejudices, and values, requiring it to moderate its radical aims and to compromise. Over the course of its history all kinds of reactionary ideological content were injected into its radical form. That ideological content, which includes poisonous ideas about the essential underlying difference between men and women and their sexuality and their gendered relation to each other, is trapped in the body of psychoanalysis as a form of practice, a practice of speech. This is serious because psychoanalysis is itself a 'talking cure' that shows us how what we say is interconnected with what we do.

The conflicts and contradictions of our class society are inseparable from our speech, as well as from our sexual life, which is also at the centre of psychoanalysis. We will try to explain in the course of this manifesto why this is so, and how it is that psychoanalysis homed in on sexuality precisely because that sexuality was seen as the intimate core of our lives.

We talk about sex, and that is what psychoanalysis is so often known for, but why? If the nuclear family was experienced as the heart of a heartless world when capitalism developed, sexuality was experienced as the most private and secret part of ourselves. But it was not only 'repressed', covered over as something shameful and pushed away as something bad, but incited, demanded of us. It was thus turned into an obsession, as well as our weakest point, an open wound, constantly irritated, which serves to dominate us in a 'heteropatriarchal' logic.

Patriarchy is always 'heteropatriarchy'. It is always 'heteronormative', that is, it makes heterosexuality compulsory as the basis of the intimate social contract at the heart of our globalised world because it enforces the power of men over women and of older men over younger men, and it excludes or barely tolerates different forms of sexuality. This is the case even when patriarchal capitalism uses a distorted version of feminist discourse against the left or turns varieties of sexual preference into a niche market.

Just as patriarchal capitalism can instrumentalize feminism and sexual diversity – absorb and distort these radical ideas and turn them against us - so it can turn psychoanalysis into its instrument to normalize and exploit our sexual lives. Our sexuality, therefore, runs the risk of being conditioned by patriarchal discourse not only in the cultural realm, but also in the psychoanalytic clinical setting. We can purge psychoanalysis of that ideological poison now, enabling it to speak for us and not instead of us or against us.

So, against psychology and psychiatry, and against most forms of psychotherapy, psychoanalysis is a psy profession with a difference. It knows how to listen to us and is not condemned to speak in our place. Therefore, instead of pretending to fix things in place, it treats the symptom of our distress as a message from the subject about their miserable condition and, crucially, about the need for change. In this way, it has the potential to be an invaluable ally of liberation movements. It is, in itself, a dialectical theory and practice of liberation.

Liberation in the clinic and culture

Psychoanalysis has been appropriated by those with power, it is true, but this does not mean that we should let it go, let it fall into their hands. We must, rather, re-appropriate psychoanalysis. In order to do this we need to grasp the dialectical relationship between its clinical work and its ever-changing historical context. The historical conditions which saw the birth of psychoanalysis, of alienation under capitalism, exploitation of life and the oppressive nature of the Western European nuclear family, were precisely the conditions that psychoanalysis aimed to understand and combat. It was in those conditions that sexuality was experienced as traumatic because it was repressed but simultaneously spoken about incessantly, provoked.

The conditions in which psychoanalysis appeared, and the ideological forces at work, entered into psychoanalysis, distorting it. There is no 'pure' non-ideological psychoanalysis, but there can be an ongoing cleansing of its theoretical elaborations, permanent unending purification of its key concepts. The complex dialectical relationship between its clinical form and ideological aspects of the theory can be constantly clarified and transcended in practice. It is a continuous process, always unfinished, of struggle against power, critique of ideology and resistance against psychologization.

Four key concepts of psychoanalysis – *unconscious, repetition, drive* and *transference* – operate as radical formal elements of the theory that allow us to resist the deeply ideological process of psychologisation. These terms have a particular meaning in psychoanalysis, but we aim to make them meaningful here to radicals who are not only seeking to change themselves but also seeking to change the world.

The unconscious, repetition, drive, and transference operate in the world and not just on the psychoanalyst's couch. We must consider these four concepts in the space of dialectical tension between the clinic as a private space of transformational work and our historical context. The four key concepts need to be reconstructed in order to make them thoroughly historical; this, to avoid the trap of 'applying' them to liberation movements and so turning them from guiding revolutionary practices to becoming tools of ideology.

We must understand that our struggles do not need to be interpreted, justified, validated and much less conducted by psychoanalytic concepts. Nor do we intend that these concepts should operate as a universe of meaning that limits and closes the horizon of freedom for which we fight. Our liberation movements must keep their path open and decide their direction and scope as they move forward and expand what they can conceive of and accomplish. They should not be guided by psychoanalysis as if by a fixed point of reference, but they can utilise it as one means among others and transform psychoanalysis as they transform everything else in their confrontation with the conditions in which we live.

We confront particular modern conditions of culture, of capitalism blended with colonialism and its necessary forms of racism and sexism and other ways of pathologising people who are unwilling or unable to adapt to this world as healthy well-behaved productive citizens. Psychoanalysis provides valuable insights into the underlying nature of subjectivity in this global culture, and into the differences that divide the peoples of the world against each other. However, its real contribution lies in the clinic, and the four key concepts, of unconscious, repetition, drive and transference that we discuss in more detail in the following chapters of this manifesto, are grounded in its clinical work.

It is in the clinic that we discover what is beyond us, how we repeat self-destructive relationships, how we are driven to do so, and how the phenomenon of transference as an uncanny relationship with the psychoanalyst operates. These discoveries in the psycho-analytic clinic do not happen outside the dominant cultural universe. They logically feed back into culture, for good or ill, and so we also have something to say about the dangers of 'applying' psychoanalysis beyond the clinic as an inevitable academic distortion of its practice.

Beyond its questionable applications, psychoanalysis needs to be recreated by us as a tool of radical work on subjectivity that is necessary if there is to be a successful over-throw of existing conditions. Dialectically understood, this tool is the result of the theoreti-cal elaborations of Freud and his followers, who enabled us to use it for radical work in the clinic and with liberation movements. What it produces is part of a creative process which enables us to make more. Our name for what it makes possible is 'revolutionary subjectiv-ity', a 'revolutionary subject'.

As in the clinic, so it is in politics; the revolutionary subject appears and disappears, comes into being, forged in struggle, and fades again when its work is done. All this will not turn us into heroic revolutionary individuals, charismatic activists, or battle-hardened leaders. What concerns us is not the formation of leaderships or personalities, but the cre-ation of a collective process of change that anticipates the kind of world we want to build, no more than that.

That will not turn us into psychoanalysts, far from it, and the end result psychoanaly-sis always aims for is to enable the human subject to kick away the ladder that they have used to reach a new place. The psychoanalytic perspective should not close our horizon. It is an opportunity, not a trap. As we bring an end to the world that creates so much misery we also anticipate the end of psychoanalysis, psychoanalysis as a revolutionary approach that is functioning as a tool and result of that historical process. We begin, in the next chapter, with the *unconscious*.

第二章
無意識：異化，理性與他者性

　　我們的鬥爭，無論它是多麼在地，都屬國際範圍，而且每一次解放鬥爭都逐步擴大關於我們是如何被分裂和統治的了解視野，若僅僅著眼於直接切近的地方關係、地區層面或甚至侷限於國家脈絡的框架之內，那麼就難以理解那些對我們所做的事情了。

　　例如，富裕國家的消費主義、失業和仇外心理只有在我們將貧窮國家的苦難、低工資和對勞動力的剝削納入考量時才能懂得箇中道理；相似地，我們需要考慮新與舊形式的殖民主義和帝國主義，才能了解種族仇恨或恐怖攻擊中的利害攸關。這也是何以智利女性主義的口號──「壓迫的國家即男性強暴犯」（'the oppressive state is a male rapist'）──能幫助我們不僅闡明政府對婦女的壓迫和暴力行為，也闡明了恐同暴行與陽剛暴力以犧牲女性化及其他被輕視的生活或存在方式為代價在群體及國家之間居於強勢宰制地位的關係形式。

　　世界上發生的一切（即使離我們很遠）是我們所言與所行的基礎。我們日常的言語與行動也涉及過去的歷史，甚至是最遙遠的、過去好幾個世紀的歷史。歷史承載著我們，所有這一切在每時每刻都存在，限制我們並引導我們朝著某個方向前進，但通常以我們沒有完全意識到的方式存在。這種限制和可能性就是**無意識**。

　　本章是關於精神分析中一個根本核心的概念。無意識生靈活現地被帶到臨床裡，而它的影響作用在日常生活裡處處都可被感受到。我們需要把握無意識在資本主義社會產生的異化[1]中以個人和政治形式呈現的方式，

---

[1]　Alienation 譯作「異化」，在作者所批判的個體心理學（individual psychol-

而我們對此的理解又是如何被「常識」（'commonsense'）[2] 所扭曲？我們也需要把握這個社會的理性是如何將我們帶進「意識自我」[3] 作爲主人的個體自我（individual self）陷阱中？而揮之不去的「他者性」（'otherness'）[4] 又是如何與語言（與我們向他人傳達我們的受苦同樣的語言）聯繫在一起的？

異化與常識

　　在這個悲慘世界中我們被異化，以致與他人分離，甚至與自己分離；

---

ogy）、自我心理學（ego psychology）及其他心理學領域中此字通常一般被理解（也被中譯）爲「疏離、疏離感」，較多指涉個體性的存在狀態，但在作者及馬克思思想和拉岡精神分析的脈絡中，此詞具有社會 - 文化 - 歷史意涵，也就是無意識的，宜譯作「異化」。作者在本章論及「異化是分離的一種形式」（'Alienation is a form of separation.'），並區分兩種不同的「異化」，包括「原初異化」（'original alienation'）——這是人皆有之，從想像的鏡象中與他者（包括自身與照顧者）遭逢而「分裂」，我們因這種「原初異化」而開展自己的路；以及特定的「文化 - 歷史的異化」（'cultural-historical alienation'）——這是在特定社會體制及意識形態剝削壓迫下的再被加劇異化，如勞動異化。

[2] 'commonsense' 譯爲「常識」，請注意作者於下一小節説明它與 'common sense'（譯爲「常理」）的巨大差別。

[3] ego 與 self 在中文世界都被譯作「自我」，但兩者在不同脈絡下各有不同的意義。作者沿著佛洛伊德到拉岡的精神分析語境，ego 明確指的是個體作爲中心的、與他人分開的、獨立的、被視爲實體、固有、本質的、理性意識的自我，是個體心理學（individual psychology）或自我心理學（ego psychology）中個體性的自我（individual self）；而 self 則指涉會經由與外界關連互動而分裂的主體的多重自我或自身、自己，在客體關係論的脈絡中又被譯作「自體」，衍生所謂「自體心理學」。爲中文讀者區辨上的方便，將 ego 譯作「意識自我」；而 self 則視上下文脈意義譯作「自我」、「自身」或「自己」，當必須譯作「自我」時加註（self），例如本章下文中 selfconsciousness 譯作「自我意識」，而 self-conscious 'ego' 則譯作自我意識的「意識自我」，以利讀者分辨。

[4] 讀者將在原文中看到 'otherness'（他者性）、'other'（異己他者、或直接譯作「他者」）、'Other'（大寫它／他者）（請注意，作者使用此詞的意義與中文地區較常耳聞的齊澤克（Slavoj Žižek）的「大它者」（'Big Other'）有細微但意義重大的不同）等詞，請見導讀説明。

而我們聽到的那些關於異化和無意識的說法，通常帶有掩蓋問題根源的意識形態作用，使得我們無法找到我們需要的幫助。我們需要以不同的方式思考無意識。

藉由國際範圍的思考、反思及採取政治行動，我們開始了解不同社會群體、國家、文化、性別和性取向的特殊他人是如何被我們視為「他者」（'other'），也了解到這種「他者性」是如何嵌入國族主義、種族主義和性別歧視形式的階級特權和侮辱而往內部作用。甚至對這個悲慘世界中的我們來說，我們被塑造成「他者」，於是他者性貫穿我們的經驗、我們的主體性、本性自身的深處；無論它究竟是什麼，都被體驗為異己的、陌生的和威脅的。這是精神分析稱之為「無意識」的重要部分。這是居住在我們的「外部」和「內部」世界的不可辨識之物。雖然它在我們的思想中，但它超出了我們的思考，它不是我們的所思。我們每個人都是與自己相裂開的、分裂的、異於自己的他者。

無意識總是逸出我們的思想，它不是簡單地僅是被埋藏而可被挖掘、思考、記憶起的東西。相反地，它是一種與我們的思想、言語、行為以及與世界關係的異化形式，這種異化形式總是有別於它們表面看起來的樣子，彷彿它們和我們是分開的。

異化是分離的一種形式。在嚴格的精神分析術語中，這是在我們與那些將我們帶到這個世界並首先照顧我們的人作必要分離之後的雙重異化形式。藉著轉身離開他們，我們也轉身離開了自己，我們往內分裂自身，所以我們可以在這個我們被「異化」的世界找到自己的道路，並使用語言將這種不安傳達給他人。然後，這個世界特定文化歷史的異化加倍強化我們的「原初異化」（'original alienation'）—— 也就是我們的內部分裂，我們作為分裂主體（divided subjects）為了生存必須與他人交流（包括談我們的痛苦）的獨特的人類本性。

在這個壓迫和剝削的社會中，我們的異化透過多個維度的分離而運作，其中包括為尋求出售勞動力在個體間的競爭、一旦我們把時間賣給雇主，就被他們掌控我們創造性勞動的成果、為了生活我們必須為別人工作，儘管我們對身體能否負荷得起感到焦慮、為了利潤所驅而剝削自然世界，以致在我們看來，自然界彷彿是與我們敵對的力量。他人、我們自己

的創造力、我們的身體和自然界，無一不與我們分離，然後被視爲威脅。常識告訴我們這是普遍而理所當然的，但常識在說謊。

常識

　　我們爲之奮鬥的「常理」（'common sense'）[5]——我們從在地知識中建立起來、透過經驗和實踐理論分析積累的創造性專門知能的那種常識——與流傳給我們或被偷渡和歪曲而往往抑制我們能力的意識形態常識（commonsense）是不同的。這種意識形態常識是我們在此關切的。這種意識形態常識系統性地挫折了我們將這種異化形式理解爲之於我們的某種「他者」（'other'）、某種無意識的努力。然而，儘管常識如此，使我們異化的他者還是存在。在這個經濟力量驅動我們得去爲他人的營利而勞動的世界，某些東西逸出意識的控制，而精神分析對於我們生活中這種總是超出我們掌握、存在於我們無意識之中的方面有很多話要說。

　　在這個過程中，佛洛伊德對無意識的發明也被平庸化，變成了隱晦深沉的圖像、某種黑暗且神祕的東西；或者，在許多心理學和精神醫學教科書中，像一座我們只能望見尖頂的冰山。心理學化的精神分析甚至告訴我們將這種無意識驅趕回隱蔽之地、忽略它，假裝它對我們的生活沒有影響。這種心理「幸福」（'wellbeing'）和「快樂」（'happiness'）的虛假形象使得自我意識的「意識自我」（self-conscious 'ego'）與無意識相對立起來，希望無意識消失。

　　這種「意識自我」已爲許多精神分析的推廣者和心理／精神相關專業的熱衷支持者所熟知，通常它被描述爲自我（the self）的理性核心，但這種理性個體自我意識的微小機制實際上根本不是關乎我們是誰的核心；畢

---

[5]　common sense 一般也譯作「常識」，但在這裡的 'common sense'（ common sense 加引號）是作者在全書唯一加引號之處，是爲了特別標示這種常識不同於本節要關注討論的意識形態常識，（commonsense），故，針對此一特殊用法，中譯爲「常理」。但請留意，作者隨後於使用的未有引號的 common sense（本章 4 次，第 3 章 1 次）以及 common-sense（出現在第 2、4 章各 1 次），在文脈中語意回到「常識」，甚至前面就接著意識形態的（ideological），也就是 commonsense。

竟，正如馬克思（Marx）教導我們的那樣，我們是「社會關係的總合」（'ensemble of social relations'），而定義我們作為人類的集體本性的社會關係網絡，並非意識自我所在之處，而在無意識。

無意識並不是藏在我們每個人與世隔絕的深處的某種晦暗隱蔽的東西，而是在我們參與並構成我們的社會關係中展開，這些關係喚起了他人、其他過去的關係，並且超出了我們的意識控制，但它們決定了我們是什麼以及我們可以控制什麼，它們形塑了我們的自我（self）和我們的自我意識。

我們想當然爾的自我意識似乎經常擁抱我們，但它不能拯救我們，它誤導了我們，它沉迷於與社會分離的自我（the self）的常識意識形態，充分利用異化，而不是去承認它、去了解它是如何被製造出來以及如何使我們能夠共同來改變它被產生的條件。

過於簡化的「自我覺察」（'self-awareness'）並沒有將我們從異化中解放出來，反倒是透過我們的「意識自我」的異化想像再複製了它，作為我們的自我（our selves）的核心、作為我們自我意識的理性中心的這種「意識自我」想像，將我們的主體性化約，讓我們相信自己該是什麼樣，使我們視每個人都是與其他人分離的個體。這種思維方式不是通往治癒的途徑，更不是革命的道路。

只要我們沒設法從那種把我們每個人立即套進意識形態上的樣子的思考中解脫出來，我們那兒也去不了，不可能去到我們已看到的自己之外的任何地方。這種關於我們自身被常識愚弄了的思考，背離了使我們成為人類的他者性，將此他者性變成了詛咒，而不是經由反對剝削和壓迫的歷史鬥爭去獲得實際持久真正治癒的實質基礎。我們的解放只能是集體的，這就是為什麼它不被那種把我們關在「意識自我」牢籠中的常識所涵蓋。

在這種常識性的思維方式中，我們僅僅是獨特的自我（self）。各種數不盡的多樣性別、膚色、文化或國籍的特殊性，許多其他方面的差異，對我們而言是外來的、有別於我們的、甚至是令人厭惡或敵對的。我們不承認我們的集體多樣性是人類共同的特性。我們也需要注意，這個自滿自足的意識自我形像如何邊緣化「特殊需要人士」（'disabled people'），將其視為受損的、不完整的。他們被這個需要正常健康、適應良好的身體來

產生「剩餘價值」（'surplus value'）的社會以及被這個功能自主的意識自我主人作爲常識標準規範形象所「失能的」（'disabled'），那些不能擔當這樣的主人角色的人常被譙罵作「瘋子」（'mad'）。

於是我們否定了作爲人類的本性，我們背離了我們內在的本性，沒有他人我們什麼都不是。當我們背離了與他人親密的關係時，對他人痛苦的團結友愛關係便被仇恨和猜疑所取代，這樣我們就掉入陷阱之中。

面對資本主義世界普遍存在的苦難，我們陷入了自以爲是、占有性和競爭性的個人化解決方案的誘惑裡，這樣的誘惑會像這個世界一樣悲慘，這個世界被囤積商品與榨取他人利益的驅動力所宰制，甚至聲稱我們那時是「快樂的」；當這種情況發生時，個人控制的、孤立的「意識自我」便與他人形成了對立。

然而，即使我們背離人性，我們也離不開作爲人類。無意識說話，從而能將我們以集體的行動聯繫在一起，這種聯繫存在一個辯證的轉向，即雖然個體性的「意識自我」不是每一個人的核心，但無意識也不是，我們在無意識中相互聯繫，在無意識中我們是社會關係的總合。無意識和意識自我都不是自我（self）的「核心」；而且，無意識也絕非我的存在中某種本質固有的東西，它並不隱藏在我們每個人的內心，它不是關乎我是什麼的那個深不可測的內核，它不是這麼一回事。

這個被我們假定爲深藏於每一個人內心的無意識，本質上是某種*外在的*（outside）指涉他者性的東西，它是由歷史、經濟、社會、文化和意識形態構成的，它是與他人相遇和分歧的空間，是與他人爭論的解釋和矛盾，是同志之間在鬥爭、說服和誤解中結盟和衝突的空間。它出現在我們與他人共享的語言領域。

無意識本身是由我們從我們生活的世界中學習的特定語言構成的。它來自外部，來自我們所見所聞，來自過去和現在的關係結構，這些關係在我們居住的空間中產生共鳴和展開。因此，它作爲一種「他者」的話語而作用，即使不總是被注意到，也總是存在。它同時是辯證的，外在的和內在的。它圍繞著我們，穿過我們。它之所以在我們之內，正是因爲它曾經而且現在仍然在我們之外，因爲我們在其中，因爲它就是我們所在的地方。

　　我們住在無意識的**外在性**（*exteriority*）。在這裡，在這個存在的外部結構領域中，似乎每一個人都必須占據一個位置，這位置要符合他／她，使他／她有別於他人，而後，當他們適應了社會，這位置要使他／她和別人一致相符。正是無意識把我們放進我們的位置，卻同時使我們感到不安，它提醒我們，我們並不只是我們想像的這樣而已，我們遠遠超過那個被化約在意識自我之內思考（卻彷彿是我們對其他世界的外交代表一般）的微小而異化的自我（selves）。

　　我們從無意識了解到，對於我們說的話，我們並沒有完全的權力，我們無法控制我們話語的意義，我們不是意義的小世界的中心，也不是與他人直接面對面關係的小世界的中心。那種我們是中心而且意識自我作為主人的錯覺，是一種和人類就是世界的中心（即對立於動物王國其他眾生，而非與他們共同生活）一樣強大的意識形態故事。這兩個關於我們處於中心（萬物存在的中心）的意識形態故事，實際上只是被基進的精神分析觀點所舉證、質疑和挑戰的一個例子，精神分析挑戰凌駕於我們及其他一切事物之上的意識自我的權力。

　　精神分析在對意識自我的批判中使我們每個人都面對選擇——是否我們仍要繼續試圖宰制自身、他人和自然界？或者要尋求一種不同的方式與之共在？——這個選擇是具有解放性與啟發性的，它讓我們發現關於權力至少三件事：第一，權力並非不可避免，它不必然是某種只能施或受的事；第二，權力沒法在不同時受苦的情況下發揮作用，因為支配他人的需要同時就預設了支配自己；第三，同樣的權力包含在使我們窒息的意識自我中、使我們壓迫他人的力量中、以及破壞我們周圍世界的力量中。

　　精神分析可以幫助我們擺脫意識自我，並在外部對抗將我們封鎖於內部的權力。戰場在外部——在自然和社會文化世界中，超出我們個體性的狹隘意識邊界。因此，透過無意識，我們從作為「環境」與世界分離的意識自我的概念轉變為基進的解放生態學——精神分析生態社會主義的概念。為此，我們必須復興這個世界，在世界中奪回我們的權力。

權力

　　什麼是**權力**（*power*）？如精神分析所設想的，權力總在意識自我強

加於自身之處；然而，它從非個人眞正所有，即使當我們相信我們擁有權力時，也並不是我們眞正地完全擁有它；相反地，權力也擁有我們並且異化我們——它透過我們或在我們身上施行控制，藉由支配我們而迫使我們不是受支配就是施加支配、藉著剝削我們迫使我們不是作爲剝削者就是被剝削者、不是作爲主人就是奴僕、不是作爲消費者就是勞動者、不是作爲販賣者就是商品。在任何情況下，由於被權力擁有，我們被異化，我們變得與自身異化，爲了成爲權力希望我們成爲的那樣的人，於是，我們不再是自己。

精神分析爲我們提供了一種關於權力的視野，它是一種在主體之外、即使施加權力者也受其支配的不可掌控之物、總是暗含著一種異質的和異化的無意識基質（unconscious substrate）的東西。這種視野對於大多數左翼多數看待權力的觀點的補充是必要的，因爲大多數左翼的觀點認爲權力是一種可以被「擁有」（'possessed'）的、在意識上對他人強加支配的東西。

的確，有權力的人（那 1% 富豪，以及許多不同私營和國有企業的統治者和大男人主義的領導者）他們喜歡故意羞辱他們的下屬。但是我們必須小心，不要把對社會的批判性分析變成一個巨大的陰謀論，而且我們知道陰謀論實際上經常充當有毒的禁令，使我們從眞正的問題（父權和殖民的資本主義體制）被岔開而轉移到拿代罪羔羊作靶子，反猶太主義陰謀論（antisemitic conspiracy theories）是最廣爲人知的例子。

馬克思主義以及許多與女權主義和反殖民運動同路線的解放理論和實踐並不是要去找出那些行使權力者的陰謀論妄想，而是要對每個人受制於多重交織權力體制的方式進行系統結構分析，這些分析與我們從精神分析中學到的東西一致。因此，我們在這裡提出的權力觀點不僅是旨在補充那些激越昂揚的解放運動，而且還要作爲對錯誤道路進行批判性分析的資源，這條錯誤道路（儘管這些運動者抱持最良善的意圖）實際上透過將政治個體化、私人化和心理學化，使得他們的鬥爭去政治化。

根本問題不在於某些人或他們的行爲，更不在他們的傾向、心理狀況或人格特質。根本問題在於結構，結構使人不知不覺地成爲那樣的人那樣地行事。結構是經濟的和象徵性的，因此它是政治的，與運作它又同時反

對它的無意識一樣具有深刻的政治性。因此，關注無意識、注意問題的根本，精神分析政治以一種更為基進的方式思考權力。那在社會關係和個人經歷中對我們而言是無意識的，卻是對我們理解世界的方式以及如何複製或嘗試改變世界具有強大的結構性影響。

　　精神分析所說的權力與異化在這個將人類的能力甚至是人類自身化約為商品的世界中普遍存在。當我們透過販賣我們的知識、我們的能力、我們的生命、我們的勞動力以競相推銷自己時，我們會與他人競爭對立。於是，我們的創造性勞動轉變成了我們的雇主所控制和販售的東西，或者我們販售自己去替雇主服務，甚至做起雇主做的事——控制和販售勞動（我們的勞動）。

　　無論是透過他人、透過事物、還是透過我們自己，我們的雇主都控制著我們，讓我們聽從他們的命令，這些命令有時也出於我們自己，我們做他們所做的事，也做了他們對我們做的事（即使他們不知道自己在做什麼），被貪得無厭的利潤追求所驅使、到了以自我毀滅性企圖（self-destructive attempts）支配他人的地步，當他們從事毀滅許多其他生命和對地球的破壞時，他們異化了我們，也異化了他們自身。

　　我們甚至擔負起貫徹雇主意志的任務，把我們想像成小雇主，這就發生在當我們被賦予某些權威（如作為顧客、業主、工頭、父母、丈夫、教師、評鑑者、官僚、警察、士兵、治療師、醫生……等）之時，這是小小的補償和安慰，至少在所有我們被奪去的、壓迫我們的權力中，有一小部分明顯地被歸還給我們，這讓我們忘記我們受到的壓迫和剝削。遺憾的是，忘記它便使得我們更易被剝削，使我們繼續被剝削，得不償失，我們獲得的微弱權力使得我們集體屈服於權力；當我們聽到說它放我們自由時，它卻是意圖設法將我們鎖在原地。

　　每個人都以犧牲自己為代價來為自己增加權力，對精神分析至關重要的這件事也是這樣發生的：我們每個人把我們自己跟我們的身體拆分開，我們扭曲了與身體的關係，我們奴役自己的身體，將它們物化，並將它們用作履行義務或滿足我們每個人的抱負的手段。這也是失能的「社會模式」（'social models' of disability）所教我們的——身體在這世界上被迫作為意識形態上「完整」（'complete'）的生產對象來運作，如果他們

不是這樣，他們就被視爲「失能」的；受到基進的特殊需要權益運動者
（radical disability activists）挑戰的這種完整而自足的身體形象與受到基
進的心理健康和「反精神醫學」（'anti-psychiatry'）運動者挑戰的完整而
自滿自足的自我（self）形象同樣具有意識形態。

　　我們每個人的意識自我持續地被用來掌管我們的身體，作爲個體時我
們在精神上被剝削，這使得作爲集體時我們在物質上被剝削，沒有意識自
我這個社群共同體中最薄弱的環節的共謀，社會剝削不可能存在。這個脆
弱點可以透過精神分析來治療，目的是重新獲得集體的權力。

　　我們的精神分析觀點認爲權力是可以由我們集體掌握的，我們可以掌
握權力並用它來逐步形塑社會和我們自己；我們並不反對權力，而是反對
將其化約爲個人層次的想像，我們支持它作爲一種創造性的力量，我們知
道，如果我們集體行使權力，權力可以使我們自由，並能爲我們創造出另
一個世界（比這更好的世界），從而抵制那種意識形態，那種使我們想像
權力始終屬於意識自我，彷彿個體是唯一的主體並且是他們行爲的主人的
宰制性意識形態。

　　對社會與對權力本質的常識性看法以意識形態運作，掩蓋了異化的根
本原因。對比之下，與這種意識形態的社會再現相反，我們聲稱，在這個
悲慘世界中，異化加上權力就是無意識。從這個意義上來說，無意識就是
政治，我們必須學會如何看懂我們的行動是如何被無意識地組織起來，更
好地以集體方式反對權力，並結束在資本主義下遍地肆虐的極端破壞性異
化形式。

在意識自我陷阱中的理性

　　某些形式的精神分析（特別是那些已經在英語世界裡成爲主流且被適
應性機構整合進去的）以意識自我爲王，並旨在恢復其臨床寶座，這種適
應性保守精神分析的目標是讓意識自我作爲主人。如此一來，佛洛伊德最
基進的觀點被背叛了，意識自我被假定爲理性的所在。

　　這種理性當然是資本主義、殖民主義和父權制意識形態所鍾愛的布爾
喬亞資產階級（bourgeois）的個體理性，這是意識自我陷阱中的理性，截

然不同於我們在反抗權力運動和解放運動中共同創造的集體理性。為了連結並創造集體理性，我們需要透過無意識來連接，在那裡找到我們自己，而不是在意識自我中迷失了自己。

　　無意識是我們擺脫個人理性的一切，有時是我們不得不寓居的必要的創造性背景，是我們的人性一個被轉向「黑暗」（'dark'）力量的面向，在布爾喬亞資產階級意識形態中，這被視為一種威脅。對那黑暗事物所持的負面印象──即象徵的種族主義，經常伴隨著這種以理想自我（ideal self）作為主人的意識形態想像──一種異性戀父權的幻覺。這種對無意識以及我們的身體和集體都持懷疑態度的意識形態，將我們限制在個人心理領域──意識自我的領域。我們被孤立在意識自我裡，為它所惑，以致於我們可能忘記無意識而致力於征服我們自己的身體。

　　於是我們每個人的任務就是控制我們的身體，讓它為資本主義服務。這就是為什麼我們征服並掌控它，我們把它當作奴隸，當作必須為自己和他人勞動的機器。然後，我們在一場正在變成生態災難的個人戲劇中，與自然本身作對，自然先是被我們視為裡面的威脅，然後又看作是我們外面的威脅。我們異化的存在狀態使我們遠離了自己的創造性勞動、猜忌他人、害怕自己的身體失控從而先發制人地不信任並破壞對自然本身。

科學

　　徹底的生態滅絕，世界不可逆轉的犧牲，始於在意識自我的祭壇上獻祭我們自己的身體，而這種獻祭到頭來又是我們異化的結果，只要當我們變成如意識自我般而遠離於本來面目的東西時，我們就會摧毀自己並摧毀整個世界。總之，當我們在意識自我的整體形式下，將我們被異化的個體性進行整體化時，這個世界將片甲不留滿目瘡痍。我們的異化也是一種「客體化」（'objectification'）──包括將主體和人際關係轉化為客體──於是*科學*（science）被轉變、扭曲，從一種實際分析理解的工具變成了一種控制工具。

　　我們明白主流心理學中那種客體化的「科學的」（'scientific'）表達。工具性的「科學」是科學理性的一種意識形態形式，基於「預測和控制」（'prediction and control'）模式，它將我們變成了客體之物，正是精神分

析所反對的主體的客體化。一旦客體化，主體就會轉變為意識自我。這個意識自我就不再是主體，它是迥異於主體之物，它是我們異化、迷失於其中之物。

我們在意識自我裡已如此地異化以致於我們不再將其視為異己之物，我們為意識自我所惑，到頭來也為其他的意識自我而迷茫。當以模仿他人為目的而不去認識他人不同於我們的價值時，我們再也無法辨別自己與他人，於是我們與群體和社群的關係就化約成模仿（mimicry），以尋求與他人相同地存在著，而不是差異共在地與他們進行創造性的辯論。在這個過程中，政治行動被化約為純粹的「認同」（'identification'），也就是模仿，這是「群體心理學」（'group psychology'）的基礎，正是這種心理基礎使得資產階級 - 個人主義者佛洛伊德對群眾如此畏懼。

我們最終將自己化約為一個個單獨、分離的個體意象，每個人都是孤立的個體，封鎖在意識自我裡面；我們徒勞地企圖透過意識自我來恢復自己，而意識自我實際上卻將我們與世界隔絕。因此，這個世界對我們而言成了異域，異化的產物，是令人感到威脅、「黑暗」、可怕的無意識，而不是在我們人類得以成為我們自己的社會關係的總合中、在集體奮鬥裡將世界重建為一個更好的、更尊重我們居住的星球的廣袤之地。

在意識自我這裡——在這個每當我們想像自己正逃離世界並保護自己的那一刻我們就變得更加異化的地方，就是資產階級和殖民意識形態常識的結晶，它是透過殖民主義、帝國主義和全球化資本主義強加給全世界的人類模式。這是一個據稱是文明的、含蓄的白人和雄性的意識自我，似乎表明著捍衛發達世界免於受野蠻侵害，但它本身就是野蠻的；它被再現為唯一的理性力量，但它的「理性」（'rationality'）卻是極其非理性的。

意識自我永遠不變的邏輯是它旨在預測和控制自然以征服和利用自然的工具性科學，其最終目的始終是為資本創造利潤。此一累及我們現今星球生態破壞的企業，牢牢地支撐著醫學精神病學和心理學學科。它與一種特殊的常態病理、破壞性刻板的陽性的理性、資本主義和殖民統治下所謂正常人的「精神疾病」（'mental illness'）合成一體。這裡正是我們要翻轉「疾病」（'illness'）的隱喻的地方，用以對抗那些經常使用這種隱喻對付我們的心理／精神相關專業掌權者。

在精神醫學中，工具理性使用疾病模式將我們的痛苦當作是一種病來處理，而對當今社會「病」（'sick'）了的此一事實卻視若無睹；這些研究只致力於實用的、有利可圖的私人和資本主義國家發展計劃，而這些發展毫不關心每個主體的獨特性，對於創造性勞動也同樣不屑一顧；這種科學把知識看作如資本般積累，好像「事實」（'facts'）是商品（經常被封箱作爲機密的商業項目進行交易）。難怪關於世界權力本質的陰謀論在這種意識形態脈絡下興盛地起來。

精神分析工作的對象是工具性科學之下的受苦主體，我們的精神分析有很不同的「科學」：它不是工具而是生態，注意到事物與我們在世界上的位置之間的相互聯繫，社會運動者不是作爲一個客體，而是作爲一個主體。

倫理

意識自我存在的常見的病理現象也滲透到精神分析領域，一個對於精神分析臨床目標的宰制性意識形態解讀，肇始於佛洛伊德本人，那就是：「凡『**它**⁶』所在，吾必取而代之。」彷彿要以布爾喬亞資產階級男性毀滅

6　它（it），指無意識，爲強調其特殊意義，中文用粗體表示。佛洛伊德此句德文引自尼采《查拉圖斯特拉》，原文是 'Wo Es war, soll Ich werden' 關於佛洛伊德此一引用及在不同語言轉譯上的詮釋存在爭議，作者此處引用的 'where it was, there ego shall be' 是多數英文版本對的佛洛伊德引用此語的轉譯，據此，作者對佛洛伊德本人的矛盾進行了批判，一般認爲這句話代表了佛洛伊德本人在前後期從對主體受無意識主導轉向由意識自我主導的轉變，拉岡本人從法文對此句重讀另作解讀，反對主體的意識自我轉向，他呼籲「回歸佛洛伊德」其實是回歸無意識並展開精神分析的重構。今日意識自我主導的精神分析仍居主流，成爲苦難世界的問題的一環，正是作者於本書嚴屬批判的。另，譯者曾就此與作者 Ian Parker 電郵往返討論，在此謹將作者的說明中譯於此提供參考：「'it' 指的是 'Id'，通常在英語中 'Id' 是德語單詞 'Es' 的翻譯，在德語中的意思是『它』，所以英語中的 'Id' 具體化了在佛洛伊德的作品中這個具不確定性指代的東西。由於佛洛伊德寫作過程中的變化，以及隨著他的觀念的改變而出現的許多矛盾，這個短句中的 'it'（它）可以指 'Id' 作爲無意識的本能部分，或者就是一般性地指無意識本身。在這裡，我們更願意從最廣泛的意義上理解『它』，即指無意識；因此，在我們對『無意識』一詞在更廣泛的社會使用中，

性虛幻的中心地位必須以犧牲在他之內及身邊（也是在我們之內及周圍）存在的他者性（otherness）[7]為代價來加以鞏固。這種強化的個人意識自我意象表達了精神分析最為布爾喬亞資產階級的面向，並暴露了佛洛伊德自己著作中一個主要的矛盾。

這種強烈的意識自我意象與那個時期許多征服自然的意象相結合，對此，生態社會主義政治已不遺餘力地作出挑戰。佛洛伊德曾提到有關精神分析的目標在於強化意識自我，對抗「它」、對抗有別於意識自我的無意識，且經常被引用的一個說法是這項工作就像是「文化的工作」（'the work of culture'），這是佛洛伊德將其比作荷蘭填海墾地的「須德海排海造陸工程」（'the draining of the Zuider Zee'）。

布爾喬亞資產階級視野下的精神分析被簡化為一種人類意識自我對抗自然、對抗「它」、對抗無意識的典型現代戰鬥工具。我們遠離這種解讀，返回精神分析的根本作為批判心理學的倫理基礎。於此，我們的目標是在「它」所在的地方成為我們，而不是驅逐它，而是在那裡找到基進進步的主體性更為寬廣的界域。精神分析目標陳述的重作聲明和重新解讀是可能的；一開始，我們要指出歐洲荷蘭的「須德海排海造陸工程」實際上是一個使人們能在那片土地上居住的開墾工作，這根本不是對自然的驅趕，而是涉及在它的上面、與它共在的新生活方式。也許，也可以透過精神分析來實現相同性質的工作。

讓我們重申精神分析是一種基進的力量，明確聲明：「凡它所在，我們相與共」。我們可以作為有歷史、有過去和未來、有興趣和欲望、有想法和共同的理想的人而存在，但現在有的只是不假思索的重複和失憶、譁眾取巧的噱頭和浮誇的場面、自動機械和數據、數字和死亡、物件和物件

一個超越我們的意義領域，不僅位於我們的『內部』，也位於包括其他人在內的社會關係中。」（譯自電郵通訊，202.06.07）。由此看，德語中的 'Id'，應譯為「它我」或「他我」，比起常見被譯作「本我」要來得更貼近德文中的涵義，也更貼近作者對無意識的描述，是一種他者性的、外部的、集體的、歷史性的、別於「意識自我（ego）」的存在。

7　他者性（otherness）意即主體非孤立個體，而是與他者的關係網絡息息相關的存在，請參考本章註 4 及本書導讀。

間的關係、商品與交換價值、資本與交易。

在資本主義日復一日自動化地運作的地方，我們的生活、我們的眞實[8]、我們的思想、我們的記憶，就必要有一種基進的「重複性」（radical 'repetition'）來開啟一些新事物，而不是同以前一樣複製它。我們必須記憶和反思，並採取行動以將我們自己從經濟和意識形態的慣性中釋放出來；這，就像殖民統治者，如果他們當中有任何人想要救贖自身，就必須了解他們在世界上的位置和他們的歷史一樣。

精神分析向我們表明，透過與無意識（以及對我們來說是無意識的種種）進行建設性、漸進的互動交往，這種「我們相與共」，是能實現的；不過，從反殖民鬥爭學到十分重要的一課是，我們不會在所有歷史和文化背景中都被固定爲同一個樣子。我們無法斷言我們心理學的任何特定方面是永恆且普遍眞實的，包括當今關於無意識的理論。

佛洛伊德的工作開闢了一條通道，通向理解他者對我們的意義、通向從隱蔽的脈絡背景創造和取材的方法、並且通向我們有意識的行動。但如果我們不想落入把「無意識」變成了一種腦袋裡的容器或是一個帶有宗教訊息的神祕領域的意識形態陷阱，那麼就需要不斷地再變造。佛洛伊德所發現的並非外於這個世界，而是座落於一特定文化和歷史時刻中，在西方世界當今的疾病診斷和治療上，精神分析有必要意識到其自身特定的文化和歷史特徵。

反對興起於西方的科學知識的破壞性意識形態（這被用作殖民主義的一部分來區隔我們並將我們變成客體），我們以這樣一種方式重新審視這一歷史發展的所有積極因素，以便更好地理解我們如何在深刻的無意識層面上與他人聯結在一起。這裡沒有那些玄奧的西方作者販售的那種「集體無意識」（'collective unconscious'）（那是那些作者爲他們的科學理性對我們所做的事尋求補償和補充），但是這裡有的是集體連結行動的機會，

---

[8]　原文 truth，在此上下文脈中譯爲「眞實」，分裂主體可能存在多重的、主觀的「眞實」，指涉主體主觀知覺、認識與解釋內外世界的狀態。但這與前言作者提及 'the real' 中譯的「實在」（也常被譯作「眞實」）是指涉主體存在，兩者是不同的（也可說是不同邏輯層次的）概念（請詳〈前言〉註 4、7 與 8）。

我們每個人都將於此發現並激活我們與他人關係中的無意識。我們必須確信，我們遠比起那個被困圍在某種科學形式和意識形態裡的個人意識所想像的要來得更多，同時，我們可以做得更多。

解放我們的不是玄奧的神祕主義，也不是帝國主義和普適化的科學教條主義。我們反全球化的西方「科學」，重視人類主體的獨特性，以及其他文明和本土文化從自己的資源中所發展出來的事物，我們知道我們必須打破西方與意識自我的鏡像，才能眞正抵達世界和我們自身，我們的未來遠超越當今父權的和殖民的布爾喬亞資產階級的個體性。

所以，反對個體性意識自我的虛假異化理性，我們全力以赴並將政治能量投入於構建進步的集體替代方案中，這些替代方案的運作是根據不一樣的邏輯——無意識的邏輯，是與它一起工作，發現我們主體性的方方面面，發現在它之中的人性。我們並不將無意識理想化，然而我們認得它在形塑我們的生成上的作用，就如我們在文化政治活動中已集體塑造了它而後被噤聲一般，那些沒被說出的、沒能被思考的種種仍然呈現在我們面前；它可能是解放的，但它仍然被隱蔽，通常不爲人所知。

在這個悲慘的世界中，我們與他人彼此相鬥，而不是與他們一起加入集體的鬥爭。我們區隔彼此，怒目相對，我們迷失了我們的本來面目，但我們還在這兒、在我們之中、在無意識裡。正是精神分析將注意力吸引到人類活動的領域，一個對於我們作爲言說的存在體（我們是以語言來交流我們彼此的希望與恐懼，並且以語言將我們對（所拒絕的）世界的批判分析和對所欲建造的另一個世界的圖像交織在一起的人類）而言，不可或缺的領域。

他者性，精神分析的

人類寓居的語言是我們存在的基礎，然而當我們說話時試圖要去控制每個字詞的意義，我們定然失敗。總有某些東西逸出，超乎我們，在這個悲慘的世界中，而這超乎我們的東西作爲一種對我們而言是「他者」的無意識卻已被意識形態地結構起來，這種他者性是我們存在的無意識面向，它總是藉由作用於我們所說的語言的另一面，以一種離奇的、不請自來的

方式向我們顯現。

　　他者性是精神分析的領地，儘管精神分析的觀點展開於歐洲，但佛洛伊德既是「歐洲人」卻又與這種文化截然不同，也許這就是爲什麼他開始了解一些無意識的東西，基進的精神分析觀點與某種極爲富含其文化和歷史特殊性的語言被文化與歷史決定的隔閡斷裂密不可分。精神分析是由佛洛伊德及其追隨者在西方文化的邊緣所創造的，其中大多數是受到反猶太主義排斥的猶太人，它本身就是這種文化下的「他者」，因此是很能站在邊緣位置上留意到資產階級「令人尊敬的」常識意識（那些當權者的意識）。

　　現今存在著對語言排除和邊緣化的其他面向，這些面向經由反對資本主義、反對父權制、反對種族主義、反對新殖民主義（neocolonialism）、反對伊斯蘭恐懼症（Islamophobia）、反對排斥特殊需要人士或反對破壞地球等抗議活動都已被昭然揭露。正是解放運動使我們能夠注意到在全球化脈絡下已經被創造的他者化（othering）、視覺圖像和無意識的象徵再現等諸多面向，精神分析本身就是透過這種全球化傳播到世界各地。

　　以女性主義運動爲例，我們注意到佛洛伊德將女性氣質稱爲「黑暗大陸」（‘dark continent’）的方式，帶有指涉女性氣質的「黑暗大陸」與無意識之間存在某種深層聯繫的含義。那麼我們就能以一種既是女性主義又是社會主義的新方式來重塑精神分析在臨床的任務以及政治鬥爭的任務。

　　作爲一項政治任務，女性主義使得男性面對一個選擇——即他們是要繼續按照他們自己的大男人氣概個人主義方式，根據某種「理性」——意識自我的理性——行使權力？還是他們要與較爲直覺的集體和照顧的存在方式（這是父權社會裡傳統又刻板地認定女性的地位）聯繫起來？換言之，我們會從所謂的黑暗大陸學到什麼？是要像佛洛伊德對歇斯底里的人做的那樣？還是我們會繼續壓迫和利用未知和神祕，就像西方對世界其他文化所做的那樣？

　　同時，反殖民和反種族主義運動旨在奪回被意識形態設定爲野蠻未開化的「黑暗大陸」，這個進步性的政治任務也在我們對精神分析的重新閱讀和轉化方式上產生深遠的影響，以使臨床也能與這些運動並肩作戰地工作。布爾喬亞資產階級理性以及強化意識自我的錯誤目標，是不可容忍的

白人優越殖民理性的症狀。

那些最先發明精神分析的猶太人含蓄地質疑這種本質性的「白人優越」（'whiteness'），現在我們要連結無意識並對白人優越的霸權進行明確的批判。我們要給白人優越「上色」（'colour'），這樣它之於我們就不再是無形的了，如此，它就不再能以這樣一種在我們內部和我們周圍成為威脅性的無意識方式而起作用了。

分裂

如果我們不了解語言運作和結構的複雜方式，我們就無法將社會關係去除白人優越或去除父權化。首先要知道的是，某些在語言的本質裡、在我們作為言說的存在體本質裡的東西，使我們分裂，因為我們沒法訴說所有的一切。主體的**分裂**（*division*）[9]乃不可避免，當我們說話時，我們必得屈從於一個我們無法完全掌握的象徵系統，因此我們成為分裂的主體（divided subjects），受到我們無意識的影響；我們的分裂是不可避免的，我們必得帶著分裂一起生活，重要的是我們如何理解這種分裂，以及我們賦予它什麼意義。

我們所知道的（也是精神分析所要工作的）是我們對分裂主體的理解充滿了意識形態的內容，對無意識本身也是一樣。意識形態中介了我們在分裂處境下的經驗，無意識作為我們訴說痛苦之地，這種處境在意識形態上被外化、延長和加劇，尤其是主體的異化分裂，這些是資本主義生活的特徵。

我們每個人都被資本主義制度及其相隨的統治形式所分裂。例如，父權制使我們分裂於異性戀雄性統治與同化於受鄙視的陰柔氣質及其他類性傾向的被統治之間；同樣地，殖民主義使我們分裂於表面看似理性的文明與膽敢反抗它的所謂「野蠻人」（'barbarians'）的那些病理化之間。

在這個異化世界裡，我們主體的分裂的意識形態表現形式，在解放運

---

[9]　關於分裂（*division*）與分裂的主體（divided subjects）的說明請見第 1 章註解 6 及本書導讀。再次提醒，「分裂」一詞有其特殊的意義，勿以一般大眾心理學或精神病理印象來解讀而造成錯解。

動的實踐中被公開駁斥聲討、消解和超越。反資本主義者、反殖民主義者、反種族主義者、女性主義者、女同性戀者、男同性戀者、跨性別者、酷兒運動者和其他許多的他者，為了將我們從個體化的權力與鞏固當權者強大宰制意象的工具性科學中解放出來，已經從事戰鬥並將持續有效地戰鬥下去。他們開闢了一條道路、一條通向無意識的精神分析道路、一條對抗權力的路徑，那些權力利用我們分裂的處境去強化和殖民及父權資本主義認同的個體意識自我來統治我們。挑戰我們的意識自我，解放運動可以讓我們每個人停止宰制自身、不再背叛我們自己。背叛與宰制是我們能加以棄絕的東西。

在我們彼此交流時，無意識經由我們的言語而存在，在我們以言說主體的關係存在之前它並不存在。它需要我們，我們所有人，這不只是我們每個人能透過對彼此所說的話而存在，也是藉由無意識能將我們聯繫起來集體行動，這對於精神分析的進步政治角色至關重要。如此，它可以幫助我們自身的復元，使我們從壓迫、抑制和鎮壓我們的集體存在與自由聯想的事物中解放出來。

主體的分裂也許是我們永遠無法擺脫的，我們沒法說這種分裂是否可以被治癒，也許是不能的，但這種分裂的痛苦可以被緩解，緩解可以來自參與解放運動，來自臨床精神分析方法對意識形態的挑戰，以及與明確的政治行動連結的精神分析的逐步重塑。在接下來的章節中，我們將更多談論進入無意識的「自由聯想」（'free association'）方法，這種方法更深入無意識，使它對我們說話，這樣我們就可以不僅僅只有一直說到它出現的作法而已。

因此，我們需要與集體鬥爭結盟並受其啟發的精神分析，這是一種批判性地處理主體分裂的意識形態再現的理論和實踐，這種意識形態再現創造並延續了無意識彷彿只是在我們的內在且對我們構成威脅的某種東西。敵人也在外面，同時我們必須在那裡與它作戰。除了臨床工作之外，還有一項政治任務是——動員無意識的力量去分析哪些力量延續意識形態的存在？又是哪些力量傾向於我們的自由？我們需要分析、言說和行動，這樣我們才能創造歷史，而不僅僅是重複它。下一章，**《重複》**（'*Repetition*'）。

UNCONSCIOUS: ALIENATION, RATIONALITY AND OTHERNESS

Our struggle, wherever it is locally, is international in scope, and every liberation struggle progressively expands its horizons to understand how we are divided and ruled. What is done to us is incomprehensible in a framework focusing only the immediate local interpersonal, regional level or even confined to national context.

Consumerism, unemployment and xenophobia in rich countries, for example, only make sense when we consider misery, low wages and the exploitation of labour in poor countries. Similarly, we need to think about old and new forms of colonialism and imperialism to know what is at stake in racial hatred or terrorist attacks. This is also how the Chilean feminist slogan 'the oppressive state is a male rapist' can help us elucidate not only government repression and violence against women, but also homophobic brutality and violent macho forms of relationship between groups and nations that predominate at the expense of other ways of life or ways of being that are feminized and denigrated.

What happens in the world, even if very far from us, underlies what we say and do. Our everyday words and actions also involve past history, even the most remote, even that of past centuries. History bears us. All of this is present at every moment, limiting us and guiding us in a certain direction, but generally in a way that is not fully conscious to us. This limit and possibility is the *unconscious*.

This chapter is about a fundamental underlying concept in psychoanalysis. The unconscious is brought to life in the clinic, but its effects are felt everywhere in everyday life. We need to grasp the way that the unconscious takes on personal and political form in the alienation that is produced in capitalist society and then how our understanding of that is distorted by 'commonsense', how rationality in this society leads us into the trap of the individual self in which the 'ego' is the master in the house, and how the 'otherness' that haunts us is bound up with language, the very same language we use to convey our suffering to others.

Alienation and commonsense

We are alienated in this miserable world, separated from others, and even from ourselves, and what we are told about our alienation, and told about the unconscious, usually has the ideological effect of covering over the source of the problem, preventing us from seeking the help we need. We need to think differently about the unconscious.

By thinking, reflecting and acting politically on an international scale we come to understand how particular others, of different social groups, nations, cultures, gender and sexualities have been rendered 'other' to us, and how that 'otherness' has worked its way inwards in forms of embedded class privilege and insult, of nationalism, racism and sexism. We are made 'other', even to ourselves in this sad world, and otherness then runs through our experience, our subjectivity, so deep that nature itself, whatever that is exactly, is experienced as alien, strange and threatening. This is an important part of what psychoanalysis names as 'unconscious'. It is something unrecognizable that inhabits our 'external' and 'internal' world. Although it is in our thoughts, it is beyond what we think. It is not what we think. We are each divided, split, other to ourselves.

The unconscious always escapes our thoughts. It is not simply something that is buried and that can be exhumed, thought about, remembered. Rather, it is a form of alienation from our ideas, words, actions and relationships with the world, which are always other than what they seem to be, as if they were separated from us.

Alienation is a form of separation. In strictly psychoanalytic terms it is a doubled form of alienation after our necessary separation from those who brought us into the world and first cared for us. By turning away from them, we turn away from ourselves, we divide ourselves internally, so we can make our way in the world, the world we are 'alienated' in and the language we use to communicate that unease to others. Then the particular cultural-historical alienation in this world redoubles and intensifies our 'original alienation', our internal division, our peculiarly human nature as divided subjects who must communicate with others in order to survive, including about our distress.

In this oppressive and exploitative society our alienation operates through multiple dimensions of separation, which include competition between individuals seeking to sell their labour power, control by our masters of the fruits of our creative labour once we have sold our time to them, anxiety over whether our bodies will carry out the work we must perform for others in order to live, and the drive to exploit the natural world for profit which then appears to us as a hostile force confronting us. Other people, our own creativity, our bodies, and nature as such, are each and all separated from us, and then experienced as threatening. Commonsense tell us that this is universal and natural, but commonsense lies.

Commonsense

There is a difference between the 'common sense' we fight for – the kind of common sense that we build from indigenous knowledge, our creative expertise by experience and practical theoretical analysis – and ideological *commonsense* that is handed down to us or stolen and distorted, used to deskill us. That ideological commonsense is what we are concerned with here. That ideological commonsense systematically frustrates our attempts to grasp the form this alienation takes as something 'other' to us, as something unconscious. However, despite common sense, the other that alienates us is still there. Something escapes conscious control in this world where economic forces drive us to work for others for their profit, and psychoanalysis has much to say about this aspect of our lives that is always out of our reach, existing as something unconscious to us.

Freud's invention of the unconscious is also, in the process, banalised, turned into popular images of murky depths, of something dark and mysterious, or, in many psychology and psychiatry textbooks, as the bulk of an iceberg of which only the top tip is visible to us. Psychologised psychoanalysis then even tells us to drive this unconscious back underground, to ignore it, to pretend that it has no impact on our lives. That false image of mental 'wellbeing' and 'happiness' pits the self-conscious 'ego' against the unconscious, wishing it away.

This 'ego' which is so well-known to many popularisers of psychoanalysis and enthusiastic supporters of the psy professions, is often described as the rational core of the self, but this little mechanism of rational individual self-consciousness is not actually the core of who we are at all. We are, after all, as Marx teaches us, an 'ensemble of social rela-tions', and that network of social relationships which defines our collective nature as hu-man beings is the site not of the ego, but of the unconscious.

The unconscious, which is not something obscure hidden in the asocial depths of each one of us, unfolds in the social relationships in which we participate and that consti-tute us. These relationships evoke others, other past relationships, and are beyond our con-scious control, but they decide what we are and what we can control. They shape our self and our self-consciousness.

Our immediate self-consciousness often seems to embrace us, but it cannot save us. It misleads us. It wallows in commonsense ideologies of the self separated from society, making the best of alienation instead of acknowledging it, understanding how it has been produced and enabling us to collectively change the conditions that gave rise to it.

Instead of liberating us from alienation, simple-minded 'self-awareness' reproduces it through the alienating images of our 'ego'. These images of the 'ego' as the core of our selves, as the rational centre of our self-consciousness, reduce our subjectivity to what we believe ourselves to be, each one of us as an individual separated from the others. That way of thinking about it is not the route to a cure, and still less to revolution.

We will not get anywhere, outside of where we already find ourselves, as long as we have not managed to free ourselves from the thought that encloses us within what each one of us already immediately and ideologically seem to be. This thought about ourselves, which is fuelled by commonsense, betrays the otherness that makes us human, turning that otherness into a curse instead of the material grounding of a practical enduring real cure through historical struggle against exploitation and oppression. Our liberation can only be collective and this is why it is not encompassed by the kind of common sense that locks us up in the prison of our 'ego'.

In this commonsensical way of thinking, we are exclusively our particular self. The other infinitely diverse particularities of gender, colour, culture or nationality, among many other dimensions of difference, appear as external, as others to us, even as repulsive or hostile. We do not recognize our collective diversity as shared humanity. Notice also how this image of the self-sufficient ego marginalises 'disabled people', people who are treated as if they are damaged, incomplete. They are 'disabled' by this society that requires normal healthy well-adapted bodies to produce 'surplus value' and also by the commonsense nor-mative image of the ego as autonomous master in the house. Those who fail to function as such masters are often condemned as 'mad'.

Our nature as human beings is thereby denied. We betray our underlying nature in which we are nothing without others. As our intimate relation to others is betrayed, loving relations of solidarity with the pain of others is replaced with hatred and suspicion, and so we fall into a trap.

We are trapped in the temptation of assertive, possessive and competitive individual solutions to the misery pervasive in this capitalist world. The temptation is to be as misera-ble as this world which is governed by the drive to accumulate goods and make profit from others, and to make the best of it, even to claim we are then 'happy'. When this happens, individual mastery, the isolated 'ego', is pitted against others.

However, even if we turn against humanity, we do not stop being human. The uncon-scious speaks and thus can connect us with collective action. There is a dialectical twist to this connection, which is that while the individual 'ego' is not the core of each human being, neither is the unconscious, the unconscious in which we connect with each other, and in which we are as an ensemble of social relations. The unconscious is not a 'core' of the self any more than the ego is, and the unconscious, furthermore, is not exactly something essential and inherent in my being, not hidden inside each of us. It is not the unfathomable kernel of what I am. It is something else.

The unconscious, which we assume to be so deep and hidden inside each one of us is, itself, something *outside* that speaks of otherness. It is made of history, economy, society, culture and ideology. It is a space for encounters and disagreements with others, explanations and contradictions that are debated with them, alliances and conflicts between comrades in struggle, persuasion and misunderstanding. It appears in the field of language we share with others.

The unconscious is itself structured by the particular languages we learn from the world in which we live. It comes from the outside, from what we see and hear, from the structure of past and present relationships that resonates and unfolds in the space we inhabit. So it functions as an 'other' discourse, always present if not always noticed. It is simultaneously, dialectically, exterior and interior. It surrounds us and crosses through us. It is inside us precisely because it was, and still is, also outside us, because we are in it, because it is where we are.

We live in the *exteriority* of the unconscious. Here, in this outer structured field of being, it is as if each individual must occupy his or her place, the one that corresponds to him or her, that which distinguishes him or her from the others, and then, as they adapt to society, that which makes him or her coincide with them. The unconscious literally puts us in our place, and, at the same time, it unsettles us, reminds us that we are not only what we imagine to be, that there is more to us than our little alienated selves reduced to thinking in our ego as if it were our diplomatic representative to the world of others.

We learn from the unconscious that we do not have complete power over what we say, that we do not control the meaning of our words, that we are not the centre of our little worlds of meaning or of immediate face-to-face relationships with others. The illusion that we are the centre, with the ego as the master in the house, is an ideological story as powerful as the one that human beings are the centre of the world, set against the other sentient beings in the animal kingdom instead of living at one with them. These two ideological stories about us as being at the centre, the centre of being, are really only one evidenced, questioned and challenged by a radical psychoanalytic perspective. Psychoanalysis challenges the ego's power over us and over everything else.

Psychoanalysis, in its critique of the ego, poses each of us with a choice, as to whether we will continue to attempt to dominate ourselves and others and nature or find a different way of being with it. This choice is already liberating, but also revealing. It makes us discover at least three things about power: first, power is not inevitable, it is not something that must be either exerted or suffered; secondly, power cannot be exerted without being simultaneously suffered, as the domination of the other's needs and presupposes the domination of oneself; thirdly, there is the same power involved in the ego that suffocates us, in what makes us oppress others and in what is destroying the world around us.

Psychoanalysis can help us to get out of our ego and to fight on the outside against the power that keeps us locked inside. The battlefield is outside, in the natural and sociocultural world, beyond the narrow conscious borders of our individuality. With the uncon-scious, then, we move from a conception of the ego separated from the world as an 'envi-ronment' to that of radical liberating ecology, of psychoanalytic ecosocialism. To do that, we must reclaim the world, and reclaim our power in the world.

Power

What is *power?* Power, as conceived of in psychoanalysis, is always there where the ego imposes itself, but it is never truly ours as individuals. Even when we believe we have power, it is not we who have it exactly and totally. Rather power is also what owns us and alienates us by exerting itself either through us or upon us, by dominating us to force us either to suffer or to exert domination, by exploiting us either as exploiters or as exploited, as masters or as lackeys, as consumers or as workers, as sellers of goods or as commodi-ties. In all cases, by being possessed by power, we are alienated, we become alien to our-selves, and then we cease to be ourselves in order to become what power wants us to be.

Psychoanalysis offers us a vision of power as something decentred from the subject, something uncontrollable that is suffered even when exerted, something that always im-plies an alien and alienating unconscious substrate. This vision is necessary as a comple-ment to most leftist views of power as something that is 'possessed', consciously exercised over others, wielded in such a way as to dominate people.

It is certainly true that there are those with power, the 1%, as well as rulers and ma-cho leaders of many different private and state enterprises, those who enjoy their deliberate humiliation of those beneath them. But we need to take care, not to turn critical analysis of society into a gigantic conspiracy theory, and we know that conspiracy theories actually often function as poisonous injunctions that distract us from the real problem, from the patriarchal and colonial capitalist system, to target scapegoats, the case of antisemitic con-spiracy theories being the most prevalent.

Marxism, and the many allied theories and practices of liberation from the feminist and anti-colonial movements are not conspiratorial delusions searching out those who exercise power, but systemic structural analyses of the ways that everyone is subjected to multiple intersecting regimes of power. These analyses coincide with what we learn from psychoanalysis. The view of power we present here is thus not only designed to comple-ment those that energise liberation movements, but also to function as a resource for the critical analysis of false paths which actually, despite the best intentions of activists, depo-liticize the struggle by individualizing, personalizing, and psychologizing politics.

The fundamental problem does not lie in certain individuals or in their actions, much less in their inclinations, their psychological profile or their personality traits. The funda-mental problem is the structure that unconsciously makes them who they are and behave as they do. That structure is economic and symbolic, and so it is political, as profoundly political as the unconscious which operates with it and against it. Psychoanalytic politics that attends to the unconscious, to what is at the root, is therefore a more radical way of thinking about power. That which is unconscious to us in our social relationships and our personal experience has a powerful structuring effect on the way we understand the world and how we reproduce it or try to change it.

Psychoanalysis speaks of power and alienation endemic in a world that reduces human capacities and even human beings to the status of things to be bought and sold. We are pitted against others as we compete to sell ourselves by selling our knowledge, our ability, our life, our labour power. Our creative labour is then turned against us as something controlled and sold by our masters or by ourselves at the service of our masters, even doing our masters' work, controlling and selling labour, our labour.

Whether through other people, through things or through ourselves, our masters control us, make us do their bidding, which is sometimes also our own. We do what they do and what they do to us, even though they know not what they do, driven by the insatiable search for profit, driven into self-destructive attempts to dominate others. They alienate us and alienate themselves as they engage in the destruction of so many other lives, and in the devastation of the planet.

We are even charged with the task of carrying out the function of our masters, to imagine that we are little masters. This is what happens when we are given some authority as clients, owners, bosses, parents, husbands, teachers, evaluators, bureaucrats, policemen, soldiers, therapists, doctors, etc. This is small compensation and consolation. At least an insignificant part of all the power that is taken from us, of all the power that oppresses us, is returned to us. This can make us forget our oppression and exploitation. The pity is that forgetting it makes us all the more exploitable, makes us continue to be exploited, losing more than we gain. The little power we receive as individuals makes us collectively surrender ourselves to power. It works to lock us in place when we are told that it frees us.

Each one empowers themselves at the expense of ourselves. This is how something crucial for psychoanalysis happens: we separate each one of ourselves from our bodies and our relation to these bodies is perverted. We enslave our own bodies, we reify them, and we use them as means to fulfil the obligations or satisfy the ambitions of each one of us. This is what 'social models' of disability also teach us; that bodies are made to function in this world as ideologically 'complete' productive objects, and if they do not they are 'disabled'. The image of the complete self-sufficient body that is challenged by radical disability activists is as ideological as the image of the complete self-sufficient self that is challenged by radical mental health and 'anti-psychiatry' activists.

The ego of each one of us is constantly used to take over our bodies. We are spiritually exploited as individuals in order to materially exploit us as a collectivity. Social exploitation would be impossible without the complicity of an ego that is usually the weakest link in the community. This vulnerable point can be treated through psychoanalysis with the purpose of regaining collective power.

Our psychoanalytic view of power is of it as something we can seize collectively. We can take the power, and use it progressively to shape society and ourselves. We are not against power but against its imaginary reduction to the level of the individual, and we are for it as a creative force. We know that power can free us and serve us to create another world, better than this one, if we exercise it collectively, thus contradicting the dominant ideology that makes us imagine that power always belongs to the ego, as if individuals were the only subjects and were owners of their actions.

Common-sense views of society and of the nature of power operate ideologically, obscuring the root causes of alienation. We claim, in contrast, and in opposition to this ideological representation of society, that alienation plus power in this miserable world is the unconscious. In this sense, the unconscious is politics, and we must learn how to appreciate how our actions are unconsciously organised, all the better to act in a collective way against power, and to put an end to the most extreme destructive forms of alienation that are endemic under capitalism.

Rationality in the trap of the ego

Some forms of psychoanalysis, particularly those that have become mainstream and incorporated into adaptive institutions in the English-speaking world, see the ego as king, and aim to restore it to the throne in the clinic. The aim in adaptive conservative psychoanalysis is to make the ego the master in the house. In this way, the most radical proposals of Freud are betrayed, and the ego is assumed to be the seat of rationality.

This rationality is, of course, the kind of bourgeois individual rationality that is so beloved of ideology under capitalism, colonialism and patriarchy. This is rationality in the trap of the ego, and very different from the collective reason we together create in movements of resistance to power and to movements of liberation. In order to connect with and create that collective reason we need to connect through the unconscious, to find ourselves there instead of losing ourselves in the ego.

The unconscious is everything of us that escapes individual reason, a sometimes necessary creative context which we cannot but inhabit, but an aspect of our humanity that is turned into a 'dark' force that is then viewed as a threat in bourgeois ideology. Negative images of what is dark, symbolic racism, often accompany such ideological images of the ideal self as master in the house, a heteropatriarchal illusion. This ideology, which is suspicious of both the unconscious and our body and collectivity, restricts us to the individual psychological sphere, the sphere of the conscious ego. Isolated in the ego, confused with it, we can forget the unconscious and dedicate ourselves to the subjugation of our own body.

The task of each of us is then to control our body and put it at the service of capitalism. This is why we subdue and master it, we treat it as a slave, as a machine that must labour for oneself and for others. We are then, in a personal drama that is becoming an ecological cataclysm, pitted against nature itself, nature viewed as a threat first inside of us, then outside of us. Our alienated state of being cuts us off from our own creative labour, suspicious of others, fearful of losing control of our own bodies and pre-emptively distrustful and destructive of nature as such.

Science

Total ecocide, the irreversible sacrifice of the world, begins with the immolation of our own body on the altar of the ego. This immolation is in turn the outcome of our alienation. Only by becoming something as the ego, something so alien to who we really are, can we destroy ourselves and destroy the entire world. In any case, there is no place left for the world when we totalize, under the total form of our ego, the individuality in which we are alienated. Our alienation is also an 'objectification' – including turning subjects and human relations into objects – and *science* is thereby transformed, distorted, from being a tool of practical analytic understanding into a tool of control.

We know the 'scientific' expressions of objectification in mainstream psychology. Instrumental 'science', which is an ideological form of scientific reason and which is based on a model of 'prediction and control', turns us into objects, an objectification of the subject which psychoanalysis speaks against. Once objectified, the subject transmutes into the ego. This ego is no longer the subject. It is something totally alien to the subject. It is something we get alienated into, lost in.

We are so alienated in the ego that we no longer see it as something alien. We become confused with the ego which in turn is confused with other egos. We can no longer distinguish ourselves from others, aiming to mimic others instead of recognising their value as something different to us. Then our relation to groups and communities is reduced to mimicry, to being like the others, instead of being different, instead of creative argumentative debate with them. In the process, political action is reduced to pure 'identification', mimicry that was the basis of the 'group psychology' that made the bourgeois-individualist Freud so fearful of the masses.

We have ended up reducing ourselves to an image of each one of us, separate, each one an isolated individual, locked inside the ego. We try in vain to recover ourselves through the ego, the ego that actually cuts us off from our world. So this world becomes alien to us, a product of alienation, a threatening 'dark' frightful unconscious instead of the wider ground of our being in the ensemble of social relations that makes us who we are and in collective struggle that may remake the world as a better place more respectful of the planet we inhabit.

The ego, in which we are all the more alienated at the very moment that we imagine that we are escaping the world and protecting ourselves, is thus, among other things, the crystallisation of bourgeois and colonial ideological common sense. It is the model of humanity that has been imposed throughout the world through colonialism, imperialism and globalized capitalism. It is an allegedly civilized and implicitly white and masculine ego that speaks as if it guards the developed world from barbarism, but it is itself barbaric. It is presented as the only rational force, but its 'rationality' is profoundly irrational.

The kind of logic the ego perpetuates is that of instrumental science that aims to predict and control nature in order to subjugate and exploit it, always with the ultimate purpose of producing profits for capital. This enterprise, which is now implicated in the ecological devastation of our planet, underpins the discipline of medical psychiatry and psychology. It is at one with a peculiar pathology of normality, destructive stereotypical masculine rationality, a 'mental illness' of so-called normal man under capitalism and colonial rule. This is where we turn the metaphor of 'illness' around against those in power in the psy professions who so often use that metaphor against us.

In psychiatry instrumental rationality uses a disease model to treat our distress as if it were an illness, blind to the fact that it is present-day society that is 'sick'. It is this kind of rationality that also underpins scientific research, research that is dedicated only to pragmatic profitable private and capitalist state programmes of development, development which cares nothing for the singularity of each subject and is equally dismissive of creative labour. This kind of science accumulates knowledge as if it were capital, as if the 'facts' were commodities, often enclosed and traded as commercial items shrouded in secrecy. Little wonder that conspiratorial theories about the nature of power in the world thrive in this ideological context.

Psychoanalysis works upon the kind of subject who suffers at the hands of instrumental science. Our own psychoanalytic 'science' is very different. It is not instrumental but ecological, noticing the interconnection between things and our place in the world, the activist not as an object, but as a subject.

Ethics

The normal pathology inherent in the ego has also penetrated the psychoanalytic field. A dominant ideological reading of the clinical aim of psychoanalysis, a reading inaugurated by Freud himself, is that 'where it was, there ego shall be', as if the destructive illusory centre of bourgeois man must be fortified at the expense of the otherness that lies in and around him, in and around us. This image of the strengthening of the individual ego expresses the most bourgeois aspect of psychoanalysis, and exposes a key contradiction in Freud's own work.

This image of the strong ego that is compounded by an image of the subjugation of nature that was very much of its time, and which ecosocialist politics has done so much to challenge. Freud's statement about the aim of psychoanalysis entailing a strengthening of the ego against what is 'it', other to it, against what is unconscious, continues with the often-cited claim that this work is 'the work of culture', something that Freud likens to 'the draining of the Zuider Zee', the reclamation of territory in the The Netherlands from the sea.

The bourgeois vision of psychoanalysis reduces it to an instrument in the typically modern combat of the human ego against nature, against the 'it', against the unconscious. Distancing ourselves from this reading, we return to the ethical grounding of radical psychoanalysis as a critical psychology in which we aim to be ourselves where 'it' was, not to dislodge it, but to find the broader compass of radical progressive subjectivity there. It is possible to reclaim and re-read that statement about the aims of psychoanalysis, and to point out, for a start, that 'the draining of the Zuider Zee' in The Netherlands of Europe was actually a work of reclamation that enabled the people to live on that land. It was not at all a driving back of nature, but involved a new way of living on it, with it. Perhaps the same can be achieved through psychoanalytic work.

Let us reclaim psychoanalysis as a radical force, asserting that 'where it was, there we shall be'. We can exist as people with history, with our past and future, with interests and desires, with ideas and shared ideals, where there is now only unthinking repetitiveness and amnesia, demagogy and spectacle, robots and data, numbers and fatalities, things and relationships between things, commodities and exchange-value, capital and transactions.

Where capitalism works repetitively and automatically, there has to be our life, our truth, our thinking, our memory, a kind of radical 'repetition' that opens up something new rather than replicates it as the same as what it was before. We must remember and reflect, and act to free ourselves from the inertia of economy and ideology. This, just as the colonial masters must learn something about their place in the world and their history if any of them are to redeem themselves.

Psychoanalysis shows us that through a constructive progressive engagement with the unconscious, with what is unconscious to us, what 'we shall be', can be, but, and this is a crucially important lesson from anti-colonial struggle, we are not condemned to be the same in all historical and cultural contexts. We cannot say whether any particular aspect of our psychology is timelessly and universally true, including present-day theories about the unconscious.

Freud's work opened a path to an understanding of what is other to us, to the way we create and draw upon a hidden context, background, to our conscious action, but it needs to be constantly reworked if we are not to fall into the ideological trap of turning that 'unconscious' into a kind of container inside the head or a mystical realm with a religious message. What was discovered by Freud is not outside the world, but is situated in a culture and in a moment in history. Psychoanalysis needs to remain aware of its own culturally and historically specific character as diagnosis and treatment of present-day ills in the Western world.

Against a destructive ideology of scientific knowledge that arose in the West, and which was used as part of colonialism to segregate us and turn us into objects, we reclaim all that was positive about this historical development in such a way as to understand better how we are connected with others at a deep unconscious level. There is no 'collective unconscious' of the kind peddled by mystical Western writers who seek to compensate and complement what is done to us by their scientific reason, but there are opportunities for collective action where each of us find and activate what is unconscious to us in our relation to others. We must be sure that we are more and can do more than what is imagined by our individual consciousness trapped in certain forms of science and ideology.

What will liberate us is not esoteric mysticism, but neither will imperialist and generalizing scientific dogmatism. Against globalised Western 'science', we value what is singular about the human subject and what other civilizations and indigenous cultures have developed from their own resources. We know that we must break the mirror of the West and of our ego in order to reach the world and ourselves. Our future is beyond our present-day patriarchal and colonial bourgeois individuality.

So, against the false alienated rationality of the individual ego, we put our bets and our political energy into the construction of progressive collective alternatives that operate according to a different logic, that operate according to a logic of the unconscious, working with it, finding aspects of our subjectivity, our humanity in it. We do not idealise the unconscious, but we acknowledge its role in shaping who we are, just as we have already collectively shaped it in our cultural-political activity and then been silenced. What is not said, what cannot be thought is still present to us. It may be liberating, but it remains hidden, usually unacknowledged.

We pit ourselves against others in this wretched world instead of joining them in a collective struggle. We separate, we confront each other, we lose ourselves in what we are, but we are still here, among ourselves, in the unconscious. It is psychoanalysis that draws attention to that realm of human activity, a realm necessary to us as beings that speak, human beings that use language to communicate our hopes and fears to each other and weave together a critical analysis of the world, a world we reject, and images of another world we want to build.

Otherness, of psychoanalysis

The language we inhabit as human beings is the ground of our being, but as we speak and attempt to control the meaning of every word, we fail. Something always escapes, is beyond us, and in this miserable world this beyond is structured ideologically as an uncon-scious that is 'other' to us. This otherness is the unconscious dimension of our being that is always in a strange unbidden way present to us through its effects as the other side of the language that we speak.

Otherness is the realm of psychoanalysis. Although the psychoanalytic perspective opened up in Europe, Freud was both 'European' and set apart from that culture. Perhaps that is why he came to know something of the unconscious. A radical psychoanalytic per-spective is inseparable from a culturally and historically determined estrangement from a certain kind of language which is also characterized by its cultural and historical specific-ity. Psychoanalysis, created at the margins of Western culture by Freud and his followers, most of which were Jews subject to antisemitic exclusion, was itself 'other' to that culture, and so very well positioned to notice what was at the edges of bourgeois 'respectable' commonsensical consciousness, the consciousness of those with power.

Now there are other excluded and marginal dimensions of language. These dimen-sions are made visible by protests against capitalism, against patriarchy, against racism, against neocolonialism, against Islamophobia, against exclusion of disabled people, or against the devastation of the planet. It is the liberation movements that enable us to notice aspects of othering, visual images and symbolic representations of the unconscious that have been created in the context of globalisation, a globalisation through which psycho-analysis itself has spread around the world.

We notice, with the feminist movement, for example, the way that Freud referred to femininity as a 'dark continent', with the implication that there was some deep connec-tion between this 'dark continent' of femininity and the unconscious. Then we are able to configure the task of psychoanalysis in the clinic and the task of political struggle in a new way that is feminist as well as being socialist.

As a political task, feminism poses men with a choice, whether they are to continue with their own macho individualist way of exercising power in line with a certain 'ratio-nality', the rationality of the ego, or whether they will connect with the more intuitive col-lective and caring modes of being that are conventionally and stereotypically assigned to the position of women in patriarchal society. In other words, will we learn something from the so-called dark continent, as Freud did with the hysterics, or will we just continue to oppress and exploit the unknown and mysterious, as the West has done with the other cul-tures of the world?

The anti-colonial and anti-racist movements, meanwhile, aim to reclaim what is ideo-logically configured as a barbaric uncivilised 'dark continent', and this progressive politi-cal task also has deep implications for the way we re-read and transform psychoanalysis so that it might work alongside those movements in the clinic. Bourgeois rationality, and the mistaken aim of strengthening the ego, is a symptom of the unbearable whiteness of colo-nial reason.

This 'whiteness' of being was implicitly put in question by those, Jews, who first invented psychoanalysis, and now we connect with what is rendered unconscious to us in such a way as to make that critique of hegemonic whiteness explicit. We 'colour' in white-ness so it is no longer invisible to us, so that it no longer operates in such a way as to be a threatening unconscious inside us and around us.

Division

We cannot colour in whiteness or de-patriarchalize social relations if we are not aware of the complex way in which language operates and is structured. The first thing to know is that there is something in the nature of language, of our nature as speaking beings, which divides us, for we cannot say everything. This subjective *division* is unavoidable. We must bend to a symbolic system we cannot completely master when we speak, and so we become divided subjects, affected by something unconscious to us. Our division is inevitable. We must live with it. What is important is how we make sense of that division and what sense we give to it.

What we do know, and what psychoanalysis works with, is that the sense we make of our subjective division is filled with ideological content, as is the unconscious itself. Ideology mediates the experience of our divided condition. This condition, in which the unconscious functions as a place that speaks of our distress, is ideologically externalized, prolonged and exacerbated in particular alienating divisions of the subject, those that are characteristic of life under capitalism.

Each one of us is divided by the capitalist system and by its accompanying forms of rule. Patriarchy, for example, divides us between heterosexual male domination and these dominated assimilated to denigrated femininity and other kinds of sexuality. Likewise, colonialism divides us between apparently rational civilisation and the pathologising of socalled 'barbarians' who dare to resist it.

The ideological expressions of our subjective division in this alienated world are denounced and neutralized and transcended in the practice of the liberation movements. The anti-capitalists, the anti-colonialists, the anti-racists, the feminists, the lesbian, gay, transsexual, queer activists and others, many others, have fought and continue to fight effectively to free us from individualised power and instrumental science which reinforces a potent dominant image of what it is to be powerful. They open up a path, a psychoanalytic path to the unconscious, against powers that use our divided condition to dominate us by reinforcing an individual ego identified with colonial and patriarchal capitalism. Defying our ego, liberation movements can enable each of us to stop dominating ourselves, betraying ourselves. Betrayal and domination are things we can leave behind.

The unconscious is spoken into being by us when we interact with each other. It does not exist prior to our relational existence as speaking subjects. It needs us, all of us, and not just each one of us, to exist through what we say to each other, but also by virtue of this, and this is crucial to the progressive political role of psychoanalysis, the unconscious can connect us with collective action. It can thus help us to recover ourselves, to free us from what oppresses, represses and suppresses our collective existence, free association.

What we may never get free of is the division of the subject. We cannot say if this division can ever be healed, perhaps not, but the pain of that division can be alleviated. Relief may come from participation in liberation movements, from the challenge to ideology that is offered by psychoanalytic method in the clinic and by progressive reshaping of psychoanalysis that connects with explicit political action. We will say more in the following chapters about the method of 'free association' that taps into the unconscious such that the unconscious speaks back to us, so that we do not merely speak it into being.

So, we need psychoanalysis allied with and informed by collective struggle, a theory and practice that critically addresses the ideological representation of the subjective division which creates and perpetuates the unconscious as if it is only something inside us and threatening to us. The enemy is also outside and we must fight there against it. Alongside the clinical work is a political task of mobilising unconscious forces while analysing which forces perpetuate ideology and which tend to our freedom. We need to analyse and speak and act so that we make history instead of simply repeating it. *Repetition* next.

重複：歷史、強迫和自由

在一個被剝削和壓迫所標記的異化世界中，在這個我們為了對剝削和壓迫做出貢獻而必須與自己異化的世界，我們忍受著異化，這對我們而言，是無意識的事。我們並不知道這股異化的力量統治著我們並且不斷地把我們放在相同的處境中，我們只知道我們無數次陷入同樣的困境，我們始終無法擺脫它。這就是**重複**（repetition）的特徵，是臨床精神分析中的一個基本概念，我們可以看到人們試圖逃避有毒和破壞性的關係，想像他們是自由的，然後與新夥伴再次重複這些模式。

我們受制於語言的重複特性，家庭的、文化的和意識形態的話語、俗語和敘事都不斷地講述著關於我們是誰以及那些我們不可能達成的事。每一次改變的嘗試都讓我們從另一條路徑繞回原地。我們在象徵和實體層面上都重複地受到對社會結構實質問題矛盾失敗的解決方案的影響。

這種對於事情一定會有所不同的幻想也掩蓋了重複和失敗的潛在的真實特性，我們相信當我們改變合作夥伴、從我們的經驗中學習或改變某些行為模式時，我們就會停止重複，但最終同樣的事情總是發生。

毫不奇怪地，在全新的情境中這種重複的逃避和不知不覺無意識的重現陳年舊有關係的循環模式，也困擾著左翼組織。這些組織也重複著有毒和破壞性的關係，以及辱罵、壓迫、排除、暴力、怠惰、冷漠、傷心和斷裂的情形。那些沒從歷史中學到教訓的人很可能真的最終會重蹈覆轍，但是，似乎即使是學了，也還會一次又一次地陷入同樣的死胡同。

我們迫切需要一種精神分析的視角來了解失敗的歷史對解放運動的影響，這些解放運動在某種自我毀滅的層面上似乎享受著重複挫敗的痛苦，我們需要探究這種重複的強迫症如何在我們的政治實踐中表現為某種病態

的現象，以及我們如何能夠自由地認識到我們正在重複什麼，進而避免失敗，或者至少是失敗得較好一些，還能真正從歷史得到學習。

關於失敗的歷史

資本主義、殖民主義和父權制有一個共同的深層結構，此結構涉及我們的主體性和我們處理某些客觀環境的能力，我們知道在鬥爭中，這些客觀環境對我們和我們的同志們具有深刻的破壞性，仿佛我們的生活是由未知和無法控制的力量所驅動的，這些力量使我們發現自己永無休止地處於相同的境地，就好像這些力量阻擋我們改變我們的生活，迫使我們重複錯誤和失敗；事實是即使我們不想重複，我們也不會停止重複，而這是左翼再清楚不過的事。

這就是無意識開始啟動、促使我們再次採取我們明知結果會很糟的方式之處。在我們的歷史構成的本質中某些東西決定、強加並結構出我們失敗的歷史，而精神分析向我們顯示了這些歷史如何在臨床內與外左右著我們。

無意識的社會結構，正如明顯有利於那些對我們享有權力的人的意識形態訊息以及誤導我們對人類行為本質的常識解釋一樣，有效地抵消了我們顛覆它們的努力。我們有必要去質問為什麼會這樣？這過程又是如何被運作的？問題在於同樣的結構甚至吞噬了我們理解它們的努力並且為其所用。它們總以某種方式令我們和複製那些我們打算改變的事相勾連，變化似乎只發生在表面。那宰制我們的，被重組並以新的面具被偽裝。如果它只在資本主義國家的層面以及在性別歧視和種族主義壓迫的權力結構中運作，這已經夠糟了，但它比那樣還糟，無意識的重複意味著這不僅僅是我們被這樣對待，我們也對我們自己這樣做。

新的組織方式往往最終還是將我們帶回到原點，這不僅是那些徒勞地試圖把他們分析過去情境的教科書套用來分析當前局勢的「老左派」（'old left'）的問題，它也涉及新的社會運動，他們想像自己已經擺脫了社會結構，但最終在新的情境下複製了他們在不知不覺中非常熟悉的那些結構。

　　在這兩種情況下，我們就好像陷入了一個沒有出路的迷宮，我們總是選定相同的策略，被困在同一個被反覆試驗的解釋的封閉場域中；然後很合邏輯地，無論我們做什麼決定都失敗。我們似乎一直在改變而致使一切維持不變。我們偉大的革命姿勢只不過是對相同不變的微小調整和重組。似乎很多時候我們只知道找新方法重複既有的東西來革新，而不是真正跳出當前情境去創造新事物。無論我們做什麼，我們最終都會做近乎相同的事情。我們做了我們必做的；我們並沒擁有我們的歷史，似乎是歷史擁有了我們。

享樂

　　這種重複是無意識的，因此它不僅攜帶著一個令人驚異的熟悉敘事，讓我們對自己的樣子感到安心，而且還帶有另一種往往令我們難以承認的東西——那就是*享樂*（enjoyment）。是的，這是真的，我們可以在我們周圍的同志和敵對陣營愚蠢失敗的策略中看到它，但是當我們陷入這種享樂之中時，就更難坦白承認它。我們不僅喜歡在事情再次變得糟糕時幸災樂禍得意地說：「我們告訴過你了」，我們還樂於等待已經知道的結果，並且關閉了對某些不可預測事情的恐懼。

　　執著於「預測和控制」的，可不僅是資產階級心理學；正是因為我們認為我們能預先知道會發生什麼，我們就注定要重蹈覆轍。縱身躍入未知的未來，這對解放運動的實踐至關重要，卻被他們多次破壞，於是就有了與權力的致命勾結，而不是對權力的真正挑戰。

　　這種享樂還有另一個面向，就是這種奇特的無意識享樂與受苦緊緊連結，這只有精神分析才能有效地描述和處理並幫助我們找到一條出路。誠然，在這個悲慘的世界中我們承受著痛苦，這是我們之所以反抗並尋求改變的原因；然而，除了將我們人類聯合在一起的這種痛苦之外，某種苦難的歷史——以一種交織纏繞的方式將我們束縛於來處的個人的和政治的苦難，為我們帶來了一種明顯的痛苦。

　　一個來自無意識的問題縈繞著我們，以至於如果我們不得不沒它過日子的話我們不知會變成什麼樣。那就是何以我們對政治敵人的指責和給自己的自責是如此強烈猶如劇毒的刺一般；它們藉著把我們置放在我們渴望

成為的位置來指出我們是誰，我們理想的這個位置使我們享受自己的痛苦。

在臨床上，令人享受的痛苦這種自相矛盾可以被解開，因為它從看似無解的矛盾在我們的言語中轉變為一種症狀，從而以這樣的方式被辯證性地結構起來，這使我們能夠找到穿越、超克它的方法。在政治領域，享樂與痛苦之間的密切連結更是強大，作為語言與情緒之間無意識地結構起來的一個結，因為沒法解開它，目前的政治實踐並不直接等同於臨床工作，所以對於享受痛苦和重複，解放運動往往缺乏能使自己重新拿回歷史、為自己去擁有、去創造而非受苦於歷史的對治方法。

我們往往不去創造我們個人的和政治的歷史，而是去忍受它，它好像時常超過了我們的控制和理解，我們只是讓自己被殘酷的決定所惑，像是由父權所形構的家庭動力或資本主義國家所捍衛的破壞性階級結構；在這兩種情況以及種族主義和其他形式的壓迫下，保密和意識形態神祕化的結合導致每個被拋出來的問題都得不到完整的分析，甚至還被拋擲到我們面前成為阻礙。

那些沒有解決的困難和矛盾會被重複，當我們生活在其中時，我們也因此受制於我們自己的重複。我們重複我們沒解決的問題。我們之所以沒解決它，是因為我們不了解它、因為我們甚至不知道它究竟是什麼、因為部分的它對我們而言是未知的、因為部分的它是被遺忘的、是無意識的。只要它沒能被憶起，就必定會被重複。

精神分析告訴我們，我們會重複我們不記得的事情，因為我們覺得它無法忍受、太屈辱、可恥、令人痛苦，甚至令人恐懼和創傷，那些我們甚至沒勇氣去記住的事，很弔詭地恰恰是我們必然重複的事。重複是一種記起為意識所不容之事的無意識作法。

我們重複我們最不想重複的——我們最嚴重的失敗、我們遭受的虐待、構成我們現在的傷口、我們被征服和制伏時的姿態、我們的失寵、我們的殖民、我們壓迫和剝削的起源。這一切，即使在與其對抗時也仍然被重複，我們的鬥爭未能使我們擺脫歷史的重複，這段歷史也是我們不斷重複的歷史。

不管我們喜不喜歡這樣，也不管我們喜不喜歡精神分析，歷史本身就

是一個試圖推翻現有秩序的嘗試和失敗的重複過程。我們沒法停止重複並一次成功到位，因爲我們不是在自己選擇的條件下創造歷史。我們在被給定的條件下行動，並根據把剝削性的異化生產和消費條件鎖定到位的不同壓迫模式而採取行動。這些模式還實現了一個重要功能——阻斷至關重要的集體自組織必要建設。

受苦

我們不被允許、不被給予空間、不被授權組織我們自己，因爲這樣的自組織會產生新的事物。對革新的禁令是一個強而有力的訊息，這訊息在意識上傳送給我們，但它也在無意識層面傳送，而在那裡就更難去注意到，因而也更難加以拒絕。這就是何以當我們遵從需求去享受時就有了*受苦*（suffering），該訊息規定一切都必須依往常繼續運作。我們的享樂和痛苦聯繫在一起的，因爲我們必須繼續被資本主義體制組織起來以實現它的目的——它的，而非我們的——並且唯有如此我們才能快樂，而之後，我們會問自己爲什麼我們不快樂？

當我們打破這個邏輯，拒絕讓資本主義體制凌駕於我們自己的欲望之上時，就會有一個強有力的訊息重複這個邏輯，一個訊息告訴我們正確的事是去接受遊戲規則、我們從體制中已經得到很多、事情可能會更糟、我們不應該反抗因爲我們會危及我們的家人、朋友和同志、我們應該爲每個部分的成功和每一次失敗感到內疚。

前一刻覺得這場鬥爭永遠不會結束，世界永遠不會改變，下一刻又覺得結局總是一樣。它們對於勞動和消費強加了一種重複的、破壞性的和自我毀滅的邏輯，越來越多的勞動和消費，但也是最多樣化的剝削和壓迫慣例。透過這種方式，階級權力、種族主義和性別歧視以及其他歧視性的意識形態實踐必須重複它們的作用以使得物質資源能夠積累、實現利潤，並將財富集中於那些被認爲最適合體現和表徵資本爲必要之物的人身上。

因此，與其去把每一次失敗都當作又一次的意外，抑或看作是對我們改變世界的希望必然被圍限於幻想之地而非現實的又一次嚴峻的提醒，我們需要的是去了解我們無意識生活更深和更危險的層面。我們重複是因爲我們學會了重複，因爲我們不知道如何採取其他行動，而不是因爲這是一

種「本能的」（'instinctive'）行為。並非本能令我們享受痛苦，失敗並不是像某種生物機體般被內建裝置在我們裡面，而是被鑲嵌於我們作為言說的存在體的歷史之中，此一歷史是環繞著階級、種族和性別向度而構建的歷史。在我們為推翻這個可悲制度而建立的組織中，這種宰制的歷史也經常不幸地被重複著。

我們的解放運動重複了我們在家庭中的生活。在精神分析臨床上，我們可以看到痛苦和享樂之間的密切關聯是如何形成於作為我們性欲功能的家庭歷史之中；而後，在政治組織中，這種密切關聯在關於地位和權力的更為公開的鬥爭中被表現出來。問題是如何擺脫跟我們知道的錯誤的社會關係形式的勾連，並為反思和行動開闢空間。透過轉化重複的強迫成為精神分析概念化的作為驅動症狀的力量，是有可能沿著更進步的方向循跡覓徑。

強迫與症狀

失敗和結構性的重複具有可理解和可識別的面向，例如，我們都很清楚，工人代表們有多麼容易屈服於雇主提供給他們品嚐殘羹剩屑大快朵頤的誘惑。下班後的時間，可以讓他們跟老闆稱兄道弟，甚至可以在聚會中一起喝酒吃飯，這使他們進入一種生活方式，這種生活方式提供了工廠或農田的同志們生活中所沒有的舒適感。

工人會被老闆引誘去要老闆想要的，甚至最終希望老闆贏，即使明顯地以犧牲工人為代價。這就是工人們會如何在他人的慾望中異化自己的欲望[1]、使用對方的話語、敵人的觀點而自尋失敗的道理。長此以往，最嚴重

---

[1] 原文 desire 一詞到了近代中文世界可譯作「欲望」與「慾望」，而兩者意義有別，在中文語境中「欲望」較指因現況不滿足而意欲追尋改變實現的意念，「慾望」較指身體耳目感官之慾念。作者在第 4 章《欲望，關於他者》一節明白分辨「欲望」不同於「驅力」、「本能」，「欲望」是最人性的面向，被創造於社會關係的總合之中，對他者有所渴望，也渴望他者對自己的認可。細品全書中作者多處提及同一個 desire 可能存在兩種相反的表現性質，在作者對照這兩種不同性質時，以「欲／慾望」表達，至於「欲望」與「慾望」，貫穿全

的後果就是資產階級結構開始嵌入工人運動，以及雇主的價值觀取得主導地位——包括虛幻的「利潤共享」（'shared interests'）和「共同利益」（'common good'）。

我們可以看到著名的馬克思主義論點的物質基礎——意識形態透過雇主的世界觀在勞動人口中傳播而發揮作用。在這裡，統治思想確實是統治階級的思想。這裡有著意識形態和結構的複製，它的重複有時是有意識的，但更多時候是無意識的。

複製

工會代表享有的特權，會使得他們作為工人運動中的官僚層級捍衛自己的特定利益。同樣地，存在著意識形態和結構的**複製**（*replication*），從而在對治這一點上問責制和職位輪調的要求就變得很重要。然而，即使採取了這些措施，也很難避免權力位置結構性決定的某些影響。殖民主義也正是以這種方式運作，這就是為什麼說工人運動被統治階級的價值觀和意識形態「殖民」，這是有某些道理的。

在殖民主義的情況下，我們看到當地的代表被侵略者收買，最終他們構成了一個特定的階層，他們跟殖民者的共同點更多於他們曾經和奴隸的共同點，我們很清楚被殖民主體的現象，他們回到他們的國家後，穿衣和吃飯都像他們的主子，把自己與當地居民區隔分開來；然而，伴隨著這種享樂而來的是痛苦，我們也知道，被殖民主體在效忠於他們的人民或他們的主子之間左右為難，他們被邀進這種勾連中而分裂、痛苦。

主體經常被分裂於是否去複製宰制性的經濟結構和意識形態之間。然而，尚有在複製之上的東西是針對享樂和受苦的精神分析方法所關注的。儘管當主體要決定他們的忠誠要放到何處時當然也有危機時刻，但重複並

書前後，譯者大致的原則是，以「欲望」表達人性的、革命性、創造性、朝向政治解放的渴望，而以「慾望」表達較指生物性、由異化驅動的、也是帶到臨床中要被消解的力量傾向，不過，這些區辨只限定於中文語境上為更清楚表達作者指涉的意義，並不是實質上二元對立的，所以，當作者在文脈中同時兩者都可能包含其中時，以「欲望」作較寬的表達，「慾望」則僅用於只在非常明顯指涉有別於「欲望」意涵的情形下。

不是意識選擇的結果。

那些危機時刻之所以如此令人痛苦，正是因為這種重複通常是無意識的、不受控制的和強迫性的，因而就必須抓住些什麼東西。強迫性重複以症狀的形式在臨床中顯化，這是主體帶在身上的一種表現衝突和痛苦的特殊症狀，這種精神上的痛苦有一個物質基礎，它是個人生活史與社會歷史之間一種怪異的無意識結合，人們在其中被告知應該如何享受以及可能會如何受苦。

因此，在當代資本主義下，日常生活中存在著雙重的重複歷程：第一個層面通常被理解為在「外部世界」（'outer world'）中運作——透過在社會和制度性的關係中重複各種形式的壓迫和剝削。因為實質的政治經濟力量也會將個人拖向自我毀滅的行為模式，精神分析對這個過程有些話值得一提。

這些力量會吸引和獎勵個人行為，這些行為再現了宰制的、階級的和地緣政治權力的實質結構，以及家庭和性別之間、身體健全者和「被失能的特殊需要者」（'disabled'）之間的權力分配。有時，那些抵制主導結構的人之間存在症狀性的矛盾，這種矛盾是以自由為名的抵抗和以暴力——即指涉壓迫的暴力性重複——為特徵的結構性反應。

這個重複歷程意識形態地運作的第二個層面，既是緊密包覆於政治經濟的物質結構領域中，也同時與那些受制於權力的個人生活世界——即所謂的「內心世界」（'inner world'）緊密連結。這是我們避難的世界，好像我們可以逃避內心的壓迫，但我們沒法做到，無法逃避到個體性的自我之中。當他們訴及在此歷程中的自身經驗時，主體被阻止說話，他們自己的立場的合法性被取消，他們的陳述被系統性地扭曲。

這裡出現的矛盾也是症狀性的，那就是在指涉壓迫的反覆抱怨和失敗與名為自由的那種渴望之間發生了衝突。因此，精神分析的臨床任務是讓主體能夠談論他們的經驗和他們的欲望，而在此，當然地，臨床成為了政治，或者更確切地說，它揭示了臨床一直以來的本質，因為個人——正如社會主義女性主義宣稱的——即是政治，或者正如我們在精神分析中說的——無意識即政治。

忘記無意識會讓我們忘記政治，當意識形態或經濟上的重複讓我們習

慣於這些重複的事物時——也就是將其固定化和當然化、使其顯現爲不可避免、看作是事物或人性必然的作用力時，這就會發生。心理學和其他科學在此處介入，爲那些被重複的事物辯護，將其合理化的、普遍化的和去政治化，以此提供我們對人性的概念。然後我們忘記了政治，因爲我們忘記了重複是歷史性的，且會被那些受限於它的人——也就是被我們、主體——所打斷。精神分析提醒我們這些主體是存在的，給他們發言權，傾聽他們對自己症狀的看法，如此，當可幫助我們將重複和症狀性地顯現出來的內容重新政治化。

正是當重複變成強迫（即臨床中精神分析治療主體強迫性重複的那種程度），它可以被濃縮爲一種症狀。請記住，症狀根本上是一種衝突，但這是一種非常特殊的衝突。這是一種欲望或願望和禁令、壓抑相抵觸的衝突。介於欲望所求的與所承載的壓擠、拒斥及抑制的力量之間的衝突，比它表象看起來的更爲複雜，而精神分析對這個複雜性的闡明也對我們如何概念化政治鬥爭產生了深遠的影響。在進步的政治鬥爭中，一種爲了自由，更進一步地，爲了一個我們所有人都將自由的世界的欲望，反對來自資本主義、殖民主義和父權制動員起來阻攔我們的各種權力形式，這就是說，壓制之下欲望升起。

然而，我們必須小心地將這逐漸出現的變革欲望視爲歷史創造的，而不是表達爲好像是從個體或群體內部噴出既已存在而人皆有之的力量；在二十一世紀這些悲慘的情形下，對自由的欲望與歷史上其他時期的這種欲望大不相同。是的，當然，在人類之中，有些東西是很有創造性但被當權者扭曲和壓制；而且，是的，很可能一直都如此。

我們現在針對當前統治體制採取對抗的這種欲望是由我們創造的，是由我們作爲歷史的存在歷史性地創造的；這些欲望現在圍繞著另一個世界的圖象接合起來，那裡將會有資源的集體管理、種族隔離的終結、婦女的賦權、差異主體的共在和對地球的保護，我們提出的訴求是對當前這個世界所拒絕我們的種種的回應。

當然，有一種對精神分析的流行印象是將每一個個體視爲具有本能力量推動釋放的壓力鍋，這種印象倒是很便利於那些希望將我們的鬥爭化約的人，他們將我們的鬥爭化約爲在這樣一個必須以多數人的需要平衡每個

人的需要的社會中一種對自然文明行為規則的不滿。然而，我們的精神分析對欲望和壓抑之間的衝突所提出的觀點其實是非常不同的。正是壓抑的形式本身產生了欲望的形式。正是被禁止的東西被創造、被激發、被挑動，從而被禁止的欲望可以以保守反對改革的或進步的方式、以自我毀滅或創造性的方式被表達出來。

　　一種被禁止的欲望可能會尋求以顛覆性的方式來滿足，這種方式藐視鎖定社會的各種壓制手段，而它也可能在資本主義中尋求一種適應性的、有利可圖的、可利用的滿足，這牽涉到壓制，而壓制在本質上就是壓抑的。同一欲／慾望[2]的兩種表達方式在個人領域與社會領域都可能彼此對立。販毒與藥物合法化運動、色情與性解放、基本教義主義與反殖民主義、黑人資本主義與反資本主義的反種族主義、生態資本主義與真正的生態學之間都存在著明顯的矛盾。

　　在所有情況下，真實總是與其受壓抑和壓制、被神祕化、退回原狀的表達形式相違，這與發生在每一個個體性的存在的歷程相同，在個體性的存在裡，欲望無可避免因壓抑手段而得要面對它的退回及合理化。就如個人在臨床裡努力理解壓抑並就他們想要的去做出決定性的選擇，在政治領域也是如此，我們集體辯論並創造全然不同於企圖操縱、利用我們的欲望並阻止我們說話和行動的壓制形式組織運作方式。

矛盾

　　當臨床情境使主體能將看似無法解決的衝突轉化為**矛盾**（*contradiction*）時，這些衝突就被濃縮為一種症狀，然後就可以辯證地處理這種症狀，從現有的行動可能性條件下，新的可能性被創造出來。這是一項臨床任務，也是一項政治任務，因為它需要將主體的生活經歷和使他們成為這樣的人的關係網絡以批判性反思的辯證性理解聯繫起來。

　　如果傳統的心理學和心理學化的（psychologized）精神分析看起來似乎是去政治性（apolitical）的，那是因為它們通常就是配合宰制和重複的政治，這並非一種真正的替代性出路，因為它與那些限制行動可能性並強

---

[2]　見註 1。

加某些禁制的現存條件沒有區別。主體的獨特性關乎政治，使我們能反對目前宰制我們並且遮蔽任何基進替代性出路的傳統保守心理／精神相關專業。這是因為心理／精神相關專業幾乎使他們的取向和色彩戳印於所有事物，他們自己關於適應的好處的理論在這個世界中幾乎所有對我們做的事情上不斷地重複。

　　當心理學家從他們已分配到的位子上說話，根據他們（專家）知道的（也是我們已經知道的）那些不斷地被重複的關於心理常態和社會規範的內容，去重新解釋他們的「個案」的生活時，那種適應性的政治就被強加於主體。在臨床上讓主體說話並明白如何透過注意和耐心地傾聽（這是精神分析中應該做到的）最終發現另一種政治，即主體的欲望和他們的重複的經驗的政治，這樣幾乎就足夠了。在這裡，精神分析的臨床空間與資本主義制度的重複運作形成鮮明對比，它不符合體制的可預測性、適應性和明顯的彈性等規範或標準。

　　主體經由可預測的方式，透過不斷地呈現他們必備的積極自信、掌控性和競爭性，藉由只是說著、思考著和感受著那些應該的事，經由使欲望和經驗靜默，並透過他們的工作和消費對資本主義壓迫性和剝削性的實質運作作出重複和複製的貢獻，以此「正常」地行動著。他們被允許，甚至被鼓勵在為他們的身分、生活方式和階級地位等類別所設限的範圍內彈性變通，這些類別可作為「市場利基」（'market niches'）而收割並賣回給他們。

　　這些意識形態和社會經濟的重複密不可分且相互支持，這越來越難解的結代表了當前新自由資本主義制度的最大優勢之一，也是反對它的人面臨的最大挑戰之一。

　　將這些物質和意識形態（即統治和抵抗的結構性與象徵性面向）聯繫起來，就是我們今天面對的根本和首要的問題——全球資本主義本質的複雜性——以及在左翼和解放組織中我們可用的解決方案的不完整和扭曲。至少，我們能清楚地看到戰鬥中兩股力量都陷入了重複的泥淖：一方面，關於權力這一面，是積累和保護資本的強迫性驅力、是剝削的成果、具有強迫執拗和重複的特徵；另一方面，關於抵抗這一面，左翼組織往往重複地陷入自己失敗的歷史，犯同樣的錯誤。

　　階級鬥爭的歷史以及不同形式壓迫中更廣泛、更基本的解放過程是這些重複和失敗歷史中的一種；還有，記住那些有時是幸運但更常是悲劇性的偶發事件，這些都完全超出我們的控制。這沒完沒了幾乎無法忍受的重複的脈絡，接著被複製到個人的生活中。個人被鼓勵去想像他們是自由的，是獨立於物質的與意識形態的雙重歷史過程，所以他們更加深刻地感受到這種失敗，他們無法接受表明他們對自己的生活幾乎沒有權力的證據；也不知道如何處理重複及其鐵律——必然和偶然、宿命和命運。精神分析致力於所有這些複雜的物質和象徵的資料。

　　在精神分析中，個體說話，試圖「自由聯想」，說出所有來到心頭上的事，而且是自由地說，沒有審查。他們試圖說一些新的、未知的東西，但沒能辦到。當他們辦不到時，他們就會聽到自己重複著同樣的老故事，那些他們被告知有關他們自己的事，那些在他們自己的生活中已經具體發生過的故事，這些故事，必須被重複地說以阻止其他故事被講述或發生。自由聯想向主體揭示了他們在言語中那些無法暢所欲言的地方，以及，更重要的，那些存在著阻塞點（阻礙言語和行動）的地方。這些阻塞點上開始浮現的就是重複的另一面，衝突的重現，一種包含欲望和壓抑兩者於其中的衝突。

　　因此，強迫而致於重複就被揭露並濃縮為一個症狀，這種症狀可以轉化為主體存在的核心的一個辯證地被組建起來的矛盾，可以開闢新的道路，為他們的言語與行動的可能性創造新的條件。這種精神分析臨床工作對政治鬥爭來說絕非完美的模式，我們也不是要建議它應被當作任何模式去運作；不過，它為臨床外與權力鬥爭的人們提供了重要的課題，透過這種方式，出現在精神分析臨床內的那種奇特的、有限的自由，就與解放運動旨於在世界創造的不可限量的集體自由形式聯繫起來。

自由性的重複，與較好的失敗

　　精神分析進步性的一課是，面對強迫性的重複[3]，我們可以開啟新的可

---

[3]　Freedom to repeat 意指具有自由意志的選擇並重複某些行為或模式；相對地，

能性，我們可能仍然會繼續受制於重複，因為我們無法否認無意識的存在，但是我們可以做出更多的選擇。我們也許沒能總是成功地得到我們想要的東西，請記住，我們是**分裂的主體**（*divided subjects*）；當然，我們甚至無法絕對確定那個去求索我們想要的東西的人就真的是我們自己。這是不可能的，至少在當前社會和未來一段時間內是不可能的，因為即使我們真能擺脫阻擋我們得到滿足的最巨大的社會障礙，我們也還是繼續被統治和異化的歷史所困擾，而這歷史形塑了我們是誰以及我們如何表述自己。然而，即使我們持續失敗，我們仍可以取得些許真正的成功，並以這樣的方式做出選擇，以便更好地了解成功與失敗之間的區別。

　　這是一個自由的空間，一個在精神分析臨床內以相當有限的方式打開的空間，一個我們可以在政治領域進一步開展的空間。這個空間不必然要排除那些被重複的。到目前為止，我們已經強調了重複的限制性面向，也就是重複相同的面向，但我們現在要將注意力放到重複的另一個面向——重複總是包含某些不同的東西。隱藏在重複中的自由空間——也同時是經常被強迫性重複束縛在個人自我的監獄中——是一個不同的空間。這是一個越來越緊張的空間，矛盾日益加劇的空間，但出於同樣的理由，它也是一個抵抗、堅持不懈的空間，而對那些被重複的而言，也是一個不可避免的位移形式或者象徵距離的空間。不是重複相同，而是重複以創造不同。

　　不同也源自於重複，重複兩次的事物第二次不會和第一次一樣，這正是因為它是第二次發生、因為已經有過第一次、因為它已經是被重複過的而不是全新的。脈絡改變了不同元素的意義，生活繼續著，重複就不僅只有相同而是微妙地、時而戲劇性地有著不同。這是一個複雜的辯證過程，在臨床治療和政治上都是如此。

　　重複可意味著堅持或強調，但這種重複也暴露其自身，顯露其特性，以致令人厭煩又無法避開，甚至是難以忍受而沒法持續下去。所有這些都會引發關於重複內容的不同感受、想法和行為。如果它持續重複自身，就可能使主體對它感到厭煩，拉開距離對它進行批判性的判斷，特別是如果

---

compulsion to repeat 則指個體被不自覺地做出強迫性的重複行為或模式。

重複發生在一個反身性 的框架之中——例如精神分析和解放運動。

能指

　　人們在生活中重複著他們話語一遍又一遍說著已重複的事。是的，這是眞的。這就是他們試圖理解的方式，他們試圖要理解生活中實體的和意識形態的情境是如何被嵌入無意識和他們對周遭事件的重複反應（無意識驅動）之中。而於此同時，隨著他們的阻塞點一次又一次地出現，他們也重複地經驗那些阻止他們把話說出來的服從關係。

　　不同的是現在（在他們自己的精神分析過程中）他們有另一個機會在臨床裡或許能讓他們說出他們以前不能說的。當這種情況發生時，他們的話語，作爲***能指***（signifiers）[4]，俾使他們能鼓舞地繼續前進，並與他們的舊生活保持一定的距離。這裡有著有限的和潛在的自由。

　　即使當人們重複時，他們的重複也不是簡單地複製相同的單字、片語和帶有意義的動作，以及我們將其概念化爲「能指」的口頭、書面或存在話語中的相同符號元素。人類世界中的每一個能指（即每一個詞、每一個行動或事物）都已經是意義系統的一部分，這個意義系統賦予我們的能指價值，使它們能被人們充分理解，從而在交流媒介和意識形態中發揮作用。這些是構成我們在不同語言中共享象徵世界的能指，是象徵世界的基石。

　　參與在精神分析臨床經驗中的「分析主體」（'analysand'）聽見了這

---

[4] 'Signifier(s)' 是象徵符號的形或音，中譯有作「能指」、「符徵」、「意符」、「符號具」等，是相對於 'signified'（被連結的概念或意義，中譯作「所指」、「符旨／符指」、「意旨／意指」、「符號義」等）的一組概念。由於人類是會以符號（最主要是語言）表達的存在主體，象徵世界就是經由符號在歷史中構成的，也就是在無意識中對人的主體性起著界定、指導的作用，但也正因爲能指與所指之間的關係會隨著時空脈絡存在變異與解構、轉變的空間，所以同一個能指的意義可被重構、也可以置換不同的能指對情境或主體自身重新定義。作者在本節説明精神分析臨床中分析主體傾聽無意識的能指而可能改變它們在個體與共同集體世界中的意義，使「個人即政治」、「無意識即政治」、「臨床即政治」成爲可能。

些能指的重複和聯繫。此「分析主體」迥然不同於精神醫生治療下的「病人」（'patient'）或心理學家治療下的「個案」（'client'）。我們精神分析的「分析主體」自己做分析，作爲分析師的我們並不給他們處遇，治癒（cure）乃掌握在他們手中。他們是主體而不是客體，他們所說的話不是由分析師作解釋，而是由他們自己。對於他們說的話，他們用更多的話來完成解釋，這些話被添加到先前的話，而這些話又必須由他們來解釋。這些話語最緊密的含義就在於它們自身，在它們之間的複雜關係中，而不是在它們之外，不是在只能憑藉分析師如占卜人或先知般解讀症狀才能預測的神祕深處。

　　我們不必鑽研到表面之下就能清楚能指在一個總是超出我們控制、對我們而言是無意識的意義系統中是如何運作的。能指運作取決於我們如何使用它們，根據它們對我們的作用，而它們一直存在於我們所說和聽到的內容中。例如，「解放」這個詞是一個能指，而我們用來定義我們是誰以及我們的集體身分的每個政治術語也都是能指，不論是「勞動者」、「女性」、「特殊需要人士」還是「原住民」。

　　能指在一個符號系統中被用來界定我們，但我們可以能動地予以重構，重構它們的意義。正如在集體政治層面上發生的那樣，在臨床中，一個分析主體聽到能指——那些被他們生活中有權力的他人賦予界定身分的能指，並抓住控制權，即使是一瞬間，也能重新塑造它們。

　　能指據其在我們所言說的矛盾、嬗變的語言中的位置而具有不同的含義，這種語言圍繞著我們，當我們改變自己和改變世界時，我們會根據這些語言採取行動。我們從試圖平反曾經以壓迫或壓制方式指涉我們的能指（例如「黑人」或「瘋子」或「同性戀」）的嘗試中很清楚這一點。我們採用這些能指並在我們進步的政治鬥爭中再次擁有它們，並以自豪而不是羞恥的態度去說出它們。

　　處於不斷變化的矛盾文化和歷史脈絡中，相同的事物、行爲和語言永遠不會全然相同。同時，特定的能指對每一個主體都具特定的意義，而「解放」（'liberation'）一詞在不同的語境下，很可能就意味著不同的意義。在臨床中，精神分析關注能指在某人生活中所扮演的特定角色。我們可以想像我們知道它們的意思，但精神分析告訴我們，我們必須以更大的

注意力來傾聽能指，以重建它們在共享的和個體的符號系統中的運作方式。

我們的歷史，無論是集體政治還是個人政治，都不是一個固定且硬性的框架，而是始終開放的，這取決於我們努力理解我們是誰以及我們想要創造的世界。我們的存在和我們的願望與重複的事物相矛盾，而重複的事物又與自身相矛盾。這些矛盾在辯證運動的過程中，造成體制系統的不穩定，或者以「休克資本主義」（'shock capitalism'）的方式利用危機來重新配置和強化其自身，或者給我們自由的空間；這取決於我們，取決於我們如何反思和行動，以及我們是否集體地行動。

意識形態的力量和政治經濟結構使同樣的事情不斷重複，因為這樣的力量與結構限制了我們的言論和行動，故我們加以抵抗。精神分析在此能幫助我們抵抗，藉由給我們一個空間來體驗和表達我們如何重複我們對自己說的話、以及我們如何重複所做的事，而使自我毀滅的行為模式永久化。這個空間是有效的，因為它允許我們對重複反思，而不僅僅是重複同樣老舊熟悉的行動模式。

因此，取代掉重複相同，臨床為不同的湧現打開了空間，使能指可以像這樣全然地不同，並對我們自己的主體性有一種非常地不同、全然獨特的意義。這種全然不同的湧現是一種勝利，一種可以為之付出無數失敗代價來換取的勝利。我們注定會重複，但我們也被驅動著去做出改變，我們精神分析師可以藉由在臨床中為不同打開一個空間，一個讓主體得以與意識形態常識及其心理學手冊建立的規則有所不同的空間，從而做出改變。

同樣，解放運動能改變世界——藉由將自己與主流意識形態區分開來、藉由想要創造一個完全不同的世界、藉由建立一個差異被珍視為成為人類的條件的世界。失敗的重複因此轉化為不同的東西。我們內在的某些東西驅使我們這樣做，這就是我們在下一章接著要討論的內容——**驅力**（*drive*）。

REPETITION: HISTORY, COMPULSION AND FREEDOM

In an alienated world marked by exploitation and oppression, a world in which we must also be alienated from ourselves in order to contribute to our own exploitation and oppression, we live with alienation as something unconscious to us. We do not know the alien forces that govern us and put us incessantly in the same kind of situations. We only know that we are in the same predicament for the umpteenth time and that we cannot finally free ourselves from it. This is the character of *repetition*, a fundamental concept in clinical psychoanalysis where we can see people attempting to escape toxic and destructive relationships, imagining they are free and then repeating those patterns again with new partners.

We are subject to the repetitive nature of language, of familial and cultural and ideological words and phrases and narratives that keep telling the same stories about who we are and what it is impossible for us to achieve. Each attempt to change leads us down another path to the same place. And we are symbolically and bodily subject to the repetition of contradictory failed solutions to socially-structured material problems.

The fantasy that something different must happen then also obscures the underlying real nature of repetition and failure. We believe that we stop repeating when we change partners, when we learn from our experience or when we modify certain behaviour patterns, but in the end the same thing always happens.

Little wonder that such repetitive patterns of escape and unwitting unconscious reconstruction in new contexts of very old relationships should also haunt left organisations. These organizations also repeat toxic and destructive relationships, as well as situations of abuse, oppression, intolerance, violence, demotivation, boredom, heartbreak, and rupture. It may well be true that those who fail to learn from history will end up repeating it, but it seems that even that learning leads again and again into the same kinds of dead end.

We urgently need a psychoanalytic perspective on what histories of failure are doing to liberation movements who at some self-destructive level seem to enjoy suffering their repetitive defeats, how this compulsion to repeat manifests itself as something symptomatic in our political practice, and how we might have the freedom to know what it is we are repeating so we might avoid failing or at least fail better and actually learn from history.

Histories of failure

Capitalism, colonialism and patriarchy have a deep structure in common that concerns our subjectivity and our ability to deal with certain objective conditions we know are deeply destructive to us and to our comrades in struggle. It is as if our lives are driven by unknown and uncontrollable forces that make us find ourselves interminably in the same situations. It is as if these forces prevent us from transforming our lives and instead force us to repeat mistakes and defeats. The fact is that we do not stop repeating even what we do not want to repeat, and this is something the left knows only too well.

This is where the unconscious kicks into action, impelling us to make again the moves we surely know will end badly. Something in our historically-constructed nature decides, imposes itself upon and structures our histories of failure, and psychoanalysis shows us how these histories carry us along inside and outside the clinic.

Unconscious social structures, as with explicitly ideological messages that benefit those who enjoy power over us and commonsense explanations that mislead us about the nature of human action, effectively neutralize our efforts to subvert them. We need to ask why that is so and how that process works. The problem is that the same structures even absorb our efforts to understand them, and use them to their advantage. One way or another, they make us collude in reproducing what we intended to transform. The changes seem to occur only on the surface. What dominates us is recomposed and disguised with new masks. This would be bad enough if it operated only at the level of the capitalist state and in apparatuses of power that repeat sexist and racist oppression, but it is worse than that. Unconscious repetition means that this is not only being done to us. We also do it to ourselves.

New ways of organising too often end up leading us back to the same place we started from. This is not only a problem of the 'old left' who search in their textbooks for analysis of past situations and vainly try to make those analyses work in the present, but it also applies to new social movements who imagine that they have broken free from social structures but end up replicating those very structures they unconsciously know so well in new conditions.

In both cases it is as if we are in a labyrinth with no way out, in which we always decide on the same strategies, stay trapped inside the same closed field of tried and tested explanations; and then, logically, whatever we decide fails. We seem to change so that everything stays the same. Our great revolutionary gestures are nothing but small readjustments and rearrangements of the same. It seems so often that we only know how to innovate by finding new ways to repeat what there is instead of really creating something new out of the current conditions. Whatever we do, we always end up doing approximately the same. We do what we must do. We do not own our history. It seems to own us.

Enjoyment

This repetition is unconscious, and so it carries with it not only an uncannily familiar narrative that reassures us about who we are, but something else that is often difficult to acknowledge, *enjoyment*. Yes, it is true, we can see it around us in the stupid failed strategies of our comrades and in rival organisations, but it is more difficult to own up to it when we are caught up in this enjoyment. We enjoy not only saying triumphantly 'we told you so' when things turn out badly again, but also rejoicing in waiting for an already known outcome and shutting away the fear of something unpredictable happening.

It is not only bourgeois psychology that is obsessed with 'prediction and control'; we are also condemned to repeat the past precisely because we think we know what will happen in advance. The leap into an unknown future that is so crucial to the practice of the liberation movements is so many times sabotaged by them, and then there is a deadly collusion with power instead of an authentic challenge to it.

There is another aspect to this enjoyment that only psychoanalysis can effectively describe and work with, and help us find a way through, which is that this peculiar unconscious enjoyment is bound up with suffering. Of course we suffer in this miserable world. That is why we rebel and seek to change it. However, in addition to what unites us as humanity, something of that history of misery – personal and political misery that is intertwined in such a way as to chain us to where we came from – brings with it a kind of suffering that is recognisably ours.

A question haunts us from the unconscious as to what we would be if we had to live without it. That is what gives accusations against our political enemies and then selfre-criminations such a potent poisonous sting. They point to who we are by placing us in the position of what we aspire to be. This position of our ideal allows us to enjoy our own suffering.

In the clinic that contradictory enjoyable suffering can be unravelled as it transforms itself in our speech from being a seemingly un-resolvable contradiction into a symptom that is then structured dialectically in such a way as to enable us to find a way through it, to transcend it. In the political realm that intimate link between enjoyment and suffering is so much more effective, as an unconsciously structured knot of language and emotion, because there is no way to solve it, as there is, at present, no direct equivalent to the clinical work in political practice. Liberation movements often lack the means to manage their enjoyment of suffering, of repetition, so they can re-appropriate their history, own it for themselves and make it instead of suffering it.

Usually we do not make our own personal and political history, but we suffer it, often as if it was out of our control and out of our comprehension. We just let ourselves be carried away by inexorable determinations such as family dynamics configured by patriarchal power or as the destructive class structure defended by the capitalist state. In both cases, and in cases of racism and other forms of oppression, a combination of secrecy and ideological mystification results in an incomplete resolution of each of the problems that are thrown up, and thrown in front of us as obstacles.

Those difficulties and contradictions that are not solved are repeated, and as we live them we are thereby subject to repetition ourselves. We repeat what we do not solve in our lives. We do not solve it because we do not understand it, because we do not even know exactly what it is, because it is partly unknown to us, because it is partially forgotten, unconscious. As it cannot be remembered, it must be repeated.

Psychoanalysis teaches us that we repeat what we cannot remember because we find it intolerable, too humiliating, shameful, distressing, even horrifying and traumatic. What we do not even have the courage to remember is paradoxically what we have to repeat. Repeating is an unconscious way of remembering what is inadmissible to consciousness.

We repeat what we least want to repeat; our worst defeats, the abuses of which we were victims, the wounds that constituted us as what we are, the gestures by which we were conquered and subdued, our fall from grace, our colonization, the origin of our oppression and our exploitation. All this is repeated even when it is fought against. Our struggles fail to free us from the repetitive refrain of our history. This history is also the history of what we keep repeating.

Whether we like it or not and whether we like psychoanalysis or not, history itself is a repetitive process of attempts and failures to overthrow the existing order of things. We cannot stop repeating and succeed once and for all because we do not make history in conditions of our own choosing. We act in given conditions and according to different patterns of oppression that lock these exploitative alienating conditions of production and consumption into place. These patterns also fulfil a crucial function; to block the crucial necessary building of collective self-organisation.

Suffering

We are not permitted, not given the space, not authorized to organize ourselves because such self-organization would produce something new. The prohibition of novelty is a powerful message that is sent to us consciously, but also on the unconscious level, where it is more difficult to notice and so more difficult to refuse. That is how there is *suffering* when we obey the demand to enjoy. The message prescribes that everything has to continue functioning as usual. Our enjoyment and suffering are tied together in the idea that we must continue to be organized by the capitalist system to fulfil its ends – its own and not ours – and that only in that way can we be happy, and we then ask ourselves why we are not happy.

When we break from this logic, refuse to allow the capitalist system to take precedence over our own desires, there is a powerful message that then repeats this logic, a message that tells us that the correct thing is to accept the rules of the game, that we have received a lot from the system, that things could be worse, that we should not rebel because we will endanger our family and friends and comrades, that we should feel guilty for every partial success as well as every failure.

At the one moment, it feels as if this struggle will never end, that the world will never change, and at the next it feels as if the ends are always the same. They impose a repetitive, destructive and self-destructive logic of labour and consumption, of more and more labour and consumption, but also of the most diverse routines of exploitation and oppression. In this way, class power, racism and sexism and other discriminatory ideological practices must repeat their function of enabling the accumulation of material resources, of the realisation of profit and the concentration of wealth among those deemed fittest to embody and represent the needs of capital.

So, instead of treating each failure as yet another surprise, yet another grim reminder that our hopes to change the world must be confined to the realm of fantasy instead of reality, we need to understand a deeper and more dangerous aspect of our unconscious lives. We repeat because we learn to repeat, because we do not know how to act otherwise, and not because it is an 'instinctive' behaviour. No instinct makes us enjoy suffering. Failure is not hard-wired into us as biological organisms, but embedded in our history as speaking beings, a history that is structured around dimensions of class, race and gender, a history of domination that is also often unfortunately repeated in the very organisations that we have built to overthrow this wretched system.

Our liberation movements repeat what we live in the family. In the psychoanalytic clinic we can see how the intimate link between suffering and enjoyment is forged in our family history as a function of our sexuality. Later, in political organisations, that intimate link is played out in more overt battles over status and power. The question is how to break from that collusion with forms of social relationship we know are wrong, and open up spaces for reflection and action. It is possible to trace a path in a more progressive direction by turning the compulsion to repeat into that which psychoanalysis conceptualises as the force that drives the symptom.

Compulsion and symptom

The repetition of failure and structure has an understandable and recognisable aspect. We know well, for example, how tempting it is for workers' representatives to succumb, to savour the crumbs of enjoyment that are offered to them by employers. Time away from work can be offered to them during which they fraternise with the bosses, perhaps even sharing drinks and meals around meetings, and this draws them into a lifestyle which provides comforts they do not have when living among their comrades in the factories or the fields.

Workers can be seduced by their bosses to the point of wanting what the bosses want, even eventually wanting the bosses to win, obviously at the expense of the workers. This is how workers can seek their own failure by alienating their desire in the desire of the other, by adopting the other's discourse, the enemy's point of view. The most serious consequence in the long term is that bourgeois structures begin to embed themselves in a layer of the workers' movement, and the values of the employers, including the fiction of 'shared interests' and the 'common good', take hold.

We can see then a material basis for the well-known Marxist argument that ideology operates through the spread among the working population of the worldview of the employers; here it is indeed the case that the ruling ideas are the ideas of the ruling class. Here there is a replication of ideology and structure, repetition of it at a sometimes conscious but more often an unconscious level.

Replication

Trades union representatives have privileges which can lead them to defend their particular interests as a bureaucratic layer within the workers' movement. Again, there is a *replication* of ideology and structure, and then demands for accountability and rotation of positions become important to combat this. However, even with these measures, it is very difficult to avoid certain effects of the structural determination of power positions. Colonialism also functions in exactly this kind of way, and this is why it somehow makes sense to speak of the workers' movement being 'colonised' by ruling class values and ideology.

In the case of colonialism, we see local representatives bought off by the invaders, and eventually they constitute a particular class layer that has more in common with the colonial masters than they do with the slaves they once were. We know well the phenomenon of colonial subjects returning to their countries and dressing and eating like their masters, differentiating themselves from the local population. With that enjoyment, however, comes suffering, and we also know that the colonial subject is torn between their loyalty to their people and to their masters, divided, anguished by the collusion they are invited into.

The subject is usually divided between replicating and not replicating the dominant economic structure and ideology. However, there is something more beyond this replication which a psychoanalytic approach to enjoyment and suffering draws attention to. Repetition is not the result of conscious choice, though of course there are times of crisis when the subject decides where their loyalty lies.

Those times of crisis are so anguishing precisely because something has to be grasped concerning this repetition, which is usually unconscious, uncontrolled and compulsive. Repetition compulsion materialises itself in the clinic in the form of the symptom, a particular symptom that the subject carries with them as an expression of conflict and pain. This psychic pain has a material basis which is a strange unconscious combination of personal life history and the history of the society in which people are told how they must enjoy and how they may suffer.

There is thus a two-fold repetitive process in everyday life under contemporary capitalism. The first aspect is usually understood as operating in the 'outer world', through the repetition of diverse forms of oppression and exploitation in social and institutional relations. Psychoanalysis has something valuable to say about this process because material political-economic forces also drag individuals into self-destructive patterns of behaviour.

These forces hook and reward individuals for behaviour that reproduces material structures of domination, of class and geopolitical power, as well as those of the family and the distribution of power between the sexes, and between the able-bodied and the 'disabled'. Sometimes there are symptomatic contradictions between those who resist dominant structures, with a resistance that speaks of freedom, and structural reactions characterized by their violence, by their violent repetition of protest that speaks of oppression.

The second aspect of this repetitive process operates ideologically, intimately bound up with the political-economic material structural domain but also intimately connected with the personal life-worlds of those subject to power, the so-called 'inner world'. This is the world we take refuge in, as if we could escape oppression inside ourselves, but we cannot, there is no escape into the individual self. As they speak of their experience of this process, subjects are prevented from speaking, their own standpoint is delegitimized and their accounts are systematically distorted.

The contradictions that emerge here are also symptomatic; that is, a conflict opens up between a repetition of complaint followed by failure that speaks of oppression and the kind of desire that speaks of freedom. The psychoanalytic clinical task is thus to enable subjects to speak, to say something about their experience and their desire, and here, of course, the clinic becomes political, or rather it reveals itself as what it always is, because the personal is, as socialist-feminism proclaimed, political, or as we say in psychoanalysis, the unconscious is politics.

Forgetting the unconscious makes us forget politics. This can happen when ideological or economic repetition accustoms us to what is repeated, petrifies and naturalizes it, makes it appear as something inevitable, as a necessary effect of the force of things or of human nature. Psychology and other sciences intervene here to offer us conceptions of humanity with which what is repeated is justified, rationalizing it, universalizing it and de-politicizing it. We then forget politics because we forget that repetition is historical and can be interrupted by those subject to it, by us, subjects. Psychoanalysis reminds us that these subjects exist, gives them the floor, listens to what they have to say about their symptoms and thus should help us to re-politicize what is repeated and manifested symptomatically.

It is when repetition becomes compulsive, the repetition compulsion at the level of the subject that psychoanalysis treats in the clinic, that it can be condensed into a symptom. Remember that the symptom is, at root, a conflict, but a conflict of a quite particular kind. It is a conflict in which a desire or wish comes up against a prohibition, repression. The conflict between what is desired and the forces that bear down on it, shutting out, re-pressing it, is more complicated than it seems, and the complication that psychoanalysis introduces into the picture also has profound implications for how we conceptualise political struggle. In progressive political struggle a desire for freedom, and for much more, for a world in which we will all be free, comes up against the forms of power that capitalism, colonialism and patriarchy mobilises against us. That is, desire comes up against repression.

We need to take care, however, to treat progressively emerging desires for change as historically created, not as expressing already-existing universal forces that spring as if from inside each individual subject or from human groups. Desire for freedom under these miserable conditions in the twenty-first century is very different from such desire at other points in history. Yes, of course, there is something in the human being that is creative and then distorted and held down by those with power, and, yes, that has most likely always been so.

The kinds of desires that we are aiming to act with now against contemporary systems of domination are created by us, historically created by us as historical beings; these desires are now articulated around an image of another world where there will be collective management of resources, an end to racist segregation, empowerment of women, inclusion of bodies of different kinds and the preservation of the planet. The demands we make are responses to what is denied us in this world now.

There is, of course, a popularised image of psychoanalysis that treats each individual as like a pressure cooker with instinctual forces pushing for release. That image is convenient for those who wish to reduce our struggle to a kind of resentment at natural civilised rules of behaviour in a society that has to balance the needs of each against the needs of the many. The point that our psychoanalysis makes about the conflict between desire and repression, however, is actually very different. It is the form of repression that itself gives rise to forms of desire. It is precisely what is prohibited that is called into being, incited, provoked, and then that prohibited desire can be articulated in reactionary or progressive ways, in self-destructive or creative ways.

A forbidden desire may seek to be satisfied in a subversive way that defies the various repressive devices that lock society into place, but it may also seek an adaptive, lucrative, exploitable satisfaction in capitalism, which involves repression, which is intrinsically repressive. The two expressions of the same desire can be opposed to each other in the individual sphere, but also in the social sphere. There are glaring contradictions between the perspectives of drug trafficking and the drug legalization movement, pornography and sexual liberation, fundamentalism and anti-colonialism, black capitalism and anti-capitalist anti-racism, eco-capitalism and true ecology.

In all cases, a truth is contradicted by its repressed and repressive, mystified and recovered expression. It is the same process as that which occurs in each individual existence where desire cannot avoid facing its recovery and justification by repressive devices. As it is with the individual in the clinic struggling to make sense of repression and struggling to make decided choices about what they want, so it is in the political realm as we collectively debate and create forms of organisation that will operate in a way very different from the forms of repression that attempt to manipulate our desires, exploit them and prevent us from speaking and acting.

Contradiction

These conflicts are condensed into a symptom when the clinical context enables the subject to transform the seemingly irresolvable conflict into a *contradiction*, and then this symptom can be treated dialectically. From existing fixed conditions of possibility for action, new possibilities are created. This is a clinical task that is also a political task, for it necessitates connecting the subject's life experiences with a critical reflexive dialectical understanding of the networks of relationships that have made them who they are.

If conventional psychology and psychologized psychoanalysis tend to seem apolitical, it is because their politics is generally geared to what is dominant and repetitive. That is not a genuine alternative because it is not distinguished from existing conditions of possibility which set restrictions on action and impose certain prohibitions in place. The singularity of the subject is a political matter, enabling us to speak against the conventional conservative psy professions that currently dominate us and cover over, obscure any radical alternative. This is because the psy professions tend to stamp their own orientation and coloration onto almost everything and because their own theories of the benefits of adaptation are repeated incessantly through almost everything that is done to us in this world.

That kind of adaptive politics is imposed on the subject when the psychologist speaks in their assigned place and reinterprets the life of their 'clients' based on what they, the professional, know and what we already know, that which is repeated incessantly, about what is psychologically normal and so socially normative. It is almost enough in the clinic to let the subject speak and to know how to listen with attention and patience – that which should be done in psychoanalysis – to end up discovering another politics, that of the subject's desire and their experience of repetition. Here the space of the psychoanalytic clinic is a space that operates in stark contrast to the repetitive functioning of the capitalist system. It does not correspond to that system's norms or standards of predictability, of adaptability and apparent flexibility.

The subject acts 'normally' by behaving in a predictable way, by being as repetitively assertive, possessive and competitive as they must be, by saying, thinking and feeling only what they should, by silencing their desire and experience, and by contributing, through their work and consumption, to a repetition and replication of the oppressive and exploitative material operations of capitalism. They are allowed, even encouraged to be flexible within the limits set for them in categories of identity, lifestyle and class position that can be harvested and sold back to them as 'market niches'.

These ideological and socioeconomic repetitions are inseparable and support each other. Its increasingly inextricable knotting represents one of the greatest strengths of the current neoliberal capitalist system and one of the greatest challenges for those who fight against it.

Tying together the material and the ideological, the structural and the symbolic aspects of rule and resistance, is the underlying and overarching problem we face today – the intrinsic complexity of global capitalism – and incomplete and distorted solutions available to us in the left and liberation organisations. At least we can clearly see the two forces in combat, both caught in repetition. On the one side, on the side of power, is the compulsive drive to accumulate and protect capital, fruit of exploitation, which takes on an obsessional and repetitive character. On the other side, on the side of resistance, are the organisations of the left that are too-often repetitively stuck in their own failed history, making the same mistakes.

The history of class struggles and the broader more fundamental process of liberation from different forms of oppression is one of repetition and failure, and also, remember, sometimes fortunate and often tragic chance events that are completely out of our control. This is the interminable almost unendurable repetitive context which is then replicated inside the lives of individuals. Individuals are encouraged to imagine that they are free and independent of this double material and ideological historical process so they feel this failure all the more deeply. They cannot bear the evidence that they have so little power over their lives. Nor do they know how they should deal with repetition and with its iron law, with necessity and with chance, with fatality and with destiny. Psychoanalysis works upon all this complex material and symbolic material.

In psychoanalysis, individuals speak, attempt to 'free associate', to say everything that comes to mind, and say it freely, without censorship. They seek to say something new, something unknown, but fail. As they fail, they hear themselves reiterate the same old stories, those they have been told about themselves, those that have materialized in their own lives. These stories must be repeated to prevent other stories from being told or occurring. Free association reveals to the subject the points in their speech where they cannot say everything, and, more significantly, where there are points of blockage, obstacles to speech and action. What begins to emerge at those points is another face of repetition, the recurrence of conflict, a conflict that contains within it both desire and repression.

So, the compulsion to repeat is unmasked and condensed in a symptom that can be transformed into a dialectically-organised contradiction at the heart of the subject's being, opening up new paths, the creation of new conditions of possibility for their speech and action. This psychoanalytic work in the clinic is not by any means a perfect model for political struggle, and we are not suggesting that it should function as any such model, but it offers powerful lessons for those who are struggling against power outside the clinic. In this way the strange limited freedom that appears inside the psychoanalytic clinic connects with the unpredictable forms of collective freedom that the liberation movements aim to create in the world.

Freedom to repeat, and fail better

A progressive lesson of psychoanalysis is that, against the compulsion to repeat, it is possible to open up new possibilities in which we may well continue being subject to repetition, for we cannot wish away the existence of the unconscious, but we can make more choices. We may not always succeed in getting what we want. Remember, we are *divided subjects*. Surely we will not even have absolute certainty that it is really us who want what we want. That would be impossible, at least in present-day society and for some time to come, because even if we were to free ourselves from the greatest social obstacles to our satisfaction, we would continue to be haunted by the history of domination and alienation that has shaped who we are and how we speak of ourselves. However, even if we continue to fail, we can achieve some real successes and make choices in such a way as to know better what the difference is between success and failure.

This is a space of freedom, a space opened up in a very limited way inside the psychoanalytic clinic, a space that we can open up even more in the political realm. This space should not necessarily exclude what is repeated. So far we have emphasised the restrictive limited aspect of repetition, repetition of the same, but we now want to draw attention to another aspect of repetition that always contains within it something different. The space of freedom that lies hidden inside repetition, and so often chained in the prison of the individual self by repetition compulsion, is a different space. It is a space of more and more tension, of increasing aggravation of contradictions, but also, for the same reason, of resistance, insistence and perseverance, and of unavoidable forms of displacement or symbolic distance with respect to what is repeated. It is not repetition of the same, but repetition that creates difference.

What is different also derives from repetition. What is repeated twice cannot be the second time the same as the first, precisely because it happens for the second time, because there has already been a first time, because it is already something repeated and not something new. Contexts change the meaning of different elements, life moves on, and repetition is then not merely the same but something also subtly, sometimes dramatically, different. This is a complex dialectical process, in clinical treatment and in politics.

Repetition can imply insistence or emphasis, but this repetition also gives itself away, reveals it, and so makes it annoying and unavoidable, even unbearable and unsustainable. All of this provokes different feelings, thoughts and behaviours regarding what is repeated. And if it continues to repeat itself, it can make the subject turn away from it, critically judge it from a distance, especially if the repetition takes place in a reflexive framework, such as that of psychoanalysis and liberation movements.

Signifiers

People repeat with their words the same things they have been repeating over and over again in their lives. Yes, that is true. Such is how they try to make sense of the way that material and ideological conditions of life are embedded in the unconscious and in their unconsciously-driven repetitive responses to events around them. At the very same time, as the blockages in their speech reappear again and again, they also repeat and experience those relationships of obedience that prevented them speaking out.

The difference is that now, in their own psychoanalytic process, they have another chance in the clinic for them to perhaps say what they did not say previously. When this happens, their words, as *signifiers*, enable and encourage them to move on and to take some distance from their old lives. Here there is limited and potential freedom.

Even when people repeat, their repetition is not simple replication of the same words, phrases and meaningful action, of the same symbolic elements of our oral, written or existential discourse that we conceptualise as 'signifiers'. Every signifier, every word or action or thing in the human world, is already part of a system of meaning that gives our signifiers value, make them understandable enough to people to function in the medium of communication and in ideology. These are the signifiers that make up the symbolic world we share in our different languages, the building blocks of that symbolic world.

The signifiers, with their repetitions and their connections, are heard by the 'analysand' who participates in a clinical experience of psychoanalysis. This 'analysand' is very different from the 'patient' treated by psychiatrists or the 'client' treated by psychologists. Our psychoanalytic analysand does the analysing. We analysts do not hand them a treatment; they take the cure into their own hands. They are subjects not objects. What they say is not interpreted by the analyst, but by themselves. Their interpretation of their words is done with more words that are added to the previous ones and that in turn must be interpreted by them. The most intimate meaning of these words is in themselves, in the complex relationships between them, and not beyond them, not in a mysterious depth that could only be divined by the analyst reading the symptom as if they were some kind of soothsayer or prophet.

We do not need to delve down beneath the surface to be able to work out how signifiers that operate in a system of meaning that is always beyond our control, unconscious to us, are operating. Signifiers operate according to what we do with them, according to what they do with us, and they are always here, in what we say and hear. The term 'liberation', for example, is a signifier, and each political term we use to define who we are and what our collective identity can be is also a signifier, whether that is as 'worker', 'woman' or 'disabled' or 'indigenous'.

Signifiers are defined for us in a symbolic system, but we can take the initiative to rework them, rework their meaning. As happens at a collective political level, so in the clinic an analysand hears the signifiers that have been given to them by powerful others in their lives to define their identity, and seizes control, even for an instant, to remake them.

Signifiers take on different meaning according to their place in the contradictory ever-mutating language that we speak, the language that surrounds us and which we act upon when we change ourselves and when we change the world. We know this well from the attempts to reclaim signifiers that have been used to speak of us in an oppressive or repressive way, such as 'black' or 'mad' or 'gay'. We take these signifiers and own them again in our progressive political struggle, and say them with pride instead of shame.

The same things, actions and words, are never exactly the same, being situated in ever-changing contradictory cultural and historical contexts. At the same time, particular signifiers are charged with meaning for each singular subject, and 'liberation' may mean something different in different contexts. Psychoanalysis in the clinic attends to the specific role that signifiers play in someone's life. We may imagine that we know what they mean, but psychoanalysis shows us that we have to listen to signifiers with greater attention to reconstruct how they operate in a shared and individual symbolic system.

Our history, whether collective-political or personal-political, is not a fixed and rigid grid but is always open, depending on our struggle to make sense of who we are and the world we want to make. Our being and our aspirations contradict what is repeated, which, in turn, also contradicts itself. These contradictions, in a process of dialectical movement, cause instability of the system, either in the way of 'shock capitalism' that uses crises to reconfigure and strengthen itself or to give us space for freedom. It is up to us, to how we reflect and act, and whether we act collectively.

The repetition of the same is perpetuated by ideological lines of force and political-economic structures, force and structures that we resist because they place limits on our speech and action. Psychoanalysis can help us here to resist by giving us a space to experience and express how we repeat what we say about ourselves, and how we repeat what we do to perpetuate self-destructive patterns of behaviour. This space is effective insofar as it allows us to reflect on repetition instead of just repeating the same old familiar patterns of action.

So, in place of the repetition of the same, the clinic opens the space for something different to emerge; the absolute difference that makes a signifier as such, and a very different absolutely singular sense of our own subjectivity. This emergence of absolute difference is a victory that can pay the price of innumerable failures, and redeem them. We are condemned to repeat, but we are also driven to make a difference. We psychoanalysts can make a difference in the clinic by opening up a space for difference, a space for the subject to be different from what the rules of ideological common sense and its psychology manuals establish.

Likewise, liberation movements can make a difference in the world by differentiating themselves from the dominant ideology, by wanting to create a totally different world, by building a world in which difference is valued as a condition for being human. Repetition of failure is thus transformed into something different. Something in us drives us to do that, which is what we turn to next, in the next chapter, *drive*.

第四章

驅力：身體，文化與欲望

某種力量驅使我們作出反抗。當我們被驅使去行動時，好像我們就是一股自然的力量，尤其當我們將創造改變時，更是如此。確實，在這些時刻，我們可以以某種方式成為一股自然的力量，我們可以在地球上與自然相處，而不是與旨在征服和剝削利用的毀滅性資本主義邏輯勾連合謀，這就是**驅力**（drive）。

當我們以適應資本主義環境的方式行事作為時，我們的行為不僅具有破壞性，而且具有虛假、人為和膚淺的一面。相反地，我們反抗的推動力似乎來自我們身體不可測的深處，來自我們自己的一種躍動、澎湃、超越語言的動物性部分。在現實中，這種推動力和言語交織在一起，透過語言解釋我們正在做什麼以及我們是誰。

語言與身體密不可分，與我們最隱秘且踰越的衝動密不可分，這些衝動總有著被壓抑的重要元素。請記住，壓抑——並不僅是壓迫我們，它也以此方式調控言語和行動，以創造並構建我們的欲望。如果我們沒能從精神分析了解這項課題，我們將仍受困於我們被交代去想望的事物上，而不是就著我們能為自己所構建的更自由的世界去作出集體的選擇。

言辭（words），與我們的存在相纏，並不僅是壓迫、禁錮、捆綁、束縛我們，它們也能鼓勵我們採取行動，將我們從枷鎖中解放出來。由此而產生的行動可以被一個可能是有作用力的、顛覆性的、革命性的、解放性的字詞來表明。它將會是與行動、與身體密切關連的一個字——可能只是「不」，或者一組詞——也許是「不，夠了！」。作為人類，我們立基於實在的身體，並被語言——文化的象徵系統——所形塑，透過此一象徵系統我們對其他人、其他的身體有所欲望。

　　驅力在身體和文化之間的邊界處湧現，這個邊界、邊緣是一個受傷的、殘缺不全的、極其敏感的地方，其特點是痛苦、羞恥、失衡與無可能性。正是在這裡，驅力以其動態的力量出現，使欲望成為可能。這些驅力是本章的主題，我們將在其中討論身體的本質，它的生與死、驅力的所在，包括性在文化之中；以及我們的欲望的本質，這與和他人的欲望密切相關。

身體，生與死的

　　我們住在我們的身體裡，但我們被與它們疏遠異化了。當我們對生命充滿恐懼——如果我們的身體不再支撐我們、如果它不能作為我們賣給別人的勞動力、如果它不能帶我們去工作——這種異化在資本主義下被強化。即使我們住在我們的身體裡，對於它們有些陌生，只有當它們停止運作時，我們才會經驗到它們是實實在在、不可思議、未知的。

　　我們永遠無法直接地認識我們的身體，我們對身體的理解是由我們用來向自己描繪它的圖像和我們用來向他人描述它的語言所構成的。身體是經由意識形態的扭曲表徵而被文化性地介導的。透過意識形態，我們對自己的認識包含了對我們的身體奇怪的異化觀念，我們的身體變成了可供他人買賣、消費和享受的物品。

　　然而，儘管存在意識形態，透過與意識形態進行鬥爭，我們還是能對我們的身體作為拒絕的所在（sites of refusal）有更多的學習。我們能以大不同於意識形態對身體扭曲表徵的方式來理解我們的身體，然後，當我們用自己的身體來說話而不是與它對立時，我們就可以找到一種方法來說出真實[1]。這是精神分析提示我們要進入的某種身體和言語——也就是我們的物質存在和能指之間奇特的、矛盾的聯繫。

---

[1]　這裡的 'speak the truth' 在語意上連接到以下段落，在精神分析臨床脈絡中被分析主體從其主觀的真實擺下壓抑真想說出的話，在這個意義上 'truth' 可被譯作「真實」、「真相」或「真話」時，都是指涉主體主觀真實的知覺。

生

在精神分析中透過言語而闡述的能指，表現爲強大作用力的言辭形式，其影響力一如在構成這個世界的宰制性意識形態訊息中，那些界定我們在這世界裡的位置的能指一般地強大。這種語言能帶來治癒，它可以治癒作用於身體的精神痛苦，因爲它能以眞實驅散令我們生病的謊言和沉默，這就是精神分析被第一批分析主體稱爲「談話治療」（'talking cure'）的一個原因。就像在我們的家庭裡以及在我們的意識自我中，那些父權的和殖民的資本主義的禁令、失憶與意識形態的神祕化，都可以被我們所說的加以消解和超越，我們說出眞實，同時，在個人 - 政治領域中，我們對權力說出眞實。這涉及到他者，是生之驅力。

有些眞實的陳述並不僅只與我有關，他者也同我一樣都受苦於企圖使我們分隔以便各個擊破我們的權力作用。我們每個人都被鎖定在個體的自我（selves）之中並承受著某種形式的壓迫和剝削。沉默和意識形態的謊言欺騙了我們、迷惑了我們、誤導了我們所有人；於是當然地，我們感到有必要尋找彼此並會合起來去言說和行動、譴責不公正和反叛、發現眞相並與權力作鬥爭。再一次，不論善或惡，我們都在驅力的國度之中。

這是生——「生之驅力」（'life drive'），是言說和行動的驅力。它是生產性的、集體的、關係的、以及性的；它不是鎖在我們裡面，而是越出我們、包覆著我們；它在我們之間也在我們之外；它使我們與他人建立聯繫，從而編織我們周圍的世界。作爲精神分析學家我們說：一切屬於主體的皆經由「大寫它 / 他者」（'Other'）[2]，皆經由作爲人類主體性標誌的他者性（otherness）。

正是在他者（other）之中，並且也是經由他者，我們的驅力使我們活著。但是，某種驅使我們越出我們自己的、無意識的、超出我們意識控制的東西，也可能在我們感到被驅動之處顯露出一種機械性；那就是當驅動我們的變成是惰性的、致命的、破壞性的和自我毀滅的東西時，驅力自身

---

[2] 關於「大寫它 / 他者」（'Other'）與他者性（otherness）請參考第 2 章註 4 以及本書導讀。

便顯現爲更危險致命的東西——即「死之驅力」（'death drive'）。

　　每個驅力都潛在地可能是死之驅力。當我們屈服於它時、當我們在它的重壓下掉落時、當我們被它的慣性沖昏了頭腦時，它致命的一面就會占上風。那些時候我們會無意識地重複相同的動作和能指。然後我們會受制於重複——重複的強迫性（compulsion to repeat），受制於自動化的和破壞性的作用力——當今，這已體現在資本主義制度之中。

　　資本，被認爲是對死之驅力的純粹滿足、將生轉換成死、消耗工人和大自然生動的存在、用來生產越來越多的金錢（死的錢）的一種過程。然而，在此同時資本運作著，並且不擇手段地以某種方式靠勞動者的活力、靠他們還呈現在我們面前的生之驅力而活著，即使它變成了追求利潤的死之驅力——資本主義的驅力。驅力的破壞性和生產性面向通常在經驗上是聯結的，彼此難以分辨，只能透過主體性和政治的基進理論，如馬克思主義和女性主義、後殖民主義和酷兒理論與精神分析等來加以辨識。

　　在這裡，若我們要掌握每個歷史時期所顯現的驅力的雙重特性，我們就需要有融合歷史的（historically-attuned）精神分析（即將精神分析概念化爲歷史構成的）。在每時每刻，驅力都是具生產性的、創造性的、建設性的生（之驅力），在我們之內而使我們能夠與他人建立聯繫、建立文化與政治組織的形式，並談論其他可能性的世界；然而，也一樣是在每時每刻，驅力也是具破壞性的、重複性的死（之驅力），違背我們自身、違背那些維持我們的社會聯繫、違背自然與文化。

　　這種驅力是在吞噬地球並腐蝕我們創造的各種不同人類文明的資本主義進程中獲得滿足的一種動力，但同時，也是促使我們抵制這種廣泛性破壞並鼓舞著那些爲自己的文化、地球、生命和反對資本主義而奮鬥的人的動力。我們必須選擇，這是我們每時每刻都面臨的選擇，尤其是現在。當我們行動時，我們的身體能與我們合而爲一；不過話說回來，我們的性格也可能被變成一部機器，那樣的話，我們異化的身體就是一台對抗我們的機器。

死

　　資本主義總是無所不用其極地剝奪我們的身體，它已藉由持續增高的

勞動分工使身體彷彿獨立於我們而運作，它已將我們與它們截然切割，它已使我們鄙視和否定它們，它已教會我們管訓和壓榨它們，它已設定我們與它們相對立。我們身體的命運與我們的生活一樣，資本主義制度占用了我們生活中的一切，將其轉變成勞動力，從而生產出越來越多的資本——也就是**驅力**（drive）。

今天，在二十一世紀晚期資本主義中，情況更糟，似乎我們為了讓我們擺脫工作而創造的機器已經把我們變成了它們的奴隸，利潤的必要性創造了額外的工作，所以我們的時間更少而不是更多。科技所打開的可能性被追求利潤的驅力所背叛，這種驅力加劇了我們的剝削和壓迫。利潤的必要性加速了生產過程，資本主義下生活的加速，意味著我們自己的身體比以往任何時候都更加被體驗為與我們分開的物件。

十九世紀以降的資本主義制度下，工業發展得如此之快，對自然和文化造成的破壞如此之大，彷彿一切堅固的東西都煙消雲散了[3]，但對勞動者的生活卻如此漠不關心。現在，隨著代表資本運作的私營公司或國有企業掌握工業和技術發展，這個過程出現了異化加速，以致留給我們的只剩我們所居住的身體、必須工作的身體、面臨毀滅的身體。確實，我們的身體被異化了，但我們能恢復它們，至少部分恢復，至少在些許片刻中暫時恢復；我們需要它們，只有將它們與言語交織在一起，與真正的言語交織在一起，我們才能行動。

我們面臨著一個矛盾的任務。一邊是驅力致命的面向，存在著許多致力於自我維護的社會結構，透過那些代表獲益者的結構來把持他們的權力，以盡可能低的工資僱用工人並獲得最大的利潤，當權者從勞動力中榨取的這種「剩餘價值」（'surplus value'），是從我們的勞動力中汲取的，但這種力量是我們生命的力量，是我們的愛和創造性的力量，所以那些擁有金錢和權力者便扭曲、工具化我們這一股照顧我們所愛的人並在世界上產生創造性影響的驅動力量。

3　語出馬克思和恩格斯的《共產黨宣言》：「……一切新形成的關係等不到固定下來就陳舊了。一切堅固的東西都煙消雲散了，一切神聖的東西都被褻瀆了，人們終於不得不清醒地面對自己真實的生活狀況，以及與同類的關係。」

　　我們人類可能共有的社群被資本主義、父權制和殖民制度所取代，我們最真實的關係被附屬於生產關係、剝削關係，由其他權力關係——男尊女卑、種族主義、以及排除那些被認為沒有生產力的人的權力關係所支撐。

　　另一邊有著生之驅力，是驅力的愛的面向。有被資本主義激發和釋放出的創造力，有創新和文化發展的可能性。就在資本主義的腹地中誕生了推翻它的力量，這些集體力量聚集在一起，使我們能夠創造性地工作，讓我們相互學習合作而不是相互對抗的價值。

　　這些是生產力，這種生產性的力量也為解放運動提供能量。問題是——我們是否繼續讓我們的主人和統治者決定我們將如何工作、如何享受以及如何為他們的享樂提供服務？還是我們是否會取得控制、是否由我們來決定我們的生活？

　　這就是現今的驅力——以一股我們無法控制的無意識動力貫穿我們並為我們的身體注入活力的驅力、一種追求創新但也可能被導向追求利潤的驅力。驅力是一種身體的力量，是生命、愛和創造力的源泉，但它已經與我們背道而馳以致於我們不僅感到受制於它，甚且是被它的邏輯所俘擄。生（之驅力）和我們的本質——像這樣的特性皆被體驗為威脅和恐懼，以致於我們經常將自己與彼此分開並封閉自己以試圖逃避。

　　資本積累並把生（之驅力）留給那 1% 的人，而對於我們其餘（99%）的人——工作的人、販賣勞力的人以及在家內勞動以支持必須販賣勞力的人，這種驅力是致於死地的。對於絕大多數生活在資本主義中的人來說，這種驅力是一種死之驅力。正是我們這種政治經濟形式的歷史發展，使得生之目標指向死。

文化，關於性的，以及更多……

　　我們體驗到我們的身體超越我們自己、超越我們意識控制的地方之一就是在性裡面；性對於包括人類在內的物種繁衍來說是如此地具有必須性，而對人類來說，性還具有一種並非出於這種必須性的愉悅（有時痛苦）的特性，驅動我們進入性的幾乎都不是出於必須性，很多人在進行性

時並沒有這種必須性，但是這種在性之中的非必需的享樂產生了一個關於身體的本質及其關係到享樂和受苦的問題，這個問題推進了精神分析的發展。

精神分析常被說是太執迷於性，但更多的情形是，精神分析幫助我們了解處於一個本身執迷於一系列有關性的強烈意識形態印象的文化中，我們是如何被性所驅動？這是一種命令我們工作的文化，並且也是禁止對經由家庭實現勞動力的再生產和維持、或是透過消費實現剩餘價值、抑或是藉由意識形態粉飾資本主義等不具功能的享樂形式的文化。於是儘管性可能被剝削，但在這種文化中，對性的禁止比要求來得多得多，而且這種禁令本身也帶有一種煽動、挑逗和要求我們享樂的相當怪誕詭異的作用。

禁令

任何我們人類的性的身體活動都存在著**禁令**（*prohibition*），存在著禁令和踰越（transgression）。性已經成為我們隱蔽的無意識要求去踰越的關鍵驅動點之一，並以這樣一種方式享受踰越，仿佛我們內心深處有某種東西必得要找到釋放。因此，我們所耳聞的應該帶來快樂的性活動，卻也經常帶來了羞恥、內疚、孤獨、嫉妒、暴力、煎熬和痛苦，這就沒什麼好驚訝的了。

性之於精神分析之所以如此重要，正是因為性是我們見到享樂與受苦如此緊密被連繫在一起之處。異化而不快樂的生活將它們更緊密地聯繫在一起——不論是在我們體驗性的現實中，抑或是在關於那些我們被告知錯過的事的幻想中。

如果沒有這些觀念我們就不可能理解我們當前關於性的經驗：無意識——超越我們並帶著我們超越意識自我，重複的活動——為我們帶來享樂和受苦，以及驅力——驅力給出生命，除此之外，性作為繁殖的源泉，就是生命的表現。我們被告知它應該在這個文化中那般地運作，但事實並非如此。它往往比我們所被告知的多得多，更多的是被禁止和煽動，被排除在意識之外，並被影射、暗示、刺激而作為一個更深的個人踰越的享樂之地。即使對於作為應該有性行為的那些人來說，當他們遵循這種既要符合文化規範同時又要踰越它們的雙重矛盾指令時，也會有愉快和痛苦。

　　這就是為什麼精神分析如此重視性的原因；人們在性中尋求庇護卻困惑於為何它常無法給他們帶來慰藉，他們被驅使到性裡，而性驅使他們進入精神分析之被發明來對治的精神官能症境地之中；而對於那些沒在性上照著被告知應該的樣子做的人來說，他們仍是受困於總是向他們施壓而迫使他們順從要求的文化，這也驅使他們進入精神分析能幫助解開的被私有化的痛苦之中。

　　例如，經常發生在核心家庭中——隱含在婚姻契約裡的——以性交易愛情；以及更為明顯的，當那些擁有權力的人（通常是男性）能利用權力要求他人（通常是女性）為他們的身體提供服務、給予他們享樂時的以性交易金錢。方程式的一邊是享樂，另一方面是受苦，通常它們被合併在一起。藉由這種方式，性就變成了勞動、並且是被商品化和剝削的，就像資本主義下的所有工作一樣。答案不是乾脆禁止這項工作，而是改變像這樣的勞動，這意味著為性工作者爭取權利而奮鬥，為一個將來不可能存在性商品化和性剝削的世界鋪設道路而奮鬥。

　　精神分析告訴我們，禁止任何事物，包括性，都不是解決方案，而是我們要將任務放在理解壓抑的結構，並解決這些結構。隨著我們集體地為我們自己創造的新結構，為欲望，為渴望他人，帶來新的可能性，也為驅力帶來新的路徑，在這些路徑上，一個人的享樂不需要由他人的屈辱痛苦來成就。

　　驅力——感覺起來似乎它是在我們裡面，但它實際上是在內部和外部的交界上；更正確地說，如佛洛伊德自己所宣稱的——是在生理的和心理的交界上。生理的是經由我們了解我們自己是誰、以及我們被告知我們的需要與欲望是些什麼而被賦予形與義；而「心理的」（'psychical'）本身——正如我們從馬克思那裡學到的——既在我們之外也在我們之內的，我們的主體性是「一切社會關係的總合」。

　　這些社會關係是由我們自己創造的文化產生的，但在我們這樣一個異化的社會中，我們並非在自己能選擇的條件下創造我們的文化和歷史。我們必須做的、以及精神分析引導我們能夠做的，是能充分理解我們人性的「第二天性」（'second nature'），文化性的第二天性的現實。

　　歷史和文化形塑並不斷地修改著驅力的領域。我們需要清楚的是，這

個驅力既不是生物學上固定的「本能」（'instinct'），也不存在單獨的生物性設置的生與死本能。確實是有關於食物、性和其他生物需求的本能過程，這是我們作為動物物種更深度進化的歷史功能，是我們動物本性的功能，但這些總是被我們有意識或無意識地予以解釋。

那驅動我們的身體的，也是跟身體（我們慣常只將它們當作資本主義下駛往勞動的車乘工具）一樣被異化的，總是受到文化的中介和形塑。沒有文化就不會有驅力，這不是一種先於文化的實際的「本能」，本質上是人性的，同我們創造的文化一樣的人性。我們沒法以我們的驅力之名擺脫文化，更不能為文化而解放自己的驅力。

這不是解放運動提出的問題，錯誤地認為驅力是一種本能的力量必須「被釋放」，是一個引導我們走上歧路的虛假問題。這使得無意識彷彿是頭殼鍋爐裡的蒸汽，而驅力會像蒸汽那樣噴發似的。不去提這種虛假化約的意識形態和偽精神分析問題，我們的精神分析與解放運動提出的問題一致，我們提出的問題是──是否這種文化應該繼續讓 1% 的人受益，讓他們緊抓蓬勃生機，而剩下的 99% 被注定只能在生存邊緣撿拾殘餘和面對死亡？抑或我們現在可以開始創造一種每個人都可以生活和興盛繁榮的文化？

解釋

驅力是從本能的*解釋*（interpretation）中產生的，它在透過語言、意識形態、文化和歷史時發生了改變、複雜化和扭曲。在此，我們同時關注驅力及其解釋，這兩者相連；語言將本能轉化成某種不再只是生物學和生理學上的東西。驅力處於生理和心理的交界。它的起源是在幻想中，而不僅僅是在身體中。它不是天生給定的東西，而是歷史的產物。我們堅持精神分析的基本前提，反對將驅力意識形態地重新定義為不變的人類本質；我們的人性透過同樣的動作轉化了驅力，同時也轉化了自身。

驅力不斷地在象徵、能指和文化的決定性作用下轉變著。這並不意味著它不是實在的（real），驅力也是實在的──它溢出言語，不能被象徵所包含或納入，它拒絕任何符號化，它表現為一種不可磨滅的力量，超出我們用以理解我們身上所發生之事的能指之外。

超出任何能被解釋的意義，驅力本身就是發生在我們身上的一部分。當它被以語言——也就是結構我們言語和行動的能指作出解釋時，它就取得生命的形式在我們的生活中得以體現。這就是象徵的實際作用。驅力的這個實在的面向，使得它出現在身體中確是它好像是一種本能的力量，一種對食物或性至爲迫切的需要。驅力的這個實在面也使得它經由一些扭曲、過度、荒謬或無用的操作（像是儀式、陳腔濫調、誇張、自動化和重複的能指）出現在我們的言語之中，在這些操作中我們受制於不覺知的意識形態重複、受制於如同一台機器的意識形態之中。

意識形態確實更像是一台機器，它有某種機械性的、致命的、抑制的東西，是一種死的驅力的顯現。它扼殺了重複中可能存在的新奇事物，並將創造力變成了令人窒息的東西。意識形態是死的生命，是以死亡爲目的的生命幻覺。於是我們在這個病態的世界裡看到了性的一個面向，性緊緊地與受苦和享樂連結起來，性的這個面向提出了關於在資本主義下的主體性本質的問題，精神分析的發展正是爲了回答這個問題。所以，再一次地，當我們討論驅力時，我們必須討論性。

性

正是在這種驅力下，我們的生理需求，尤其是**性**（*sex*）需求，被重構爲社會的需求。這些需求都作爲家庭結構、私有財產和國家的功能而被創造、表達和壓制的。文化和歷史制度並不是簡單地排拒自然傾向，而是在依賴它們之外，同時也吸收、利用和改造。

例如，當物種本能的繁衍基礎得到支撐而後被社會或家庭制度的生活所指導時，這種生物學過程就轉變成了人類的性慾，從與生殖的錨定中鬆開，並在驅力層面上變得多樣化和複雜化。這就是色情如何滲透到消費、廣告、文化產業和魅力型領導中。精神分析表明，即使是科學工作、宗教信仰和政治理想，也包含理想化、昇華或合理化的性慾元素。

性本身被轉化爲對權力的中繼與反叛的社會節點（nodal points of society）之一，這是精神分析以性作爲中心的另一個原因——性作爲階級社會中社會關係的歷史構成症狀的核心而起著作用。這些宰制關係（但同時也是鬥爭和衝突關係）都是圍繞並基於性作爲軸心來表達的。父權制與資

本主義密不可分，消費主義和資本主義的貪婪揭示了高度性慾化的占有傾向。

沒有任何一個人（man）是孤島一座，但資本主義驅使他（he）[4] 想像自己是個孤島，並想像愛一個人的唯一方法就是擁有他們。而女性——經常被化約爲男性所擁有的客體物件，也可能犯同樣的錯誤。恰如一位智慧的共產主義小說家所言：喜歡是最好的擁有形式，擁有是最壞的喜歡形式[5]。

我們的性欲望不僅是我們最爲動物性的一面，也是我們人性中最人性化、最具人性特徵的一面。人類文化源自某種性的文化新陳代謝，正是在他們作爲有性別與性的存在的條件下，人類才成爲社會存在。他們的社會化是一個過程，藉由此過程，性被象徵化、維持和超越，它成爲文字、語言的一部分，成爲欲望、愛、友誼、團結、社會關係、文化慣例、政治行動和其他由我們的欲望激發的象徵性實踐的一部分。

沒有獨自的、先於存在的生和死之驅力，也不存在有特定的性驅力，但在這個文化裡驅力與性掛鉤，將其視爲我們最個人、最私密和隱蔽的部分。於是，無論是否試圖閃避，每個人都被性文化所吸引，都被吸引進商品的性慾化中，以使它們更有吸引力，使它們賣得更多。

我們的性被統治工具化，而不是作爲一種解放的方法。在這些情形下，精神分析的解答不能簡單地是要求更多的性，那是對佛洛伊德立場的誇大扭曲，這個誇大扭曲的印象吸引了所謂「佛洛伊德馬克思主義者」中的一些人，他們試圖透過將佛洛伊德和馬克思結合起來以使精神分析基進化，只是有時太快而且太簡化了。

正如我們已經解釋過的，無論是在精神分析臨床的個人層次還是在政治鬥爭的集體層次上，我們的任務並不是要去釋放既有的衝動以使我們快

---

[4]　作者於與譯者的電郵討論中表示，這裡原文的 man 指的是每一個人，他刻意使用 'man' 及 'he'，意圖暗示資本主義與男性陽剛特質作爲常識意識形態的性別觀點，這在本章末將會提到。

[5]　語出 1988 年諾貝爾文學獎得主葡萄牙籍作家 José Saramago 1997 年小說 *The Tale of the Unknown Island*.

樂。相反地，是要去拒絕那些我們被告知應該去想望的東西、是要去創造條件讓我們可以更好地選擇對我們所有人都有益的東西。不是去簡單地要求更多的性，而是我們需要去解決如何與爲什麼在性裡享樂變得和受苦相連？以及性作爲生命源泉是如何運作得好像它本身也是死之驅力的一部分而變得與我們對立？爲了使驅力再次回歸生命，我們需要將它接合到最人性的現象——欲望。

欲望，關於他者的

　　欲望是人性的，因爲它被創造於社會關係的總合之中，在這之中使得我們每一個人成爲人性的主體。雖然驅力會使我們將自己視爲世界的中心、自然的主人，並表現出一種重複且有時是自我毀滅的形式，但欲望與他人有著密切的聯繫。欲望具有一種特別的辯證性質，即我們對他人的欲望和我們被驅使從他人那裡獲得的欲望。我們渴望從他人那裡得到的認可，這使我們與他們聯繫在一起，並且我們在他們身上尋找某種將我們拉向他們、渴望他們的東西。

　　這是社會關係中享樂和受苦的來源，於是它也驅使我們將文化構建爲一種共享的媒介、一種象徵的媒介，透過此媒介我們可以與他人分享我們的種種，參與到有別於我們的事物中。這種驅力和拉力運作於人際面對面關係的層面和組織層面並且將社區（包括全球）聯繫起來構建共同的理想。它是社會中個別的性愛的原動力，它給這種欲望賦予了價值，也是解放運動建立的國際網絡中團結的動力。我們在這裡重新構建這種團結是爲了提醒人們關注它的此一面向，而不是用精神分析來殖民它。我們的欲望，政治性的團結，被意識形態地栓在資本主義下的性上，而這正是精神分析要幫助我們理解的面向。

　　驅力在我們獨特的主體性形式中已經被轉化爲欲望。作爲言說的存在體，我們處於一個象徵的領域——一個集體的交流媒介、一個我們真正成爲人的共享空間。在這裡，我們對他人的欲望被反射成最多樣化和最複雜的關係形式，這種關係雖然在我們內心深處被體驗著，但也受到我們之間他人的制約。

象徵界——作爲獨立於我們的事物，很容易地、並且經常地變成一種近似機器的力量，這種力量因我們自己的異化形象意識形態地重複而加劇。在我們將性慾象徵化時，異化和意識形態化是兩個必然承擔的風險。宛似一種不可磨滅的驅力和無法抑制的慾望的性需求，其文化功能與意識形態的扭曲、性的曲解緊密關連，與被象徵性地構建的異化的性關係緊密關連，這種性關係的象徵性構建以一種不僅允許文化再生產，同時也顧及那些盛行於資本主義制度的統治和破壞關係得以延續的方式進行。

市場

在資本主義中，透過意識形態化和異化，生被變成了死——死的驅力，交流變成了人的物化和商品化——也就是人的創造性勞動和人的慾望對象。東西和商品篡奪人的位置並行使人們的權力和權利，例如自由流通的權力和權利，對世界上很大一部分人口而言這是被剝奪了的。在資本主義中，尤其是在新自由主義資本主義中，被物化了的對象物比人類主體本身更像是「主體」，資本主義使主體爲對象物服務，它將*市場*（*market*）利益置於人類利益之上，它使得資本以其占有、積累、競爭和破壞性的傾向統治並定義了人類的驅力。

被異化了的需求成爲資本主義包羅萬象的市場的驅動力，性慾望被納入這個市場中，性別逐漸變成了商品化形式的有害場域，例如父權制下的色情業，女性變成可以被買賣、擁有和剝削、享受和交換金錢的物品，在這裡欲望幾乎沒有位置，這裡只有驅力和表現爲本能的東西，只有意識形態的動物本能表現而非人性的欲望。

欲望降爲驅力這種對實在的化約，以及驅力降爲本能這種意識形態的化約，將我們創造性的人類活動、我們與他人的象徵性中介關係，都給變成了以客體的、僵化的、機械自動的和無意義的方式運作的東西。我們的身體和我們身體的一部分變成了我們迷戀或恐懼的啞、聾和盲的生物性過程的異化場所。因此，基進的特殊需要權益運動者提請人們關注「聾」、「啞」和「盲」等詞運作爲承載意識形態上劣等人的能指——有時甚至是被化約爲客體而非主體——是低劣於「正常的」身體，低劣於那個我們被告知要爲了工作、爲了替我們的雇主創造「剩餘價值」所應當擁有的「正

常的」身體。

這些過程將我們排除在外，排除了主體，但產生了想像。就好像自然和自我的圖像的交流可以獨立於象徵性結構歷史構成的社會關係（symbolically-structured historically-constituted social relations）來傳遞。也好像是我們所經驗到的，以常識的一個面向就直接反映什麼是眞實。

今日，市場被強加為唯一的眞實。一切都必須被商品化、出售、購買和開發利用，這種普遍的商品化是資本主義的特徵，但商品化的性別印象的產生也是父權制的一種作用。父權制在資本對我們與事物和人的關係的影響上也具有決定性的作用。被資本主義和父權制所主體化了的現代性主體，以競爭、占有、囤積和破壞性的方式連結這個世界和其他人，就像典型的大男人主義情人對待女性那般。這就是驅動大男人主義企業家的動力，不幸的是，有時也驅動著社會運動中英雄主義式的運動領袖。

男性至上主義

我們不應該對於擁護資本家的新自由主義極右派雄性模式的極度陽剛化和厭女元素感到驚訝。當前的資本主義形式需要*男性至上主義*（machismo）作為一個主體的前提。對這種男性至上主義和其他父權制的表現作鬥爭是一種主體性地削弱資本的方式。正是因此（也還因為更多其它的理由）女性主義對當前的權力部署構成了威脅，現今恰如既往，女性主義透過將現代資本主義社會的父權資產階級核心家庭投影到史前時期，出奇地喚起佛洛伊德透過原始部落壓迫性的父親神話形象所再現的。它是一個意識形態的深層移動，而現在它也揭示著性慾化男性至上主義的資產階級意識形態本質。

女性主義不僅威脅到資本主義主體的基礎和性別的商品化，它還危及構成資產階級核心家庭的個人政治意識形態的社會紐帶，它堅持認為這些紐帶是對人類眞實需求的虛假想像，是象徵性地合法化壓迫的反映。這就是為什麼女性主義與更廣泛的女同性戀、男同性戀、雙性戀、跨性別、酷兒、雙性人及有關的鬥爭，是服務於解放運動的精神分析所不可或缺的盟友。

精神分析並沒有界定我們應該怎樣去愛以及我們該愛誰才對，它也沒

特殊化性別該是什麼樣，或什麼種類的身體該與其他的身體發生性關係。驅力和欲望遵循著複雜路徑，對每個主體都是獨特的，所以，一項緊迫的政治任務是去創造多種可能的條件，讓要有性的人或選擇不要有性的人都能夠定義自己並做自己決定做的事。精神分析的目的不是讓人們固守於他們被告知的性是什麼，而是一種自我探究的實踐，以使我們能夠改變我們和誘餌般擺在我們面前的任何一種「好處」（'good'）的關係。

精神分析可以幫助我們改變與世界的關係，或者透過重新考慮我們周圍的事物而以不同的方式處理我們的驅力，或者為我們的欲望開闢新的空間，所有這些對於解放運動都至關重要，解放運動也必須改變與他們所要改變的世界的關係。為了達成他們的目標，運動者必須深刻地改變他們與周圍環境以及與其他人的關係，藉由建立相互之間的橫向關係，藉由嘗試基進的民主形式並藉由編織網絡的行動和團結，他們從一開始就不斷嘗試這樣做。

解放運動創造了改變世界的行動網絡，而且至關重要的是，團結網絡逐漸擴大了他們的行動領域，包括那些沒有直接涉入但希望成為世界變革的一部分的所有人。團結是對他者的愛——不論他者遠在天邊或近在眼前，它是具有象徵性作用的，而不僅僅是幻象。這是實現驅力成為一種闡述社會關係和一種文化的力量的空間，在這種文化中，我們對他人的欲望乃以從他人接收到對我們的一種承認和認可的這種方式來形構——承認和認可我們不只是動物，我們的身體不只是機器，我們是人。

在本章中，我們專注於我們的親密關係與文化領域，以及精神分析對驅動我們作為人類的本性的洞察。在此，精神分析理論直接參與解放運動的工作，向它們學習並給予它們一些額外的概念工具來理解文化如何作用，理解它是如何以具創造力的建設性方式運作，又是如何扭曲而變成同資本主義那樣具有壓迫性和破壞性的東西。

在下一章中，我們將回到精神分析臨床上，我們將詳細闡述我們對驅力的無意識重複運作的具體做法，以及這些是如何被嵌入權力關係之中。臨床之中之所以有這種權力，是因為這個社會存在著一種權力關係的特殊組構。精神分析臨床就在這個世界之中，就在這個我們非常想改變的世界之中，它透過**移情**（transference）來工作。

DRIVE: BODY, CULTURE AND DESIRE

Something compels us to rebel. When we are impelled to act it is as if we are a force of nature, and all the more so when we will make a difference. Indeed, in these moments, we can somehow be a force of nature; we can be with nature on this earth instead of colluding with the devastating capitalist logic which aims to subdue and exploit it, this is *drive*.

When we behave in a way adapted to the capitalist environment, our behaviour is not only destructive, but also has a false, artificial and superficial aspect. Instead, our impetus to rebel seems to come from the inscrutable depths of our body, from an animal part of ourselves that palpitates, surges forth beyond language. In reality, this impetus is intermeshed with speech, with an accounting for what we are doing and so also with who we are through words.

Language is inseparable from our body, from our most secret and transgressive impulses, which always have crucial elements already repressed. Repression, remember, does not merely press down on us but regulates speech and action in such a way as to create and structure our desire. If we do not understand that lesson from psychoanalysis we will still be trapped in what we are told we want instead of making collective choices about the kind of freer world we can construct for ourselves.

Words, entangled with our being, not only oppress, imprison, chain and immobilize us. They can also encourage us to act in order to free us from our chains. The resulting act can then be explained by an effective, subversive, revolutionary and perhaps liberating word. It will be a word, perhaps just 'no', or words, perhaps 'no, this is enough', intimately connected with action, with the body. What we are as human beings is grounded in our body as real, and shaped by language, by the symbolic system of culture, through which we desire others, and desire other bodies.

The drive springs forth at the border between the body and culture. This border, this edge is an injured, mutilated, extremely sensitive place, characterized by pain, shame, imbalance and impossibility. It is here where the drives emerge with their dynamic force that makes desire possible. These drives are the subject of this chapter, in which we speak of the nature of the body, its life and death, of the place of the drive, including for sex, in culture, and of our desire which is intimately connected to the desire of others.

Bodies, of life and death

We live in our bodies, but we are alienated from them. This alienation is intensified under capitalism when we fear for our lives if our body lets go of us, if it cannot function as labour power that we sell to others, if it cannot take us to work. Even though we live in our bodies, there is something strange about them, and it is when they cease to function that we experience them as something real, uncanny, unknown.

We can never know our body directly. Our understanding of our body is structured by the images we use to picture it to ourselves and the language we use to describe it to others. The body is mediated culturally by ideological misrepresentations. What we know of ourselves through ideology includes strange alienating ideas about our bodies, our bodies turned into objects to be bought and sold and consumed and enjoyed by others.

However, despite ideology and through combating ideology, we can also learn something more about our bodies as sites of refusal. We can then know something of our bodies that is very different from ideological misrepresentation of them, and then, when we speak with our body rather than against it we can find a way to speak the truth. This is something that psychoanalysis cues us into, the peculiar contradictory connection between bodies and words, our material being and signifiers.

Life

Signifiers elaborated through speech in psychoanalysis take the form of words with powerful effects, as powerful as the signifiers that tell us what our place in the world is in the dominant ideological messages that structure this world. The word can be healing; it can heal psychic pain that has effects on the body, because it can be true and thus dispel the lies and silences that make us sick. This is one reason psychoanalysis was called, by one of the first analysands, a 'talking cure'. The prohibitions, amnesia and ideological mystifications of patriarchal and colonial capitalism, such as those of our family and those of our own ego, can be neutralized, transcended by what we say. We speak the truth, and in the personalpolitical realm, we speak truth to power. It involves others, life.

There are true statements that concern not only me. Others suffer like me the effects of power that tries to divide us in order to defeat us one by one. Each of us has been locked in to our individual selves and suffers some form of oppression and exploitation. The silences and lies of ideology deceive us, confuse us and mislead us all. It is logical then that we feel impelled to look for each other and meet to speak and act, to denounce injustice and to rebel, to discover the truth and fight against power. Here again, for good or ill, we are in the realm of the drive.

This is life, this 'life drive', drive to speak and act. It is productive and collective, relational, and sexual. It is not locked inside us, but it exceeds us and overflows us; it is between us and outside of us; it makes us bond with others and thus weave the world around us. Everything that is of the subject, we psychoanalysts say, goes through the 'Other', through the otherness that is the mark of human subjectivity.

It is in the other and through the other that our drive makes us live. But something of this drive which takes us beyond ourselves, which is unconscious, beyond our conscious control, can also take on a mechanistic quality in which we feel driven. That is when what drives us turns into something inert, deadly, destructive and self-destructive. The drive then manifests itself as something more deadly, as a 'death drive'.

Every drive is potentially a death drive. Its deadly aspect prevails when we surrender to it, when we drop under its weight, when we get carried away by its inertia. Those are the times we unconsciously repeat the same actions and signifiers. Then we are subject to repetition, compulsion to repeat, subject to an automatic and destructive force, today embodied in the capitalist system.

Capital, conceived as a process, is pure satisfaction of the death drive, conversion of life into death, consumption of the living existence of workers and of nature to produce more and more money, dead money. However, at the same time, capital works and somehow lives with the vital energy of the workers, with their life drive that is still what is present to us, even when it transmutes into the death drive of the drive for profit, capitalism. The destructive and productive aspects of drive usually appear empirically united, indiscernible from each other, and can only be distinguished through radical theories of subjectivity and politics; theories such as Marxism and feminism and post-colonial and queer theory, and psychoanalysis.

Here we need historically-attuned psychoanalysis, psychoanalysis conceptualised as constituted historically, if we are to grasp the two-fold nature of drive as manifested in each historical period. In every moment drive is productive, creative, constructive, life, what it is within us enabling us to build links with others, to build culture and forms of political organisation, and to speak of other possible worlds. However, also at every moment, drive is also destructive and repetitive, death, that which is turned against our-selves and against those social links that sustain us, against nature and against culture.

The drive is what achieves satisfaction in the capitalist process that devours the planet and corrodes the various diverse human civilizations we have created. It is also, at the same time, what is impelling us to resist this widespread devastation and moving those who fight for their cultures, for the planet, for life and against capitalism. We must choose. This is the choice we face at every moment, and especially now. Our body can be at one with us when we act, but then our nature can be turned into a machine; then our alienated body is a machine turned against us.

Death

Capitalism has always done whatever it takes to strip us of our bodies. It has made them function as if independently of us through an ever-increasing division of labour. It has sharply divided us from them; it has made us despise and repudiate them; it has taught us to discipline and exploit them; it has set us against them. The fate of our bodies is the same as our lives. The capitalist system appropriates everything that lives in us to transform it into labour power and thus produce more and more capital, *drive*.

Today, in late stage capitalism in the twenty-first century, it is worse. It is as if the machines that we have created to relieve us from work have turned us into their slaves, and the imperative to make profit creates extra work, so we have less time instead of more. The possibilities that technology opens up are betrayed by the drive for profit, a drive that intensifies our exploitation and oppression. This imperative to make profit speeds up production processes, and that acceleration of life under capitalism means that even more than ever our own bodies are experienced as things alienated from us.

Under capitalism in the nineteenth century the development of industry proceeded so fast and it did it so destructively for nature and for culture, and with so little care for the lives of workers, that it was as if everything that was solid melted into air. Now, with industrial and technological development that are in the hands of private companies or state enterprises that work on behalf of capital, there is an alienating acceleration of this process such that all that is left to us are the bodies we inhabit, bodies that must work, bodies faced with ruin. It is true that our bodies are alienated, but we can recover them, at least in part, at least for moments. We need them. It is only with them interwoven with speech, with true speech, that we can act.

We are faced with a task which works at a contradiction. On the one hand there is the deadly deathly face of drive. There are social structures in place that are dedicated to their own self-maintenance, structures personified by those who benefit from them to hold onto their power, to employ workers at the lowest possible wages and to make the maximum amount of profit. This 'surplus value', that which those in power extracts from the workforce, is drawn from our labour power, but this power is that of our life, that of our love and our creativity, and so those with money and power pervert, instrumentalise, what drives us all to care for our loved ones and have a creative impact in the world.

Our possible human community is replaced by the capitalist, patriarchal and colonial system. Our truest relations are subordinated to the relations of production, relations of exploitation that are shored up by other relations of power, of men over women, and of racism and exclusion of those who are deemed not productive.

On the other hand, there is a drive for life, the loving face of the drive. There are the creative forces that are provoked and unleashed by capitalism, possibilities for innovation and development of culture. Within the very belly of capitalism are born the forces that will overthrow it, the collective forces that are gathered together in order for us to work creatively, and that allow us to learn from each other the value of working with each other rather than against each other.

These are the forces of production, the productive forces that also provide the energy of the liberation movements. The question is, whether we continue to let our masters and rulers determine how we will work and how we will enjoy and how we will service their own enjoyment, or whether we will take control and whether it will be us who will decide on our lives.

This is the drive today, a drive that runs through us and energises our bodies in an unconscious dynamic that is out of our control, a drive for innovation that is also channelled into a drive for profit. The drive is a bodily force that is the well-spring of life, of love and creativity, but has been turned against us so we not only feel subjected to it, but captured by its logic. Life and our nature, and nature as such are then experienced as threatening and frightening, and so we often separate ourselves from each other and close in on ourselves to try to escape.

Capital accumulates and gives life to the 1% while for the rest of us, those who work, those who sell their labour, and those who labour in the home to support those who must sell their labour, the drive is deathly. The drive is a death drive for the vast majority of those who live in capitalism. It is our historical development of this form of political-economy that makes it that the aim of life is death.

Culture, of sex, and more

One of the places where we experience our bodies taking us beyond ourselves, beyond our conscious control is in sex, and this sex which is so necessary to the reproduction of species, including the human species, also, for human beings takes on an unnecessary pleasurable, and sometimes painful, character. What drives us to sex is not at all necessary, and there are many who do without it, but this unnecessary enjoyment in sex poses a question about the nature of the body and its relation to enjoyment and suffering that drove the development of psychoanalysis.

It is often said that psychoanalysis is obsessed with sex, but it is more the case that psychoanalysis helps us to understand how it is that we feel driven to sex in a culture that is itself obsessed with a certain intensely ideological series of images of what sex is. This is the culture that demands that we work, and that prohibits forms of enjoyment that are not functional either to the reproduction and maintenance of the work-force through the family or for the realization of the surplus-value through consumption or for the cosmetic embellishment of capitalism through ideology. Although sex can thus be exploited, more is prohibited of sex in this culture than is demanded of it, and that prohibition itself has the bizarre uncanny effect of also inciting, provoking and demanding of us that we enjoy.

Prohibition

There is no sexual bodily activity for us human beings without *prohibition*, prohibition and transgression. Sex has become one of the key points at which we are driven by the hidden unconscious demand to transgress, and to enjoy transgressing in such a way that it is as if there is something deep inside us that must find release. It is then not surprising that the very sexual activity that should, we are told, bring pleasure, also often brings shame, guilt, loneliness, jealousy, violence, anguish, pain.

Sex has been so important to psychoanalysis precisely because it is a place where we see enjoyment and suffering so closely linked together. An alienated unhappy life links them together all the more closely, whether in reality as we experience sex or in fantasies about what we are missing, what we are told we are missing.

It is impossible to understand our current experience of sexuality without a conception of the unconscious, that which is beyond us and takes us beyond the ego, and of repetitive activity that gives us enjoyment and then also suffering, and of the drive; the drive gives life, and is an expression of life when sex operates, among other things, as the wellspring of reproduction. We are told that it should operate like that in this culture, but it does not. There is always more to it than we are told, more that is prohibited and incited, pushed out of consciousness and alluded to, hinted at, provoked as a place of deeper personal transgressive enjoyment. Even for those who have sex as they should, there is pleasure and pain when they follow this double contradictory injunction to conform to cultural codes and to go beyond them.

This is why psychoanalysis makes such a big deal about sex; people seek refuge in sex and puzzle over why it so often fails to bring them comfort. They are driven to it, and it drives them into the neurotic conditions that psychoanalysis was invented to treat. And, for those who do not have sex as they are told they should, they are haunted by a culture that is still always pressing on them the demand to conform to what is demanded of them, and that too drives them into the privatised suffering that psychoanalysis can help unlock.

Take, for example, the trading of sex for love which so often happens inside the nuclear family – implicit in the marriage contract – and the more explicit trading of sex for money when those with power, usually men, are able to use it in order to command others, usually women, to service their bodies, to give them enjoyment. On the one side of the equation is enjoyment, and on the other is suffering. Often they are combined. In this way, sex is turned into work, and commodified and exploited, as all work under capitalism is. The answer is not simply to prohibit this work, but to transform work as such, and that means fighting for sex workers to have rights, paving the way for a world in which such commodification and exploitation of sex would be impossible.

Psychoanalysis teaches us that the prohibition of anything, including sex, is not a solution, but rather that our task is of understanding structures of repression as such, and tackling those structures. With new structures that we collectively create for ourselves come new possibilities for desire, for desiring others, and new paths for the drives, paths in which the enjoyment of one does not require the humiliating suffering of others.

The drive feels as if it is inside us, but it is actually on the border of inside and outside; more correctly, as Freud himself declares, on the border of the physiological and the psychical. What is physiological is given shape and meaning by who we understand ourselves to be, and what we are told our needs and desires are, and the 'psychical' itself is, as we learn from Marx, as much outside us as inside us, our subjectivity being 'an ensemble of social relations'.

Those social relations are produced by the culture we ourselves create, but in an alienated society such as ours, we make our culture and our history in conditions that are not of our own choosing. What we must do, and what psychoanalysis guides us to be able to do, is to be able to comprehend the reality of the 'second nature' of our human nature, the second nature of culture.

History and culture shape and incessantly modify the realm of the drive. We need to be clear that this drive is not biologically wired in 'instinct', nor that there are separate biologically wired-in life and death instincts. There are indeed instinctual processes concerning food and sex and other biological needs that are a function of our deeper evolutionary history as an animal species, of our animal nature, but these are always interpreted by us, consciously or unconsciously.

That which drives our body, and which is as alienated as the bodies that we routinely treat as if they are mere vehicles to drive to work under capitalism, is always mediated, shaped by culture. There is no drive without culture. This is not actual 'instinct' which precedes culture, but something quintessentially human, as human as the cultures we create. We cannot free ourselves from culture in the name of our drives; much less liberate ourselves from our drives in favour of culture.

This is not the question raised by liberation movements. It is a false question leading us down false paths, to a mistaken idea of the drive as an instinctual force that must be 'released'. That makes it seem as if the unconscious is inside the head like steam in a cooker, and is if the drive will burst forth like steam. Instead of this false reductive ideological and fake-psychoanalytic question, our psychoanalysis is in tune with the question posed by the liberation movements. The question they pose is whether this culture should continue to benefit the 1%, allowing them to grab life and condemn the remaining 99% to mere survival and death, or whether we can now begin to create a culture in which everyone might live and flourish.

Interpretation

The drive is what results from the *interpretation* of instinct, from its alteration, complication and perversion as it passes through language, ideology, culture and history. We are concerned here with drive and its interpretation, the two linked together. Words transmute instinct into something that is no longer just biology and physiology. The drive is on the border of the physiological and the psychical. Its origin is in fantasy and not only in the body. It is not something given naturally, but a historical product. We maintain that fundamental premise of psychoanalysis against the ideological reframing of drive as something of unchanging human nature. Our humanity transforms the drive by the same gesture by which it transforms itself.

The drive is incessantly transformed under the determination of the symbolic, of signifiers, of culture. This does not mean that it is not real. Drive is also real; it overflows words, it cannot be contained or channelled by the symbolic, it resists any symbolization, it appears as an implacable force, outside the signifiers we use to make sense of what is happening to us.

Beyond any sense, the drive is itself a part of what is happening to us. It takes form in our lives, as life, when it is elaborated in language, in the signifiers that structure our speech and action. It is here a real effect of the symbolic. This real aspect of drive is what makes it appear in the body as if it were indeed an instinctual force, an imperative need for food or for sex. This real aspect of the drive also enables it to appear in our speech through disturbed, excessive, absurd or useless operations such as rituals, pet words, exaggerations, automatisms and repetitive signifiers in which we are subject to senseless ideological repetition, to ideology as a kind of machine.

Ideology is indeed rather like a machine. There is something mechanical, deadly, mortifying about it. It is a kind of manifestation of the death drive. It smothers what novelty there might be in repetition and turns creativity into something deadening. Ideology is dead life, the illusion of life whose aim is death. It is then that we see one of the faces of sex in this sick world, sex intimately linked to suffering as well as to enjoyment, the face of sex that posed questions about the nature of subjectivity under capitalism that psychoanalysis was developed to answer. So, once again, when we talk of drive we must talk about sex.

Sex

It is in drive that our biological needs, for *sex* among other things, are reconfigured as social needs. These needs are both created and expressed and repressed as a function of the structure of the family, private property and the state. Cultural and historical institutions do not simply exclude natural tendencies, but absorb, use and modify them, in addition to relying on them.

For example, when instinctual reproduction of the species underpins and is then informed by social or family institutional life, this biological process is turned into human sexuality, which is released from its reproductive anchor, as well as diversified and complicated at the level of drive. This is how eroticism can permeate consumption, advertising, the culture industries and charismatic leadership. Psychoanalysis shows that even scientific work, religious beliefs and political ideals involve idealized, sublimated or rationalized erotic elements.

Sex itself is transformed into one of the nodal points of society, as relay and rebellion against power. This is another reason why sex is central to psychoanalysis; sex operates as the historically-constituted symptomatic kernel of social relationships in class society. These relations of domination, but also of struggle and conflict, are articulated around and based on a sexual axis. Patriarchy is inseparable from capitalism. Consumerism and capitalist voracity reveal highly sexualized possessive tendencies.

No man is an island, but capitalism drives him to imagine that he is, and to imagine that the only way to love someone is to possess them. Women, who are so often reduced to the level of objects to be possessed by men, can also make the same mistake. As has been said by a wise communist novelist, liking is the best form of ownership and ownership is the worst form of liking.

Our sexuality is not only the most animal aspect of us, but also the most human, the most characteristic of our humanity. Human culture results from a certain cultural metabolism of sexuality. It is in their condition, as sexual and sexed beings, that human beings are social beings. Their socialization is a process whereby sexuality is symbolized, maintained and transcended symbolically, and it becomes word, part of language and so of desire, love, friendship, solidarity, social relationships, cultural institutions, political action and other symbolic practices animated by our desire.

There is no specific sexual drive, any more than there are separate pre-existing drives for life and for death, but the drive in this culture hooks into sex as something most personal and private and hidden about us. In this way, everyone is hooked into the culture of sex, whether they intend to avoid it or not, and into the sexualisation of commodities to make them more alluring, to make them sell more.

Our sexuality is instrumentalized by domination instead of being a means of liberation. Under these conditions, the psychoanalytic answer cannot simply be to demand more sex. That is a caricature of Freud's position, a caricature that has attracted some of the so-called 'Freudo-Marxists', those who have tried to radicalise psychoanalysis by making a combination of Freud and Marx that was sometimes, only sometimes, too-fast and simplistic.

As we have explained, the task is not to release pre-existing urges to make us happy, neither at the level of the individual in the psychoanalytic clinic nor at the level of the collective in political struggle. Rather, the task is to refuse what we are told to want, to create the conditions in which we might better choose what will be good for us all. Instead of simply demanding more sex, we need to work through how and why enjoyment becomes connected with suffering in sex, and how sex as a wellspring of life is turned against us, to function as if it were itself also part of the death drive. To turn the drive back towards life again, we need to articulate it with that most human of phenomena, desire.

Desire, of others

Desire is human because it is created in the ensemble of social relations that make each of us into human subjects. While drive can impel us to treat ourselves as the centre of the world, masters of nature, and takes on a repetitive and sometimes self-destructive form, desire is intimately connected with others. Desire has a peculiarly dialectical quality of being a desire for others and a desire that we are driven to obtain from others. The recognition that we desire from others binds us to them, and we seek in them something that pulls us towards them, to desire them.

This is the source of enjoyment and suffering in social relations, and it then also drives us to build culture as a shared medium, a symbolic medium through which we might share what we are with others, to participate in something that is other to us. This drive and pull operates at the level of interpersonal face-to-face relationships and at the level of organisations and the construction of shared ideals which bind a community together, including globally. It is mainspring of individual sexual love in societies that have given value to that kind of desire, and of solidarity in the international networks that the liberation movements build. We reframe that solidarity here in order to draw attention to an aspect of it, not to colonise it with psychoanalysis. Our desire, political solidarity, is ideologically chained to sex under capitalism, and it is that aspect that psychoanalysis helps us to understand.

Drive is already transformed into desire in our distinctive forms of subjectivity. As speaking beings we are in a symbolic realm, a collective medium of communication, a shared space in which we become truly human. Here our desire for others is reflexively transformed into the most diverse and complex forms of relationship, which, though experienced as lying deep within us, are also conditioned by others, between us.

The symbolic realm, as something independent of us, can so easily and often turn into a machine-like force which is exacerbated by ideological repetition of alienating images of ourselves. Alienation and ideologization are two risks we must take when we symbolise sexuality. The cultural functioning of sexual need as if it were an implacable drive and an irrepressible desire is intimately bound up with ideological distortion, perversion of sexuality, bound up with alienated sexual relations that are structured symbolically in a way that allows not only for the reproduction of culture, but also for the perpetuation of relations of domination and destruction such as those prevailing in the capitalist system.

Markets

In capitalism, through ideologization and alienation, life is turned into death, death drive, and communication is turned into reification and commodification of human beings, human creative labour and human objects of desire. Things and commodities usurp the place of people and exercise powers and rights of people, such as that of free circulation, of which a large part of the world's population is deprived. In capitalism, especially in neoliberal capitalism, fetishized objects are more 'subjects' than human subjects themselves. Capitalism puts subjects at the service of objects. It puts the interests of the *market* before those of humanity. It makes the possessive, accumulative, competitive and destructive tendencies of capital govern and define human drives.

Alienated needs become the driving force of the market that encompasses everything under capitalism. This market includes sexuality. Gender grows into the poisonous site of forms of commodification, such as pornography under patriarchy, with women turned into objects to be bought and sold, to be owned and exploited, to be enjoyed and exchanged for money. There is little place here for desire, but only for the drive and for what appears as instinct, what appears ideologically to be mere animal instinct rather than something human.

The real reduction of desire to drive and then the ideological reduction of drive to instinct turn our creative human activity, our symbolically-mediated relation to others, into things that work in an objective, rigid, automatic and meaningless way. Our bodies, and parts of our bodies, are turned into alienated sites of dumb, deaf and blind biological processes which we fetishize or fear. Radical disability activists have thus drawn attention to the way that the 'deaf', 'dumb' and 'blind' operate as ideologically-loaded signifiers of beings less than human – sometimes even reduced to objects rather than being subjects – less than the 'normal' body we are told we should possess in order to work, to produce 'surplus value' for our employers.

These processes leave us out, exclude the subject, but produce the imaginary. It is as if communication of images of nature and the self could be relayed independently of symbolically-structured historically-constituted social relations. It is also as if what we experience as an aspect of common-sense directly reflects what is real.

The market is today imposed as the only reality. Everything has to be commodified, sold, bought and exploited. This generalized commodification is characteristic of capitalism, but the production of commodified images of gender is also a function of patriarchy. Patriarchal power is decisive as well for the tendencies that capital imprints on our relations with things and people. Modern subjects, subjectivated by capitalism and patriarchy, relate to the world and others as competitively, possessively, accumulatively and destructively as the prototypical macho lover does with women. This is what drives the macho entrepreneur, and, unfortunately, sometimes the heroic activist leader in a social movement.

Machismo

We should not be surprised at the hyper-masculinized and misogynist element of the male model of the pro-capitalist neoliberal ultra-right. The current form of capitalism requires *machismo* as a subjective prerequisite. Fighting against this machismo and the other expressions of patriarchy is a way of subjectively undermining capital. It is for this, and for much more than this, that feminism constitutes a threat to current arrangements of power, which, now as before, mysteriously evoke what Freud represented through the mythical figure of the oppressive father of the primitive horde, projecting back into prehistory the patriarchal bourgeois nuclear family of modern capitalist society. It was a deeply ideological move, but it also now reveals something of the nature of sexualised macho bourgeois ideology.

Feminism not only threatens the subjective foundation of capitalism and the commodification of gender. It also endangers the personal-political ideological social bonds that structure the bourgeois nuclear family, insisting that these bonds are deceptive imaginary figurations of real human needs and reflection of symbolically-sanctioned oppression. This is why feminism, along with the broader lesbian, gay, bisexual, transgender, queer, intersex and associated struggles, is an indispensable ally of psychoanalysis in the service of liberation movements.

Psychoanalysis does not define how we should love and who we should love, nor does it specify what sex should be like or what kinds of bodies should have sex with other bodies. Drive and desire follow complicated paths which are singular to each subject, and a pressing political task is therefore to create multiple possible conditions in which those who have sex, or those who choose not to have sex, are able to define themselves and do what they decide. Psychoanalysis is not designed to attach people to what they have been told sex is, rather it is a practice of self-inquiry that enables us to change our relationship with any or every 'good' that is held out in front of us as bait.

Psychoanalysis can help us change our relationship with the world, either by reconsidering what surrounds us, dealing in a different way with our drives, or opening new spaces for our desire. All of this is crucial for liberation movements that must also change their relationship with the world they want to change. To achieve their goals, activists must profoundly transform their relationship with their immediate environment and also with other people, which they constantly try to do, from the beginning, by establishing horizontal relationships with each other, by experimenting with radical forms of democracy and by weaving networks of action and solidarity.

The liberation movements create networks of action to change the world and also, crucially, networks of solidarity that progressively expand their domain of action, to include those not directly involved, but all those who desire to be part of change in the world. Solidarity is love for those who are other, far away, as well as those who are close. It is symbolically effective, not merely imaginary. This is the space for the realisation of the drive in such a way that it becomes a force for the elaboration of social relations, and of a culture in which our desire for others is configured in such a way as to receive from others an acknowledgement and recognition that we are not mere animals, our bodies not mere machines, that we are human.

In this chapter we have focused on our intimate relationship with the realm of culture, and on the insights psychoanalysis provides into the nature of what drives us as human beings. Here psychoanalytic theory participates directly in the work of the liberation movements, learning from them and giving to them some additional conceptual tools to understand how culture works, how it can operate in a creative constructive way, and how it becomes perverted and turned into something as oppressive and destructive as capitalism.

In the next chapter we turn back to the psychoanalytic clinic, and we will elaborate our specific approach to the unconscious repetitive work of the drives, and how these are embedded in power relations. There is this power in the clinic because there is a peculiar constellation of power relations in this society. The psychoanalytic clinic is in this world, of this world that we so much want to change; it works through *transference*.

移情：權力、抵抗與分析

欲望和權力的結構性現象從一個領域「轉移」（'transfer'）到另一個領域，即**移情**（transference），這在精神分析中具有技術性的意義和用途。但要注意，因爲結構，被結構化的關係模式，會在整個社會領域複製和重複，並傳遞到我們的組織和家庭中。

精神分析聚焦於與他人的個人關係（包括在家庭中構建的關係）的方式被轉移到臨床上，重複在分析主體用來設定和理解他們和分析師的關係（或缺乏關係）的能指之中。於是，這種化約的意義解讀──這種被轉移的結構性現象是有關早年愛的經驗重複在和精神分析師的關係中──也是受到一種意識形態的普適化（ideological generalization）的影響。

精神分析師經常試圖將他們自己在臨床中移情的特定理解「應用」到社會和政治權力關係的其他領域，這些關係因此被以臨床性地分析、神祕化和心理學化，忽略了它們需要特別的分析和行動（政治性分析與行動，從而幫助我們更好地理解精神分析治療本身的性質）的事實。當佛洛伊德的觀點變成了假裝能包羅和理解一切的世界觀時，就會發生了將精神分析「應用」到臨床之外的領域的錯誤嘗試，此外，它包含了一種對社會是什麼和應該是什麼的看法，並要求一種正是我們所拒絕的特定的道德立場。

這種將精神分析擴大「應用」的相同誘惑也發生在當治療被概化之時──也就是當它在變成一種特殊的專業學科並與其他競逐的心理／精神相關方法（如精神醫學、心理學和心理治療）等競爭並採用其語言後，超過它的能力範疇之時。

精神分析實際上既不是一種世界觀也不是一門專業化從被用來概化的學科，但不難理解許多從業者被他們自己對精神分析在知識和專業能力上的不夠厚實，而被引誘去想像它應可如此這般地發揮作用。這些從業者忘

記了治療的一個基本原則，即分析主體才是分析的人，是分析主體（而非精神分析師）有一些重要的事情要對自己說。

　　給予分析主體一個發言權並且肯認他們在他們所說的話中的位置，可能對他們的生活以及他們與他人建立的各種關係產生決定性的、有時是解放性的影響。同樣地，當精神分析師繼續說話而不是主體說話時，會再生產壓迫性邏輯。現在我們需要關注臨床的權力，重現某些類型的關係——也就是對這種權力的抗拒／抵抗（resistance）形式，以便修通／克服（work through）[1] 它們。我們需要關注精神分析作為個人和社會關係的資源和意識形態模式的作用，這是從事著解放運動基進、危險且具革命性潛力的精神分析家必須留意到的事。

權力，在臨床中及關於臨床的

　　臨床在這個社會中擁有權力，因為人們在那裡尋求庇護，他們在那裡找到機會以一種他們以前從未有過的方式說話。分析師，作為他們的受苦與享樂的見證者，聆聽他們說話，鼓勵他們訴說，以使無意識在他們面前更多地出現。正是在臨床中，分析主體在能指之間建立和聆聽那些他們過往可能從未建立、聽見和感動的聯繫。即使是那些從不進入臨床的人也會猜想那裡面正發生著一些怪異的事。有時，人們會因為所談論的內容而感覺受威脅——尤其是當他們身邊親近的某個人正在談論——並且可能正在向另一個人（精神分析師）談論他們時。有時，臨床作為表達個人想法的私密空間，被那些想要完全知道和掌握主體所說的內容的當權者視為一種威脅。

　　臨床的力量——一種潛在的顛覆性力量，是會被濫用的，因此基進的

---

[1]　'resistance' 在精神分析一般中譯專業術語為「抗拒」，而在政治性上則譯作「抵抗」或「抵制」，而 work through 在精神分析一般中譯專業術語為「修通」，而在政治性上意為「逐步處理、解決困難的問題」，可譯作「克服、處理、解決」，由於本書的論述位於精神分析與革命政治的交織處，為表達兩種論述的接合，故於內文中並陳這兩層涵意，惟當 'resistance' 出現在章節標題處時，為求精簡，以本書強調之別於主流的政治性意涵「抵抗」作呈現。

精神分析的任務是保護那個空間，並且藉由解放而不是壓迫來接合其基進的潛力。這項任務對精神分析師而言，最爲首要與最起碼的要求是他們避免說服、暗示或操縱分析主體，這就回過來又需要極其謹慎和相當大量的沉默。

　　精神分析師大多保持沉默，並且不假裝知道他們的分析主體的話是什麼意思。臨床中精神分析師的權力乃關乎那個特定空間所界定的界限、每時每刻被移情到這空間的事情，以及讓分析主體更清楚得見意識和無意識間交界的機會。分析師的任務不應涉及對無意識內容的猜測，好像他們只是在心裡打開了一個盒子般；更不是根據假想的知識向分析主體提供建議。精神分析師了解有關語言的性質，但並不了解有關他們的分析主體使用自己的能指去構建自己的幻想以及和自己與他人的關係的獨特方式。

客觀性

　　臨床上的話語，不能用像心理學或精神醫學假想爲客觀的科學知識那樣，來假設精神分析的知識而能得到澄清、理解和回答。在這個主觀性是臨床之必要成分的特殊領域中，**客觀性**（*objectivity*）是很不一樣的。主流的心理／精神相關專業人士緊抱虛假的科學形象，從而試圖在與人類的工作中貫徹實施這種科學形象。這些專業，以及與他們所治療的人分隔開的專業人士們，犯了雙重錯誤，首先是他們對自然科學的錯誤觀念，其次是他們試圖把錯誤觀念強加執行於他們自己的臨床工作中。

　　正是在我們作爲人類反身性的分裂主體的本性之中，「客觀性」並不排斥主觀性，它**不**（*not*）是在主觀性的對立面，不是像零和遊戲那般。這是精神分析與每一種解放理論以及我們在臨床中的實踐有關的另一個關鍵課題。主流的心理／精神相關專業試圖達到的「客觀性」的虛假觀念，實際上正是他們無法逃避的主觀性面向的表達，它就是主觀性的一個版本，但卻是一個異化的、無意識的版本。它是主觀性的一種特別扭曲的形式，但它不承認自己是這樣。他們試圖逃避這點，但失敗了。

　　傳統的心理／精神相關專業人士自認的那種「客觀性」（也就是他們所謂中立，對處於困境中的人保持距離的立場），根本不是這回事，它實際上充滿了由他們拒絕納入考量的特定立場和經驗所構成的主觀性。當他

們將治療人視同物件般彷彿是可「被修理」（'treated'）的機械時，他們
踩上這樣的立場——好像他們是掌握所有必要知識的大師，而他們可憐的
病人一無所知。心理／精神相關的治療工作本身，並非僅是基於無關乎人
的客觀知識，而是已經涉及連結了兩個人相牽引的驅力、享樂和欲望，涉
及了專業人士與所謂的客觀知識間的一組主觀關係，以及專業人士認為自
己是主體而對被視為客體的病人工作的一組權力關係。

　　主觀性內部構成了心理／精神相關專業人士假定知識的客觀性。因
此，當精神分析指出他們的掌握是脆弱的，而且他們也是分裂的主體時，
這些「客觀的」從業人員們就更加感到受威脅。精神分析向我們展示了我
們如何始終與知識相關連而運作著，而不是完全掌握它，而這種與知識的
關係需要以一種主觀性的形式來把握。正是在這種與知識的關係中，我們
傾注了我們的希望和恐懼、我們的異化、以及我們有能去訴說，並傾聽在
臨床對我們說話的他人。

　　與精神醫學家和心理學家不同，精神分析師對在臨床與他們交談的個
別主體沒有任何特殊的知識，也不應假裝這樣做。他們所聆聽的言說的存
在體是一個主體而非一個客體，不是知識的客體。精神分析師必須剔除自
己對分析主體擁有任何知識的宣稱，以及對他們控制的任何權力慾望。在
精神分析實踐中第一個必須放棄的權力慾望，恰恰是他們假定的知識（也
是分析主體所假定的知識）本質上對指導、說服和建議的慾望。

　　分析主體不應被精神分析師說服或故意操縱和支配，就像他們日常中
精神科醫生、心理學家、心理治療師、父母、朋友、同事、老闆、教師、
傳道者、理論家、知識分子、政治家、記者、公關人員、企業家或廣告商
等對他們做的那樣。

　　人類社會的每個構造裡都可以找到對權力的慾望，在積累資本的人和
願意（如果不自覺地）將自己變成商品的人之中，它成了一種致死的驅
力，它在渴望統治他人的種族主義者中運作，在那些自願（如果不自覺
地）將自己變成受害者的人中運作。而在解放運動中，權力的慾望則運作
於那些尋求擺脫官僚機制的剝削和壓迫，但卻要成為大家的代言人而不是
促進人們為自己說話的那群人之中。這種象徵性結構的慾望和權力形式，
在精神分析臨床中受到分析主體所質疑和挑戰。

精神分析打開了一個空間，在這個空間中，權力和對權力的慾望可以被轉移並在臨床上治療。這也是爲什麼在臨床中的移情至關重要。那些「被轉移」（'transferred'）至臨床中且使分析主體經驗性可見（或者說是在他們用以結構自我解釋的能指中所聽見）的，是在分析主體生長的社會結構內部定義著他們的一種特殊的慾望和權力的糾結。

家庭

在所有具有象徵性保障的社會結構中，最強大的就是*家庭*（*families*）。在這種現代西方而今已全球化了的機制版本中，家庭被濃縮成一個具有明顯散播性別刻板化功能的機制。這種機制是父權核心結構矩陣（patriarchal nuclear structural matrix），作爲一種模範形式、一種社會結構，它的強大不是因爲家庭眞的都以這樣的形式存在（儘管有些人確實是生活在一個由母親、父親、也許有兄弟姐妹的核心家庭），而是因爲在意識形態上它被運作爲一個刻板的標準規範結構。

這種模範形式被標舉爲一種令人嚮往的理想，而對於如果是生活在沒有母親、或沒有父親、或沒有兄弟姐妹、或者沒有血緣關係的照顧者和小孩們的家庭中就相形感到匱乏，正因爲這種家庭印象是一種強大的神話力量，使得似乎所有幸福的家庭都是一個樣；而更悲哀的是看到精神分析師們透過所謂的「伊底帕斯」情結（'Oedipus' complex）的「正常」（'normal'）或「異常」（'abnormal'）發展歷程理論，把這視爲一個理想的家庭形象。

伊底帕斯——那個在希臘戲劇中被丟到荒野等死的孩子，在一連串非常奇特的情況下，最終在不知不覺中謀殺了他的父親並娶了他的母親，這故事爲特別保守的精神分析師們布置了一組特定的家庭關係矩陣，這個故事把戲劇布置在男孩與父親的競爭，以及對母親的愛的基礎上，那樣的關係如果被套進臨床作爲標準規範模式，那麼精神分析就眞落入了「伊底帕斯化」（'Oedipalisation'）的意識形態形式了。而發生在女孩身上的事情則被視爲一個神祕的謎，保守的精神分析師對女性氣質的看法，最好的呢，是視其爲一種神秘的事物——一個「黑暗大陸」（'dark continent'）；而最糟的呢，是視其爲僅僅是個物件——只是陽性的伊底帕斯戲劇場景的

一部分。

　　夠了，因為大多數精神分析師其實早已超越這一點，認識到這種家庭模式的侷限性了；我們解放運動者必須鼓勵他們，幫助他們完全擺脫家庭意識形態。我們能做的就是堅決持續地強調，這個矩陣建立了人們認同的強大理想，因此臨床工作必須涉及解決這些理想常常構成人們對性愉悅和痛苦本質的無意識幻想的方式。正是這種矩陣經常在臨床中以移情的形式再次出現，而精神分析工作使我們能夠超越這一點。我們的精神分析旨在朝向另一個世界，一個不同而不是相同的世界。

　　問題是，同樣的情形一再反覆。伊底帕斯式的父權核心矩陣成為情感投注的政治經濟結構模型，然後來到精神分析中被討論，並似乎證實了伊底帕斯情結，這合乎邏輯，因為它們與其意識形態矩陣有著千絲萬縷密不可分的連繫。它們可以在臨床中被「修通／克服」（'worked through'），但沒法全然擺脫。解構和克服這種家庭意識形態是解放運動的任務。

　　當分析主體離開他們的分析時，臨床內分析主體和分析師關係中凝聚的特殊形式的權力可以很容易地再次「轉移」（'transferred'）出去，這是移情引發的一個問題。這種「轉移」在每次分析主體離開會談後發生，可能繼續以他和分析師的關係中所構建的那些方式，在臨床之外的世界去體驗關係。

　　這種轉移有時發生在分析完成時，即使當它已經成功地使分析主體能過著不那麼痛苦的生活，這時，分析主體很可能將移情理想化並繼續到處尋找它，想要宣揚精神分析，彷彿它是對所有人和一切事物有效的方法，這是精神分析的「應用」的陷阱，但這個陷阱之所以更深是因為它是基於強烈的情感經驗、生活關係，而不僅僅是理論，不僅僅是將精神分析理論轉成世界觀。

　　精神分析臨床之所以如此力量強大，不僅僅是因為它將理論付諸實踐。臨床是一個經驗的共鳴容器，精神分析師在其中構建治療條件，使得分析主體存在的結構性條件得以再現和凝結，分析主體不只是要直接跟精神分析師交談以處理治療中所發生的事，也要處理與一切因他們而顯現的事物的間接關係，他們對自己的記憶、他們的童年、他們的家庭矩陣，以及在這個矩陣中形成的政治經濟結構賦予某種形式的理解。

於是，所有這些象徵性的資料都在移情之內——即過去經驗複製於臨床之內——並構成了分析主體的治療和說話的條件；因此，它們與親密的身體關係如此密切相關。

精神分析臨床並不因它爲主體打開了一個他們過去從未能這樣說話的空間就排除了身體和性，或是忽視了身體與結構及權力的關係；恰恰相反地，因爲事實上這些問題是精神分析的核心，因爲個別的主體乃藉由他們的身體，經歷著他們的痛苦、煎熬以及他們的享樂。

無論是否在現實世界中刻意地上演，這種痛苦和享樂具有性方面的意義，它在幻想中上演，正是這種幻想在分析中被具體化且被說出，精神分析提供了一個可以將這些問題用語言說出的地方，從而主體可以在移情中處理這些問題是如何構建的。

這些在日常生活中不斷地被上演、被忍受、被噤聲或被神祕化的敏感議題，可以透過精神分析對語言的關注來仔細處理。在臨床中，人們把慾望說出來，而不是只在幻想中上演，它不是僅僅被度過和感受著，而是被包容、被思考和被探問。透過這種方式，分析主體聽到並對他們如何打造慾望和權力之間關係說出眞話，也說出他們與他者、別人及社會結構的身體關係的眞相。

幻想

這種分析主體與自身的慾望和權力在臨床的移情中的交會，作爲個人政治性象徵結構的複製和反映，能使分析主體遇見自己的無意識和對這些結構在*幻想*（fantasy）層次上所進行的不知覺的解釋。反對把幻想視爲個體內部湧現並被文明所控制的精神分析誇張刻畫，我們堅持認爲這些幻想是被主體所建構的。它們是由主體精心製作的，是內部組織的，由符號組成的情節，具有意義並提供由慾望驅動的現實解釋。再一次地，反對將幻想看作是個體腦袋中不斷湧現的力量然後被文明所控制那種誇張諷刺的精神分析刻畫，我們堅持幻想是*被建構*（constructed）的。它是某種被主體精緻化的、在內部組織的東西，是一種由有意義的能指組成的情節，並提供由慾望所驅動對現實的一種解釋。

幻想是一種慾望的展演，它總是包括一個被描述爲在享樂和痛苦之中

分裂的***主體***，以及在無意識層面上想像會爲他們帶來滿足的***客體***；幻想在臨床的移情中是一個舞台，它包括了分析師作爲這些他者們和給主體帶來刺激並引起焦慮的客體們的替身，這就是爲什麼分析師在移情中被分析主體賦予權力的原因，這種權力是幻想的一部分，是已經將主體束縛住的權力的複製。

精神分析臨床的權力是幻想內容的作用，受慾望展演的影響，當然也受到將知識歸功於分析師的影響。分析主體假設分析師擁有關於他們的知識，對他們瞭若指掌，但在分析過程中發現事實並非如此；這也發生在臨床之外其他的生活情境中，某些人例如親戚、伴侶、魅力理論家或政治領袖，似乎對我們知之甚詳，至少直到我們幻想消失而感到失望並擺脫他們之前，他們擁有對我們生活的巨大影響力。臨床的不同之處在於移情——即一種權力的「轉移」——允許分析主體以他們用來構建和說自己是誰的能指，去反思和談論那個演出關係的片刻裡所發生的種種。

精神分析臨床是一個談論和思考幻想而不僅僅是度過它的空間，象徵的結構與主體之間的內在聯繫——即有關結構在主體的著根（the subjective rooting of the structures）——由此向分析主體揭露開來。透過這種方式，分析主體與權力直接面對，可以對權力說出他們的眞實——關於他們存在的、欲望的眞實，而分析師有倫理責任來處理這種欲望，指導治療，而不是指導分析主體。這是一種特別的權力，是透過移情構建而在臨床中復甦的權力，這必須被謹慎地處理，用來自分析主體對此權力的精確解讀，然後從權力裡解放出來。

我們再三強調，分析不是藉由分析師給出的巧妙解釋來進行，分析主體才是分析的人，是分析主體解釋移情，分析師引導治療，以使分析主體能夠抓住權力來指導他們自己，能在作爲談話治療的精神分析中對權力說出眞話。

分析師不能直接回應分析主體所期待於他們的事，在分析主體詳細闡述必須訴說的內容之處，分析師必須消音與留白。儘管分析師將自己設定爲慾望的對象，但這只是作爲對話者，作爲被談論的人，他們側身於慾望，以便分析主體可以更好地注意到慾望是如何上演的，以及結果是什麼樣的。分析師能在移情中使用慾望，然後消解它們於現身之處，使其被摒

除、被取消、被遺忘；分析師們知道，讓幻想在現實中實現而不是在言語中闡述，是濫用權力，動得太快、主張走捷徑行動，都將使分析主體原地打轉，而受制於最初導致他們進入分析的同樣的權力形式。

　　精神分析師避免身體的接觸，因為正是這種滿足——對分析主體可能是直接立即的滿足——會破壞了分析關係。性在分析中具有致命的雙重效應，透過性，移情會變成了對權力的盲目行使，由此，精神分析術語中理解為移情的作用也被破壞，分析主體不但沒能藉由言語從移情中解放出來，反而陷入了移情的曲解版本中。當分析主體無意識地將分析師假定為對他們存在的深處有所知悉時，分析師作為被授予權力的人實際上變成了大師，而跨了這決定性的一步超越了言語而進入身體滿足的分析師則是一個精於控制——精通於以性控制為樂的人。這是一條將享樂和痛苦結合在一起的捷徑，而不是解開兩者之間的紐帶。

　　透過臨床中的移情，權力和慾望形式的重複呈現出一種詭譎的面向。它之所以詭譎，正是因為它結合了主體性的兩個相互矛盾的方面：被權力激發和壓抑的欲望、以及被欲望維持和顛覆的權力。請記住，欲望乃是經由它所被禁止的方式而成形，這就是為什麼在幻想中慾望的上演總是包含了焦慮和內疚，以及經由踰越而獲得滿足的原因之一。

　　正是在這個意義上，權力激發並且壓制欲望，欲望維持權力並假裝超越它。權力與欲望，又涉及政治與個人的互動，體現了意識與無意識的分離、鴻溝、聯繫與衝突，也正是由於這一切，臨床中的移情相當詭譎。

　　移情將存在於分析主體的個人 - 政治關係元素外顯出來，通常是存在於過去以及他們的家庭中，這些不斷重複的家庭關係可被有意識地向精神分析師描述。它還喚醒那些被壓抑排除在意識之外的無意識元素，這種壓抑對父權制下被賦予其極重要意義的性的慾望形式有所影響。這種壓抑的和父權化的慾望牽涉到權力，透過在主體的生活中無意識地重複而不斷地顯現它自身，並暈染及人們在臨床移情中的許多內容。

　　在臨床中，當移情在言語中形成、在能指中運作，也就有了機會能循著欲望探跡索隱。它在某個時刻變得有意識起來，且仍然在無意識的層面上運作著，幻想不會在精神分析中就消融不見，但我們可以更好地認識到，作為分析主體，我們正用它在做些什麼。

真實

　　並非一切都能被訴諸言語，精神分析臨床中出現的**真實**（*truth*）——那種經由移情成爲可能的主觀的眞實——仍然分裂於瞬間意識和持續無意識運作之間。眞實被「半說」（'half-said'），但這已經足夠爲欲望開闢新的道路。移情是一個陷阱，同時也是爲主體顯現出從陷阱逃出的機會，它精確地重現過去關係的形式，所以未來的關係可以有所不同。

　　分析在一個必要的變革性辯證過程中將批判和變革聯繫起來，透過這個過程，理解正在發生的事情的同時也是我們憑藉這種理解做一些不同的事情的時刻。政治分析和精神分析就是這種情況。我們的存在可以透過簡單的言語和思考行爲改變，透過解釋我們的症狀，了解一些被壓抑的眞相，這些眞相回歸並塑造了我們的自我。

　　對性的壓抑，以及經由父權社會關係對個別主體形塑性的方式，對臨床而言至關重要，藉由某種症狀、問題、痛苦和記憶缺失（遺忘、只記部分）和重複的形式它們造成被特徵化的主體特定類型的規訓結構。欲望的壓抑和父權正常化經由在資本主義下對人們及其需求的馴化、統治和剝削，以及他們對與種族主義和殖民主義一樣專斷的秩序形式的接受，使某種主體化（subjectification）成爲可能。所有這一切在其表現形式上可能是有意識的，但在其原因和邏輯上可能是無意識的。

　　我們可以透過將個人存在的關鍵形式移情到精神分析診所中，也可以直接透過社會存在來意識到主體化的無意識面向，例如參與解放運動和其他在現代社會中起到「臨床」作用的轉化實踐。許多轉化實踐在現代社會中像在診所中一樣發揮著臨床作用，不僅限於精神分析實踐，也不總是在診所內進行。

抵抗，在臨床中及關於臨床的

　　臨床是權力關係再生產的場所，而精神分析將這些權力關係概念化爲移情，因而我們知道，作爲心理／精神相關專業人員，我們最佳企圖——對移情形式中的權力加以「解釋」或過急地希望它離開——終究會落得悲

哀、會失敗；相反地，正是爲了讓分析主體可以對權力說出眞話，作爲精神分析師，我們指導治療──並且只使用我們的權力來指導它，分析主體必須是在移情中那個說話的人，這樣他們才能更好地消解移情的力量。這和解放運動非常相似，權力不能是被傳遞的，而必須由自己去把握。解放運動和分析主體都只有經由他們自身以及爲自己去認識他們所做的事，才能達成他們的使命。如果這種理解和自我理解是眞實的，那麼理解世界的過程就會同時改變它自身。

　　在精神分析臨床中，移情的力量給了權力一種主體的形式，以此方式將權力消解。正是從這個意義上說，有權力的地方就有抗拒／抵抗，這意味著有必要掌握臨床內外抗拒／抵抗的本質。

臨床

　　什麼是**臨床**（*clinic*）？「臨床」不僅在診療室的物質建築內部運作，而且由於精神分析話語在當代社會的傳播，在它之外具有存在的象徵性面向。這使得精神分析在那些能夠支付治療費用的人中享有特殊的聲譽，也同時有充分的理由引發沒法支付治療費用的人的懷疑。由精神分析生產的知識和權力可以被討論或拒絕，也可以被壟斷和利用、可承受痛苦和羨妒、可被摻雜和庸俗化、以及可使它分散和民主化、或可被顛覆和轉變爲完全不同的東西。知識和權力是意識形態和文化財富的一部分，它們在階級鬥爭和解放我們自己的其他集體嘗試中處於危急關頭。

　　我們需要清楚移情在臨床中的特殊權力，在分析主體這邊，透過表達他們用來反映和他們交談的分析師的存在的特定能指來重新建立依賴感，這被指導治療的精神分析師所使用，但這種移情效應不僅限於精神分析的臨床。

　　這就是精神分析話語在全球範圍的影響，以至於許多其他形式的治療無論是身體的還是心理的、醫學的還是靈性的，都受到那種分析主體把知識歸功於精神分析師的影響。這種假想的知識──這種在精神分析中，它之所以存在只爲消解它自身的知識，卻是許多醫生和心理／精神相關專業人員權威和聲望的主要基礎。

　　畢竟，移情並不全都是佛洛伊德的發明，而是被他概念化和使用的，

進步的精神分析師知道如何以能消解它的方式來使用它，精神分析總是利用一種既存的移情權力，在一個與另一人相關的小空間中，顯現權力關係複製的濃縮效果，而以一種特定的方式引導它。精神分析乃植基於既存的歷史構成實踐之上，這些實踐來自宗教傳統和薩滿治療；當然，也來自醫學所提供的對身體疾病近乎神奇的治療力量。

　　與其他實踐不同，精神分析必須承擔特定的責任來處理好移情，並確保離開它的路徑與進入它的路徑同樣被清楚詳細地說明。這些可能無法為分析主體仔細說明，之所以這樣是因為分析主體對此是無意識的，但這些要為精神分析師清楚地說明，以作為他們訓練期間吸收關於社會結構和語言的一部分知識。我們將精神分析與解放運動的理論和實踐相接合，這也意味著我們應擴展佛洛伊德自己對精神分析師培訓的規準，納入對權力的分析，以及臨床在既存權力機制中的位置分析。

　　佛洛伊德本人很清楚，除了基本的醫學和「心理學」知識外，精神分析訓練中最重要的要求是歷史和文學的知識，這更使得分析師能夠將他們的工作建立在他們自己的文化以及他們的分析主體的文化之中。今日的精神分析師也需要有政治性解放原理的基本基礎，只有這才能使他們認識到他們在移情中指導治療的權力與他們在社會權力體制中的地位之間的差異，在某些文化中這種社會權力體制賦予他們的臨床特權的地位。

　　這也意味著精神分析師應該承認，還有許多其他形式的實踐，如政治性的，甚至是靈性的，在這些實踐中，主體性得到反映和轉化。遠非將精神分析當成一種福音似的世界觀，彷彿它是通往個人救贖的唯一途徑那樣，精神分析必須認識到它只是許多駕馭權力且與「移情」方法類似的不同實踐中的一種。精神分析與大多數其他的關懷形式的關鍵差異在於，我們在使用權力分析主體性的同時，我們也分析權力；或者更確切地說，我們精神分析師透過讓分析主體作出解釋並以此分析權力，來使用權力指導治療。

無結構

　　如果我們不分析權力結構，我們就注定會重複它們，這與女性主義的論點有所連結，即盼望權力會消失不見、假裝革命組織和社會運動內部不

存在結構性不平等，只是允許那些有權力的人以一種隱蔽的形式繼續享受它；「**無結構**」（'*structurelessness*'）的幻覺，亦即政治分析中所謂的「無結構暴政」（'tyranny of structurelessness'），就是對這種企圖假裝群體中不存在權力的事實的一種描述方式；例如，依照性別劃分權力，只是給男性保持控制權而使女性在試圖指出存在某些錯誤時沉默無聲的又一次機會。

對移情的處理，我們堅持不應該由分析師去作「解釋」（'interpreted'）堅持治療應以促使分析主體自己能夠注意到移情、解釋它並反抗它的方式來催化，這也是與女性組織的一個基本原則有關，這一原則總結為「立足點」（'standpoint'）一詞；分析師作為擁有權力者其立足點往往傾向於忽視特權、地位和結構，而分析主體作為移情中受制於權力的一方，其立足點則是一種允許（甚至攪動）他們去意識到它。

正是這種對立足點的敏感——使主體能夠從他們自己的立足點而不是從他們的意識形態知識或被別人給定的位置來說話——而不是任何性別歧視的譏諷漫畫式女性圖像（那引導分析師把目標放在「歇斯底里化」（'hystericise'）分析主體）。是的，女性抱怨她們的地位，而且她們有充分的理由這樣抱怨，卻為此被病理化。在無能為力的位置上，她們看到了關於這個世界的某些事。無論是出於女性還是男性，歇斯底里的抗議已經被病理化太久了，這正是精神分析要公義對待的。這種歇斯底里是對抱怨、反抗的進一步激發，定位他們的抱怨並更好地理解他們在移情中的抱怨是一種「意識覺醒」（'conscientisation'）的形式；以這種方式，分析主體會意識到無意識和重複運作的權力結構，這些權力結構在臨床之外控制著他們的生活。

精神分析中的歇斯底里化（hystericisation）讓人們可能獲得一種如同在解放運動中追求的覺醒。這些運動也以某種方式讓人們「歇斯底里化」，允許他們表達自己和被傾聽，這反過來又幫助他們意識到壓迫他們的力量，深化傳統上所謂的「階級意識」（'class consciousness'）並發展他們抗議和反叛的精神。在這裡，歇斯底里不是一種失序，而是一種對真實的體驗，也是對權力唯一合乎邏輯和合理的反應，這意味著精神分析起源自歇斯底里一詞，仍在實踐中持續耕耘它，這可以為我們的鬥爭和解放

運動帶來更多額外的益處和用途。

　　我們的奮鬥不僅是要爭取控制生命生產和再生產的生物性及技術經濟性工具，還要爭取控制表達與關係、存在與經驗、意識與欲望、知識與權力的象徵性工具，這些工具可以私有化或社會化、意識形態化或去意識形態化，用於統治和操縱或用於抵抗和解放，這就是精神分析臨床的情形，這使它不斷地擺盪於其破壞性、顛覆性的動力與適應性、常規化（normal-ization）和心理學化（psychologization）的偏誤之間。

　　精神分析的臨床是具矛盾性的，正是精神分析作爲一種辯證的實踐，熟悉自身的矛盾，所以最適合用來處理矛盾。然而，精神分析的矛盾就是社會的矛盾，精神分析的臨床並不在我們歷史決定的社會之外，它是這個社會及其矛盾的一部分。於是，對作爲一種社會關係形式的「臨床」而言，就有一個結構性的話語實踐框架，可以伴隨著其他解放運動一起被構建與再生產，移情可以是一種強化痛苦的私有化或將治療與政治性的抗拒／抵抗聯繫起來的方式。

　　無論是保守地使用還是服務於革命，移情都預設著與資本、父權、殖民和其他壓迫性的權力不可分的象徵性結構的重複，這些結構就是在臨床中被重複的，因此，它們再現了被轉移到臨床的個人想法、感受、個人分配的角色和人際關係。

分析，關於權力與抵抗的

　　移情允許我們能夠認出結構，然後去質疑它或認可它、突顯它或增強它、擴展或限縮對它的抗拒／抵抗，以使我們可以對那些被重複的事物採取對抗或屈從；以一種或另一種方式在結構中行動，這是可能的，但一勞永逸地擺脫它，徹底地將我們從壓迫我們的東西釋放出來，而永不重複地走上一條全新且清楚的道路，是我們辦不到的。

　　過去永遠不會完全離我們而去，我們總是被困在其中，我們必須不停地穿越它才能繼續前進，這就是爲什麼精神分析治療雖然可以終止，但也是一個在治療終止後繼續的不停息的過程，這也是爲什麼當一個革命進程以一個簡單的政治勝利作爲結束時，它會失敗。

　　革命可以是而且應該是文化性的和永久性的，因爲結構的重複不會停止，並且與人類文化不可分離，這也是佛洛伊德認爲文化的不安、文明的不滿是難以超克的原因之一。我們知道它並沒有被克服，儘管包括許多心理學家在內的一些人並不這樣想，而是想讓我們分享他們勇敢的新世界，向我們兜售我們可以「快樂」，同時讓人們適應這個悲慘的世界，彷彿這只是把東西丟回它們的環境、置諸原地、任其在混亂惡劣的天候中自生自滅的一件小事。

　　人們很容易想像我們生活在一個沒有不滿的文明中，生活在一個不再被過去阻礙和困住的當下，生活在一個已經不再不斷重複精神分析中的移情現象所命名和運作的象徵結構的生活中。這種錯覺對於那些從中得到好處的人而言更具誘惑，這些人透過對其過去和未來的意識形態想像來確保這種運作，彷彿事情總是保持不變，彷彿沒有逃脫的可能。我們在這裡指的是那些擁有權力並行使權力的人，這種權力對我們施加過多的壓迫，這種權力將可避免的不滿加諸於我們在文明中不可避免的不滿之上，這種權力使人們在譴責不滿並談及欲望時遭受到來自破壞者的威脅。

　　那些受權力支配的人是注意到權力運作的主體。在這裡，女性主義政治中的「立足點」爲我們在精神分析中所說的內容提供了聲音，使我們能夠更好地對抗「無結構暴政」（也就是存在著純粹無中介的「溝通」（'communication'）的幻覺、意識形態政治矛盾的逃避想像）。在日常生活、臨床和政治中，總是存在結構的。

　　我們處於象徵結構中，我們注定要與之應對。移情只是在精神分析臨床的狹小的特定空間中處理它的一種方式，在這個非常有限的空間中，移情使個體生活中能指和行爲模式的結構性重複被凝結、駕馭以及「修通／克服」（'work through'）成爲可能。

　　因此，主體可以用精神分析一定程度地解放自己，但不只是可以用精神分析，也絕不能只用精神分析，就其解放力而言，它本身總是不夠的。誠然，臨床中移情的修通／克服被概念化爲權力和欲望一個非同尋常的奇異結合，爲言論和運動的有限的自由打開了空間；但是，這種在臨床中開啟的自由，其潛力只能實現於臨床之外——在個人-政治的活動中，當私領域的成爲公共的、集體的、眞正具變革性的、採取*行動*（action）之時。

TRANSFERENCE: POWER, RESISTANCE AND ANALYSIS

The 'transfer' of structural phenomena concerning desire and power from one realm into another, *transference*, has a technical meaning and use in psychoanalysis. But beware, for structures, structured patterns of relationship, are replicated and repeated across the social field, and down into our organisations and into our families.

Psychoanalysis focuses on the way that personal relations with others, including relationships structured in the family, are transferred into the clinic, repeated in the signifiers the analysand uses to configure and comprehend their relationship, or lack of relationship, with their analyst. This reduced meaning, in which the transferred structural phenomena concern early love experiences repeated in relation to a psychoanalyst, is then also susceptible to an ideological generalization.

Psychoanalysts are often tempted to 'apply' their own particular understanding of transference in the clinic back out into other realms of social and political power relationships. Those relationships are thus clinically analysed, mystified and psychologized, ignoring the fact that they need particular analysis and action, political analysis and action which then help us better understand the nature of psychoanalytic treatment itself. The mistaken attempts to 'apply' psychoanalysis to realms outside the clinic occurs when the Freudian perspective turns into a worldview that pretends to encompass and understand everything; it then involves a vision of what society is and should be, and demands a particular kind of moral position, one that we reject.

The same temptation to 'apply' psychoanalysis happens when the treatment is generalized, when it goes beyond its field of competence, after having become a professional disciplinary speciality competing with, and adopting the language of, rival psy approaches, such as psychiatry, psychology and psychotherapy.

Psychoanalysis is really neither a worldview nor a specialized and then generalized discipline, but many practitioners are understandably lured into imagining that it should function as such by their own precarious claim to knowledge and expertise. These practitioners forget a fundamental principle of the treatment, which is that it is the analysand who analyses, that it is the analysand and not the psychoanalyst who has something significant to say about themselves.

Giving analysands a voice and acknowledging their place in what they say can have decisive, sometimes liberating effects on their lives and the kinds of relationships they establish with others. Similarly, there are oppressive logics that are reproduced when the psychoanalyst continues to speak instead of the subject. We need to focus now on the power of the clinic to bring to life certain kinds of relationship in order to work through them, the forms of resistance to this power. We need to focus on the role of psychoanalysis as a resource and ideological model for personal and social relationships, something radical, dangerous and potentially revolutionary psychoanalysts working with liberation movements need to beware of.

Power, in and of the clinic

The clinic has power in this society because people seek refuge there, and they find in that place opportunity to speak in a way they have never spoken before. The analyst, as witness to their suffering and enjoyment, hears them speak, encourages them to speak, and so makes the unconscious more present to them. It is in the clinic that the analysand makes and hears connections between signifiers that they may never have made, heard and be moved by before. Even those who never go into the clinic suspect that something strange is happening there. Sometimes they feel threatened by what is spoken about, especially if someone close to them is speaking, and may be speaking about them to another, to the psychoanalyst. Sometimes, the clinic as a private space for speaking private thoughts is viewed as a threat by those in power who would like total knowledge and control over what their subjects are saying.

The power of the clinic, a potentially subversive power, can be abused, and so the task of radical psychoanalysis is to protect that space and articulate its radical potential with liberation instead of oppression. The first and the least that this task requires of psychoanalysts is that they refrain from persuading, suggesting or manipulating the analysand. This in turn requires extreme caution and a good deal of silence.

The psychoanalyst is mostly silent, and does not pretend to know exactly what their analysand's words mean. The power of the psychoanalyst in the clinic is concerned with the boundaries that define that peculiar space, with what is transferred into it at every moment and with the opportunity to make the border between consciousness and the unconscious more visible to the analysand. Their task should not be concerned with divining what lies inside the unconscious, as if they were simply opening a box in the mind, and much less with advising the analysand on the basis of supposed knowledge. The psychoanalyst has knowledge about the nature of language, but not about the specific singular way that their analysand is using their own signifiers to structure their own fantasy and their own relationships with others.

Objectivity

Words in the clinic cannot be clarified, understood and answered with a supposed knowledge of psychoanalysis as it would be with the supposedly objective scientific knowledge of psychology or psychiatry. *Objectivity* is very different in this peculiar realm of the clinic where subjectivity is a necessary ingredient. The mainstream psy professions cling onto a fake image of science, and then attempt to implement that image of science in their work with human beings. These professions, and professionals separated from those they treat, make a double mistake, first in their mistaken idea about natural science and second in their attempt to enforce it in their own clinical work.

It is in the nature of our reflexive divided subjectivity as human beings that 'objectivity' does not exclude subjectivity, is *not* the opposite of subjectivity, as if it were a zero-sum game. Here is another key lesson of psychoanalysis that is relevant to every theory of liberation as well as to our own practice in the clinic. The false ideal of 'objectivity' that the mainstream psy professions try to attain is actually an expression of the subjective sphere from which they cannot escape. It is a version of subjectivity, but an alienated, unconscious version. It is a peculiar distorted form of subjectivity that does not recognise itself as such. They try to escape it, and fail.

What the traditional psy professionals think of as their 'objectivity', their supposedly neutral, distanced stance towards those in distress, is nothing of the kind. It is actually suffused with subjectivity, structured by their particular position and experience, position and experience that they refuse to take into account. The stance they take when they treat people like objects, as if they are mechanisms that can be 'treated', is of a master in command of all the knowledge that is necessary, knowledge that their poor patients know nothing of. Psy treatment itself is not only something impersonal based on objective knowledge, but already involves two personal links that embroil drives, enjoyment and desire; a subjective relationship of professionals with the purportedly objective knowledge and a power relationship of professionals who do think of themselves as subjects working on their patients as objects.

Subjectivity internally constitutes the objectivity of the supposed knowledge of psy professionals. And so, these 'objective' practitioners feel all the more threatened when psychoanalysis points out that their mastery is fragile, and that they too are divided subjects. Psychoanalysis shows us how we always operate in relation to knowledge, never in complete command of it, and that this relation to knowledge needs to be grasped as a form of subjectivity. It is into that relation to knowledge that we pour our hopes and fears, our sense of alienation, and our ability to speak and to listen to others who speak to us in the clinic.

Unlike psychiatrists and psychologists, the psychoanalyst does not have any special knowledge about the singular subject who speaks to them in the clinic, and should not pretend to do so. This speaking being they listen to is a subject and not an object, not an object of knowledge. The psychoanalyst must deprive themselves of any claim to knowledge about the analysands as well as of any desire for power over them. The first desire for power that must be renounced in psychoanalytic practice is precisely one inherent in their supposed knowledge, knowledge supposed by their analysands, the desire for instruction, persuasion and suggestion.

Analysands should not be convinced or deliberately manipulated and dominated by the psychoanalyst as they are daily by psychiatrists, psychologists, psychotherapists, parents, friends, colleagues, bosses, teachers, evangelists, ideologues, intellectuals, politicians, journalists, publicists, entrepreneurs or advertisers.

Desire for power is found in all the fibres of this human society. It becomes a deathly drive among those who accumulate capital and among those who willingly, if unconsciously, turn themselves into commodities. It operates among racists who desire domination over others, and among those who willingly, if unconsciously, turn themselves into victims. And, in the liberation movements, desire for power operates among those seeking escape from exploitation and oppression in the bureaucratic apparatuses that then represent and speak for others instead of enabling people to speak for themselves. Such symbolically-structured forms of desire and power are questioned and challenged by the analysand in the psychoanalytic clinic.

Psychoanalysis opens a space in which power and the desire for power can be transferred and clinically treated. This is also why transference in the clinic is crucial. What is 'transferred' into the clinic and made experientially-visible to the analysand; heard by them in the signifiers they use to structure an account of themselves, is the peculiar knotting of desire and power that has made them who they are inside the social structures into which they were born.

Families

Among the most potent of the symbolically-warranted social structures are *families*. In the modern Western, and now globalised version of this apparatus, the family is condensed into a mechanism with clearly distributed gender-stereotypical functions. This mechanism is the patriarchal nuclear structural matrix, which is powerful as a model form, a societal structure, not because it actually exists as such – though some people do indeed live inside a nuclear family consisting of a mother, a father and, perhaps, a brother and sister – but because it operates ideologically as a stereotypical normative structure.

This model form is held out as an ideal for people to aspire to, and to feel lacking if they are living in a household with no mother, or no father, or no siblings, or with carers and children to which they have no blood-tie. It seems as if all happy families are alike precisely because this image of the family is a potent mythical force, and so it is all the more sad to see some psychoanalysts treat it is an ideal in their theories of 'normal' or 'abnormal' developmental journeys through what they call the 'Oedipus' complex.

Oedipus, who in Greek theatre, was left for dead, and then, through a very strange set of circumstances, ended up unwittingly murdering his father and marrying his mother, lays down the matrix for a particular set of family relationships, and especially so among conservative psychoanalysts. This story, and those relationships, also lay down the basis for a drama of rivalry of the boy child with his father and his love for his mother, and if it is used as a normative model in the clinic, then it does, indeed, amount to form of ideological 'Oedipalisation' of psychoanalysis. What happens to girls is viewed as a mystery, and conservative psychoanalysts treat femininity, at best, as something mysterious, a 'dark continent', and at worst, as a simple object, as part of the scene of the Oedipal drama of masculinity.

Enough of that, for most psychoanalysts have moved beyond that, recognise the limitations of this model of the family, and we liberation activists have to encourage them, help them break from familial ideology altogether. What we can do is to insist that this matrix sets up powerful ideals with which people identify, and so the clinical work must include tackling the way those ideals often structure the unconscious fantasy that people have about the nature of sexual enjoyment and suffering. It is that matrix that is often brought to life again in the clinic in transference, and psychoanalytic work enables us to move beyond that. Our psychoanalysis aims for another world, something different rather than the same.

The problem is that the same comes back again and again. The Oedipal nuclear patriarchal matrix becomes the emotionally-invested model for political-economic structures, which are then addressed in psychoanalysis and seem to confirm the Oedipus complex, which is logical, since they are inextricably linked with its ideological matrix. They can be 'worked through' though never completely left behind in the clinic. Dismantling and overcoming them is a task of liberation movements.

This is a problem posed by transference, for the peculiar forms of power condensed in the relation between analysand and analyst inside the clinic can then very easily be 'transferred' out again when the analysand leaves their analysis. This kind of 'transfer' happens each time an analysand leaves a session, and then may continue to experience relationships in the world outside the clinic in similar ways to those that have been constructed in relation to their analyst.

This kind of transfer sometimes happens when the analysis is completed, even when it has been successful in enabling the analysand to live a life without so much distress. It is then that analysands may come to idealise the transference, and continue to look for it everywhere, want to evangelise about psychoanalysis as if it were an effective means for everyone and everything. Here is a trap of the 'application' of psychoanalysis, but a trap that is all the deeper because it is based on an intense emotional experience, a lived relation, rather than just theory, rather than just the turning of psychoanalytic theory into a worldview.

The clinic in psychoanalysis can be so powerful because it is more than just putting theory into practice. The clinic is an experiential resonating container in which the psychoanalyst constructs the conditions for the treatment in such a way that they allow for the reproduction and condensation of the structural conditions in which the analysand's existence has been formed. The analysands are not only dealing with what happens in the treatment and speaking directly to the psychoanalyst, but also relate indirectly to what all this represents for them; a certain form is given to their understanding of their memories, their childhood, their family matrix and the political-economic structures which are formed in this matrix.

All this symbolic material is then inside the transference – the replication of the past inside the clinic – and constitutes the conditions for the analysand's treatment and speech, which are, as such, intimately connected with an intimately close bodily relationship.

The psychoanalytic clinic does not exclude the body and sexuality, and neither does it neglect the body's relation to structures and power because it opens a space for the subject to speak as they have never been able to speak before. Quite the reverse, for in fact these questions are central to psychoanalysis, for the individual subject lives out their pain and suffering, as well as their enjoyment through their body.

This suffering and enjoyment has a sexual dimension, whether or not it is deliberately enacted in the real world. It is enacted in fantasy, and it is this fantasy that is crystallised and spoken about in the analysis. Psychoanalysis provides a place where these matters can be put into language, and the subject can thereby work through in the transference how these matters have been constructed.

These sensitive issues, which are constantly enacted and suffered and silenced or mystified in everyday life, can be carefully addressed through attention to language by psychoanalysis. Here in the clinic desire is spoken about rather than simply enacted. Instead of being just lived and felt, it is contained, thought about and questioned. In this way the analysands hear and speak the truth of the relation they have forged between desire and power, the truth of their bodily relation to others, to other people and to social structures.

Fantasy

The encounter with desire and power in transference in the clinic as the replication of and reflection upon personal-political symbolic structures enables the analysands to encounter their unconscious and their unwitting interpretation of these structures at the level of *fantasy*. Again, and against caricatures of psychoanalysis which treat fantasy as a force bubbling up inside the head of the individual and then being contained by civilization, we insist that this fantasy is *constructed*. It is something elaborated by the subject, something internally organized, a kind of plot composed of signifiers that make sense and offer an interpretation of reality powered by desire.

Fantasy is a staging of desire that always includes a *subject*, defines who they are as divided in their enjoyment and suffering, and *objects* which they think, at an unconscious level, will bring satisfaction. Fantasy is a stage which, in transference in the clinic, includes the analyst as stand-in for these others and the objects that give a thrill and also cause anxiety to the subject. This is why the analyst is accorded power by the analysand in the transference, a power that is part of the fantasy, a replication of the power that has already held the subject in thrall.

Power in the psychoanalytic clinic is an effect of what happens in fantasy, of the staging of desire, but also of the attribution of knowledge to the analyst. The analysand supposes that the analyst has knowledge about them but, in the course of the analysis, discovers that they do not. This is something that also happens outside the clinic, in other life situations in which certain people, such as relatives, partners, charismatic theorists or political leaders, seem to have great knowledge about us and therefore also great power over our lives, at least before we are disappointed and free from them, when our fantasy dissipates. The difference in the clinic is that this transference, a 'transfer' of power, allows the analysand to reflect on and speak about what is happening at the very moment the relationship is being enacted in the signifiers they use to structure and speak about who they are.

The psychoanalytic clinic is a space to speak and think about fantasy instead of just living it. The internal link between symbolic structures and the subject, the subjective rooting of the structures, is thus revealed to the analysands. In this way the analysands come face to face with power and can speak their truth to power, the truth of their existence, of desire, while the analysts have an ethical responsibility to handle this desire, to direct the treatment, not to direct the analysands. This is power of a special kind. Power structured through the transference, brought to life in the clinic, must be handled carefully, with the release from this power coming from the accurate interpretation of it by the analysand.

We repeat, the analysis does not proceed through clever interpretations being given by the analyst. It is the analysand who analyses, and it is the analysand who interprets the transference. The analyst directs the treatment so the analysand can seize the power to direct themselves, to speak truth to power in psychoanalysis as the talking cure.

The analysts cannot respond directly to what the analysands expect of them. They must be absent and appear as a void in which the analysands elaborate what needs to be said. Although the analysts configure themselves as an object of desire, it is only as interlocutors, those who are spoken to about it. They sidestep desire, so that the analysand can notice better how it is being staged and what the consequences are. The analyst is able to utilise it in the transference and then to dissipate their presence there, to be discarded, annulled, forgotten. The analysts know that to allow fantasy to be enacted in reality instead of elaborated in speech would be abuse of power. To move too fast, to advocate a short-cut to action, would be to leave the analysand in the same place, subject to the same forms of power that led them into analysis in the first place.

The psychoanalyst eschews bodily contact precisely because that kind of gratification, gratifying perhaps at an immediate level for the analysand, destroys the analytic relationship. Sex in the place of analysis has a deadly double effect through which the transference is turned into a blind exercise of power and, as a consequence, the transference understood in psychoanalytic terms is also destroyed. Instead of releasing themselves from the transference through speech, the analysand then becomes trapped in a perverted version of the transference. The analyst as one who was accorded power as one the analysand assumed unconsciously to know something about them in the depths of their being is really turned into a master, and the analyst who takes this fateful step beyond speech into bodily gratification is one who enjoys their mastery, mastery expressed through sex. This is a short-cut that knots enjoyment and suffering together instead of untying the bond between the two.

The repetition of forms of power and desire takes on an uncanny dimension through transference in the clinic. It is uncanny precisely because it combines two contradictory aspects of subjectivity; desire excited and repressed by power as well as power sustained and subverted by desire. Remember that desire is given form through the way it is prohibited, and that is one reason why the staging of desire in fantasy includes elements of anxiety and guilt as well as satisfaction through transgression.

It is in this sense also that power excites and represses desire, and desire sustains power and pretends to push beyond it. Power and desire, moreover, involve interactions between the political and the personal, as well as make manifest the separation, the gaps, the connections and the conflicts between consciousness and the unconscious. It is also for all this that transference in the clinic is uncanny.

Transference externalizes elements of personal-political relations in the analysand's existence, usually in the past and in their family, family relationships that have been repeated and can be consciously described to the psychoanalyst. It also brings to life unconscious elements that have been shut out of consciousness by repression, repression that bears upon what is so heavily-invested with meaning under patriarchy, a form of sexual desire. This repressed and patriarchalized desire involves power, constantly makes itself present through being unconsciously repeated in the subject's life, and stains much of what they transfer into the clinic.

As the transference takes form in speech, in the signifiers that make it operate in the clinic, there is also the opportunity to track what is happening with desire. It is, at one moment, made conscious, and it still operates at an unconscious level. Fantasy is not dissolved in psychoanalysis, but we can come to know better what we, as analysands, are doing with it.

Truth

Not everything can be said, and the *truth* that emerges in the psychoanalytic clinic, the kind of subjective truth that is made possible by transference, is still divided between what is immediately momentarily conscious and what continues to operate unconsciously. The truth is 'half-said', but that is enough; that opens up new paths for desire. Transference is a trap and the opportunity for the escape from the trap it represents for the subject. It repeats the shape of past relationships precisely so that future relationships might be different.

Analysis links critique and change in a necessary transformative dialectical process through which understanding what is happening is simultaneously the moment when we are, by virtue of that understanding, doing something different. This is the case for political analysis and for psychoanalysis. Our existence can be transformed by the simple act of speaking and thinking about our symptoms, of interpreting them, of knowing something about the repressed truth that returns and makes us who we are.

Repression of sexuality, and the way sexuality is thus given shape for each individual subject by patriarchal social relations, are crucial for the clinic because they contribute to the disciplinary constitution of a specific type of subject characterized by certain kinds of symptoms, problems, sufferings and forms of amnesia, of things forgotten and halfremembered and repeated. The repressive and patriarchal normalization of desire enables a certain subjectification by enabling the domestication, domination and exploitation of people and their needs under capitalism, as well as their acceptance of forms of order as arbitrary as those of racism and coloniality. All this may be as conscious in its manifestations as unconscious in its causes and logics.

We can become conscious of the unconscious aspect of subjectification through the transference of key forms of our personal existence into the psychoanalytic clinic, but also directly through our social existence, for example by participating in liberation movements and in other transformative practices that function 'clinically' in modern society. Many transformative practices operate clinically, as they do in the clinic, not only psychoanalytic ones, and not always inside the clinic.

Resistance, in and of the clinic

The clinic is a site for the reproduction of power relations, but psychoanalysis conceptualises those power relations as transference, and so we know that our own best attempts, as psy professionals, to 'interpret' that power in the form of transference or to wish it away too fast will come to grief, will fail. Instead, as psychoanalysts, we direct the treatment, and only use our power to direct it, precisely in order that the analysand may speak truth to power. The analysand must be the one who speaks within the transference so they may better be able to dissolve its power, very much as the liberation movements cannot be handed power but must seize it for themselves. Both liberation movements and the analysand can only achieve their mission by knowing by themselves and for themselves what they are doing. The process of understanding the world simultaneously transforms it if that understanding and self-understanding is true.

The power of transference in the psychoanalytic clinic gives subjective shape to power in such a way as to undo it. It is in this sense that it is true that where there is power there is resistance. This means that it is necessary to grasp the nature of resistance both inside the clinic and outside it.

Clinic

What is a *clinic?* The 'clinic' operates not only inside the material architecture of the consulting room, but has a symbolic dimension of existence outside it by virtue of the spread of psychoanalytic discourse in contemporary society. This gives a peculiar prestige to psychoanalysis among those who can pay for treatment, and it evokes suspicion, for good reason, among those who cannot. The knowledge and power attributed to psycho-analysis can be discussed or rejected, but also monopolized and used, suffered and envied, adulterated and vulgarized, as well as distributed and democratized or subverted and transformed into something completely different. Knowledge and power are part of the ideological and cultural wealth that is at stake in class struggles and other collective attempts to liberate ourselves.

We need to be clear that the peculiar power of transference in the clinic, the recreation of a sense of dependency on the part of the analysand through the voicing of the particular signifiers they use to reflect upon the presence of the analyst to whom they speak, is utilised by psychoanalysts who direct the treatment, but this transference effect is not only confined to the psychoanalytic clinic.

Such is the impact of psychoanalytic discourse globally that many other forms of healing, whether physical or psychical, medical or spiritual, are affected by the kinds of knowledge that are attributed to psychoanalysts by their analysands. This supposed knowledge, which in psychoanalysis exists only to dissolve itself, is the main foundation of the authority and prestige of many physicians and psy professionals.

Transference was, after all, not invented wholesale by Freud, but conceptualised and utilised by him, and progressive psychoanalysts know how to use it in such a way that it can also be dissolved. Psychoanalysis always draws on an already existing kind of transference power, the effect of the replication of power relations condensed in a small space in relation to one other figure, but channels it in a particular way. Psychoanalysis is grounded in existing historically constituted practices from within religious traditions and from shamanic healing, and, of course, from the power of the medical doctor to provide almost magical cures to physical ills.

Unlike other practices, psychoanalysis must take a particular responsibility to handle the transference well, and to ensure that the paths out of it are as clearly elaborated as the paths into it. They may not be clearly elaborated for the analysand, they could not be because they are unconscious of it, but they are clearly elaborated for the psychoanalyst as part of their knowledge about social structure and language that are absorbed during training. Our articulation of psychoanalysis with the theory and practice of the liberation movements also means that we should extend Freud's own specifications for the training of psychoanalysts to include an analysis of power, and of the place of the clinic within existing apparatuses of power.

Freud himself was clear that alongside basic medical and 'psychological' knowledge, the most important requirements in psychoanalytic training were knowledge of history and literature, this all the better to enable the analyst to ground their work in their own culture, and in the culture of the analysand. Psychoanalysts today also need a basic grounding in the principles of political liberation. It is only that which will allow them to recognise the difference between their power to direct the treatment within the transference and their position within regimes of social power that accord their clinic some privileged status in some cultures.

This also means that psychoanalysts should acknowledge that there are many other forms of practice, political and even spiritual, in which subjectivity is reflected upon and transformed. Far from evangelising for psychoanalysis as if it were a worldview, and as if it were the only route to personal salvation, psychoanalysis must recognise that it is but one of many different kinds of practice that harness power, and that do so in ways that are cognate with 'transference'. The difference, the critical difference that marks out psycho-analysis from most other forms of care is that we analyse power at the same time as we use it to analyse subjectivity, or rather that we psychoanalysts use power to direct treatment in a way that allows the analysand to interpret and thus to analyse power.

Structurelessness

If we do not analyse structures of power we will be condemned to repeat them, and there is a connection here with the feminist argument that wishing away power, pretend-ing that structural inequalities do not exist inside revolutionary organisations and social movements, simply gives licence for those with power to continue enjoying it, but in a hid-den way. The illusion of *structurelessness*, the so-called 'tyranny of structurelessness' in political analysis, for example, is one way of naming the fact that attempts to pretend that a group is free of power, power structured along lines of gender, say, is just one more op-portunity for men to retain control and for women to be silenced when they try to point out that there is something wrong.

The handling of the transference, and the insistence that it should not, as a rule, be 'interpreted' by the analyst, but that the treatment should be facilitated in such a way as to enable the analysand themselves to notice it, interpret it and so rebel against it, also con-nects with a basic principle of feminist organisation. This principle is summed up in the term 'standpoint'; the standpoint of the analyst as one with power is a standpoint that tends to overlook privilege and status and structure, whereas the standpoint of the analysand as the one who is subjected to power in the transference is one that allows, even incites them, to become aware of it.

It is this sensitivity to standpoint – enabling the subject to speak from their own standpoint rather from ideological knowledge of them or position accorded to them by oth-ers – rather than any sexist caricature of women, that leads the analyst to aim to 'hystericise' the analysand. Yes, women complain about their position, and have good reason to, and are then pathologised for that. They see something about the world from their position of powerlessness. Hysterical protest, whether by women or men, has been pathologised for too long, and it is psychoanalysis that does it justice. This hystericisation is a progressive incitement to complain, rebel, localise their complaint and understand better how their complaint in the transference is a form of 'conscientisation'; the analysand in this way be-comes conscious of structures of power that operated unconsciously and repetitively, that drove their lives outside the clinic.

Hystericisation in psychoanalysis makes possible a kind of awareness such as that sought by liberation movements. These movements also 'hystericise' people in some way by allowing them to express themselves and be heard, which in turn helps them to become aware of the power that oppresses them, to deepen what has traditionally been called 'class consciousness' and to develop their spirit of protest and rebellion. Hysteria is not a disor-der here, but an experience of truth and the only logical and sensible response to power. This means that psychoanalysis, which arises from the hysterical word and still cultivates it in its practice, can be of additional interest and use for our struggles alongside and inside liberation movements.

We fight for the control not only of the biological and technological-economic means of production and reproduction of life, but also of the symbolic means of expression and relationship, of existence and experience, of consciousness and desire, of knowledge and power. These means can either be privatized or socialized, ideologized or deideologized, used for domination and manipulation or for resistance and liberation. This is the case of the clinic in psychoanalysis, which has therefore constantly oscillated between its disruptive, subversive impetus, and its deviations towards adaptation, normalization and psychologization.

The psychoanalytic clinic is contradictory, and it is psychoanalysis as a dialectical practice, attuned to its own contradictions, that is best equipped to handle that. The contradictions of psychoanalysis are, however, the contradictions of society. The clinic of psychoanalysis is not outside our historically determined society. It is part of this society and its contradictions. There is then a structured discursive-practical frame to the 'clinic' as a form of social relationship that can be constituted and reproduced alongside other movements for liberation. Transference can be a way of intensifying the privatisation of distress or of connecting treatment with political resistance.

Whether used conservatively or in the service of revolution, transference presupposes the repetition of symbolic structures inseparable from capital, patriarchy, coloniality and other oppressive powers. These structures are what are repeated in the clinic. They are thus what reproduces the ideas, feelings, personal assigned roles and interpersonal relationships that are transferred into the clinic.

Analysis, of power and resistance

Transference allows us to recognize structure and then question or ratify it, distend it or reinforce it, expand or contract resistance to it, and so we can fight or resign ourselves to what is repeated. It is possible to act in one way or another in the structure. What we cannot do is to get rid of it once and for all, definitively free ourselves from what oppresses us, never repeat it again and move on a totally new and clear path.

The past is never completely behind us. We are always stuck in it and we must go through it incessantly to continue moving forward. This is why psychoanalytic treatment, although terminable, is also an interminable process that continues after the termination of the treatment. That is also why a revolutionary process fails when it thinks it ends with one simple political victory.

The revolution can and should be cultural and permanent because structural repetition does not cease and is inseparable from human culture. This is one of the reasons why Freud considered the unease in culture, discontent in civilization, to be insurmountable. We know that it has not been overcome, although some, including many psychologists, believe otherwise and want to make us share their brave new world, peddling us the illusion that we can be 'happy', while adapting people to this miserable world as if it were simply a case of slotting back objects into their environment, leaving it as it is, allowing it to continue to destroy itself until it disappears in climate chaos hell.

It is tempting to imagine that we live in a civilization without discontent, in a present that is no longer blocked and trapped in the past, in a life that has already ceased to constantly perform the repetition of a symbolic structure that the phenomenon of transference in psychoanalysis names and works with. This illusion is even more tempting among those who benefit from it and therefore ensure its operation in the present and through ideological images of its past and future, as if things could be always the same, as if there was no escape. We refer here to those who have power and exercise a power that imposes a surplus of repression on us, a power that adds avoidable discontent to our inevitable discontent in civilization, a power that is threatened by those who undermine it when they denounce discontent and speak of desire.

Those subject to power are the subjects who notice its operations. Here 'standpoint' in feminist politics gives voice to what we speak of in psychoanalysis, enabling us better to counter the 'tyranny of structurelessness', the illusion that there is pure unmediated 'communication', imaginary ideological evasion of political contradiction. There is always structure, in everyday life, in the clinic and in politics.

We are in the symbolic structure and we are condemned to deal with it. Transference is just one way to deal with it in the narrow particular domain of the psychoanalytic clinic. In this very limited space, transference makes it possible to condense, harness and 'work through' the structural repetition of signifiers and behavioural patterns in the life of an individual.

So, the subject can free themselves to some degree with psychoanalysis, but not only with psychoanalysis, and never with psychoanalysis alone. That is always insufficient in itself in its liberating power. It is true that working through the transference in the clinic conceptualised as a peculiar singular knotting together of power and desire opens the space for limited freedom of speech and movement. But the potential for this freedom opened up by the clinic can only be realised outside the clinic, in personal-political activity, when what is private becomes public, collective, and truly transformative, subject to *action*.

第六章

主體的轉化：理解的時機與行動的時刻

　　現今我們生活在一個被結構成巨大全球化市場的世界中，它產生了各種形式的精神分析理論和實踐，這些理論和實踐本身被私有化、商品化，變成了只有少數人付得起費用的昂貴私人治療。在這個每一種解放理論和實踐都曾在某個時刻被轉變成學術商品、被扭曲並違背社會運動的資本主義社會中，這應該不會令我們感到驚訝。正如我們需要將各種潮流的批判性思維從大學和書店的禁錮中拯救出來一樣，我們也有必要記住精神分析的起源，了解它的真相，不要讓有權力的人從我們這兒奪走它作為批判心理學的解放潛力。

　　我們生活在一個需要精神分析但卻不可能實現的世界。它通常被實現為貧乏和扭曲毀損到了幾近顛倒的地步，終致使它比它原本可能成為的少得太多甚至是相反，它沒能成為一種革命性的理論和實踐，而是被化約為一種適應性的技術。此外，它的實踐被侷限於個體，並退化到保守主義所標榜的私人實踐——這個關於性和性別以及其他更多反動思想的中繼驛站之內。

　　在當今私有化保守形式的精神分析裡，我們在本宣言中描述的四個關鍵現象已被扭曲，被變成障礙而不是機會：無意識——我們集體存在的不言自明的根基，被以這樣的方式異化成一種威脅，並使個人意識的工具理性享有特權。我們在不同情境、不同結果中重複行動的能力，從本作為反思性自由的源泉被轉成了重複強迫行為的精神官能症牢獄。我們創造性的生活中驅動著我們的東西被轉成一種機械般的力量對我們作對，並使我們受制於死亡驅力。而移情被隔絕在臨床裡，沒能向我們展示社會權力是如何運作，反而變成了外部世界依賴關係的模式。所有這些都與精神分析完

全無關，其所呈現的不是它的眞實，而只是它的不可能性。

　　事實上，精神分析之不可能性的情況並不只是它本身，它們不只是存在於其本身，不只在其內、在其缺陷和錯置之中。更甚的缺陷和錯置在於──對那些缺乏經濟資源來付費的人、那些必須一直勞動而沒能有片刻對欲望作思考的人、那些受苦於異化而對他們的存在和對文明的不滿失去興趣的人來說，精神分析都是不可能的。

　　除此之外，精神分析治療對於那些可以輕易地購買它、消費它並在最終丟棄它的人來說，也是不可能的。它就像是另一種商品、像是其他奢侈品、像是任何一種嗜好諸如網球、高爾夫、遊艇、瑜伽、風水、慈善和藝術收藏等一般。最後，精神分析對許多人──尤其是那些參與解放運動的人來說，也被變得不可能了，他們的敏感度使他們無法接受被訓練過、爲聆聽異化言論而被付費的人的實踐的商品化，以及把對酬金的戀物癖闡述成行使專業知識、象徵地位和權力的自我辯護。

　　在這份關於作爲「批判心理學」最基進的可能形式的精神分析宣言中，我們的任務正是使解放運動成爲可能。更精確地說，我們的任務是在歷史中定位精神分析的實踐，以使我們可以將它與解放運動必要的進步性工作聯結起來，並與適應性的心理／精神專業所應許的虛假未來作鬥爭。我們必須在臨床中將精神分析視爲一個轉變的空間，把精神分析轉向人類的解放，而不是試圖將個人重又置回這個悲慘社會，我們必須把它轉變爲朝向大同主義／共產主義（communism）[1]的觀念與實踐的過渡。這項任務

---

[1]　在此，作者以小寫 communism（而非大寫專有名詞 Communism）表達其政治理想，究其字首 commun-（也就是 common-）意即公共、共同體，而字尾 -ism 涵意爲運動實踐的思想信仰，也就是「主義」；所以，'communism' 的原意指的就是「以社區、社群和社會作爲共同體的思想信仰」，這確實表明作者在宣言中貫穿全文反對高舉意識自我的個體主義意識形態，肯認無意識他者性作爲人類同體共生存在基礎的政治主張及立場；在中文語境中，禮運大同篇「天下爲公、世界大同」的政治思想與作者思想最爲相契，可以譯作「大同主義」，而作者也確實是馬克思思想的信仰者，在與譯者來回討論中作者清楚表明其對重新拿回社會曾經共有的資源的倫理立場，如果將 communism 意義等同於大寫的 Communism 直接譯作「共產主義」，是完全符合作者之意的；事實上「大

的一部分是要從過去圍繞主體性的鬥爭中，提取那些正因想改變世界而眞正關懷疾苦的精神分析師們歷史性進步的理論和實踐。

歷史與革命的時刻

精神分析處於心理／精神相關專業的邊際上，經常被許多尋找答案、尋找他們痛苦的原因和出路的人將它與精神醫學、心理學和心理治療相混淆；精神分析實際上是完全不同的東西，它實際上根本不是心理／精神專業，而是一個有潛力的解放理論和實踐，這意味著我們必須把和解放運動相聯繫的基進精神分析與精神醫學的精神分析、心理學的精神分析和心理治療性的精神分析區分開來。

將它與那些虛假朋友們區分開來的最好方法就是透過歷史分析；而且，這種分析也與精神分析的基進主義相一致，正如我們將看到的，眞正基進的精神分析本身就是一種歷史分析形式，它準確地轉向過去，以便能夠將我們個人和集體導向未來。

我們必須在我們的精神分析工作中持續關注我們實踐中被壓抑的歷史記憶、關注佛洛伊德左派的基進歷史、關注精神分析與社會主義運動的聯盟。我們不能忘記馬克思主義和佛洛伊德學說在奧地利和蘇聯啟發革命的教育經驗，以及精神分析對二十世紀下半葉西方文化政治革命與印度支那[2]抵殖民革命（anti-colonial revolution）結盟的貢獻，還有阿根廷和其他國家精神分析師的承諾和被迫害。我們必須記住歐洲大陸的免費精神分析診所，並且感謝現在於巴西街頭和公共廣場上提供的免費精神分析。我們必須讓移情再次以一種眞正的精神分析來運作，而不是作爲一種把錢付給某個假裝知道我們以爲我們曉得無意識裡躺著什麼東西的人而引起的依賴

同主義」與「共產主義」在中文世界一些重要的文獻（例如，孫逸仙先生的《民生主義》中，是意義等同的。在此，爲精確把握作者意旨，又同時考量中文世界之內因國際地緣政治有不同的地方歷史過程，對如果直接譯作共產主義可能引發簡化的、固定的、想當然爾的理解，在本章中並陳「大同主義／共產主義」。有關這部分的討論，請見本書導論。

2　即中南半島。

表現。

不意外地，這些運動還伴隨著所謂的「反精神醫學」（'anti-psychiatry'）運動，這是因為許多基進運動者認識到精神醫學是一種精通醫療技法的實踐，它把人們變成病人，成為舊精神病院精神醫師的奴隸，讓他們接受禁閉和殘酷的身體治療（physical treatments）。精神醫學受到了攻擊，這是正確的，因為它顯然是一種粗暴殘酷的實踐，儘管現代精神醫學尋求化學藥品的治療方法以使人們適應資本主義，但它實際上延續了前資本主義封建領主的話語和實踐，這些專制的領主在使自己適應於資本主義的同時，重複著最惡劣的古典父權制對婦女的性別歧視凌虐以及對原住民族的殖民種族主義迫害。

精神醫學是他們武器庫中的一個強大工具，精神醫師們肆無忌憚地為那些統治者服務，對人們的階級、種族、文化、性別或政治位置進行病理化，折磨他們並用他們做實驗。當佛洛伊德──一個精神醫師──發明精神分析時，他必得與精神醫學決裂，這是一個重大的歷史突破，必須一次又一次地重複，才能在今天的反資本主義、女性主義和反殖民鬥爭中發揮作用。

拜精神分析不可能性之賜，精神醫學發展起來。這種不可能性在醫學精神病學的治療重新框定中被遮蔽且複製，其中我們的痛苦的不同面向被分出不同的成分加以特殊化成為不同類型的病理。醫學和精神病學的診斷藉著將人一個個包裹在他們的病裡而將我們分隔開來，使我們忘記了在這個社會中發生在我們身上的事情的共同起源。我們是被這個政治經濟體制、資本主義、父權制和殖民主義作用所致病的，當我們感到沮喪或痛苦時、當我們感到空虛或受到迫害時、當我們聽到別人聽不到的聲音時、當我們無法工作或專注於任何事情或以漸進的建設性方式與他人建立聯繫時，我們別無選擇地只能活在今天這個悲慘世界裡。

病

我們需要將我們的*病*（*illness*）視為我們所過的生活的一種症狀，而不是個人的病理跡象。這種痛苦，無論多麼嚴重，都與醫生治療的真正身體問題大不相同。我們不是問題，我們的「病」──我們在這裡借用這個

詞來隱喻我們的痛苦——只是一個跡象，同時也可能是對治眞正問題的藥。

我們需要將主體的這種病轉變爲一種武器，將其稱爲對抗權力的武器，以我們談論對另一個世界的欲望並針對此欲望集體行動來修通／克服它，這就是精神分析本將使之成爲可能的——如果不是它自身已變得不可能，如果它不像現在這般退化，如果它不是成爲另一種暗示、意識形態化、避世、隱退隔絕於個體性、心理學化、精神病理化、逃避衝突、服務於既定世界社會再製的適應和調控的工具。事實上，在所有關於主體性的心理／精神相關方法中，精神分析最能鑑識「社會再生產」（'social reproduction'）在爲資本服務的殖民和家庭結構的實質複製中所扮演的角色。

在這些普遍存在的種族主義、異性戀和一再貶低那些被排除在權力之外的人的情況下，精神分析之不可能性隨著將痛苦降低到個人層次而加劇。越來越無能爲力、貧窮和狹隘的個人領域在集體場域匯集力量，最終成爲資本主義的壓迫和破壞過程對我們主體性造成的所有負面影響必須被解決的地方。然而，在這裡，各種形式的心理學，包括各種形式的精神分析心理學，都與醫學精神病學的精神分析（medical psychiatric psycho-analysis）一起運作。

確實，精神醫學經常被心理學家摒斥，他們自認比精神科醫師更善解人意、更敏感、更體貼和更尊重人類，並且非常清楚醫學和資本主義之間的共謀（例如，已經被證實的，在製藥產業的權力以及在藉由化學手段完成勞動力復健的工作等情形）。於是，心理學假裝取代精神醫學，精神醫學被以更明顯地複製前資本主義的專業統治和奴役關係而運作著，在這種關係中，那些受苦的人被當作「病人」（'patients'）。但是，這種更現代的心理學，則冒稱精神分析理論更好地爲快速適應性認知－行爲的處遇提供訊息，透過以更高的效率和速度爲它服務、經由使我們適應它、使它變得可被忍受、避免我們的病打擾它、將我們重建爲勞動者和消費者，從而複製了資本主義。

勞動和消費，是人類生產和實現資本的主要功能，應該用不著用精神分析去催化，精神分析的主體不是資本主義，並非每個人都需要一直工作

或將購物作爲一種休閒方式。最適合資本的主體是心理學的那種——大體上適應且表面看起來自由的個體、能自我控制的人——也就是最好的勞動者和消費者。

心理學「健康的」（'healthy'）主體是精神醫學「生病的」（'sick'）主體對稱和對立的理想反射。正是從「疾病」（'disease'）——藉由否認並神祕化疾病所揭示的眞實，「健康」——一種常態、資本主義病態的常態——被構成。這就是爲什麼心理學家經常將精神科醫師視爲他們眞正的主人，以及爲什麼精神分析的心理學版與精神醫學版一樣危險。

精神醫學前資本主義的精神分析、爲精神醫學所利用的精神分析、資本主義心理學的精神分析、以及教科書中吹捧爲心理和行爲理論的適應性版本，它們的主體被化約爲異化的隔絕孤立的身體或個別性的心智。相比之下，基進的精神分析——既不心理學化也不精神病化的精神分析，其主體恰恰是不能被化約爲心智或身體的存在。我們的主體——人類的主體，不是資本主義社會異化的客體，更不是準封建殖民的精神醫師治療的奴隸客體。

我們的主體——作爲一個**主體**（*subject*），外在地與這些客體、與它們的異化、與心智和身體、與資本主義和殖民主義相關連著，我們的主體可以是反資本主義和反殖民主義的，可以透過它對權力說出的眞實來表達其潛力，並可能成爲後資本主義的存在模式。目前的權力機制幾乎不可能實現這種潛力，但可以讓歷史來說話，無論是臨床內個體主體的歷史，還是鬥爭的歷史，都揭露了心理／精神專業在複製而非挑戰權力上的角色。

心理／精神相關專業人士應許的虛假未來

精神醫學許諾治癒所謂的「精神疾病」（'mental illness'），而心理學則許諾治療適應不良的思想和行爲，它們的從業人員在異化的實踐中接受訓練，往往難以爲受壓迫者尋求發聲；那些實務工作者中的一些人打破了專業規訓，加入解放運動，例如半個世紀前的「反精神醫學」運動和當今的「批判心理學」。

一定得要提的一位是革命精神科醫師法蘭茲‧法農（Frantz

Fanon），他在撰寫有關白人種族主義的文章後加入阿爾及利亞反殖民戰爭，那時他繼續擔任醫生，對他仍然認爲的「精神疾病」進行傳統的身體治療，不過他最終將精力全都投入到解放運動中。另一個令人注目的例子是伊格納西奧・馬丁 - 巴羅（Ignacio Martín-Baró），他批評了他那個時代的心理學理論和實踐，提出了一種替代性的「解放心理學」，並爲拉丁美洲人民（特別是薩爾瓦多人民）的解放而戰，最後因此被武裝軍隊暗殺而死。必須說的是，馬丁 - 巴羅在他的鬥爭中有時會使用傳統的心理學方法，比如民意調查，他從未停止過在他所質疑的同一個心理學領域中教學和研究。

當今的「批判心理學家們」（'critical psychologists'）也處在類似的矛盾中，寫著他們所在的學科的問題，但經常繼續在大學任教支領薪資，當這些心理專業人士面臨現實世界的解放鬥爭時，矛盾就突顯得非常尖銳。

心理治療

正是在這裡，我們心理／精神相關專業的第三個虛假朋友——*心理治療*（*psychotherapy*）進到了框架中，這是一種處理痛苦的方法，精神分析經常被與之混淆。精神分析之經常被混淆有很多理由，不只是因爲許多心理治療師借鑑佛洛伊德學說的各種版本，也因許多精神分析師出於策略性原因，在僱用他們的機構裡自稱爲心理治療師，有時也稱爲「精神分析心理治療師」（'psychoanalytic psychotherapists'）或「心理動力諮商師」（'psychodynamic counsellors'）；此外，混淆更被加深的原因是最基進的精神分析形式確實具有「療效」（'therapeutic effects'），然而，這些作用並不是精神分析臨床的目的，它的目的（正如我們已看到的）是一種解放，而不僅僅是一種適應性治療或在壓迫情境下的一絲緩解。

精神分析不是心理治療，儘管如此，它是具某種治療性（therapeutic）的。精神分析與心理治療的區別在於，精神分析處理的是主體的、世界的以及主體和這個世界相關聯的矛盾。因此，更重要的是要了解心理治療掩飾這個現實的矛盾本質的運作方式。是，就如同有一些「批判的精神科醫師」（'critical psychiatrists'）一樣，確實是有一些基進的心理治療師，但

如果他們眞的基進，那麼他們就會打破他們的心理治療實踐。今日踐行精神分析之不可能性是心理治療假裝安撫、假裝解決的一個問題。

　　心理治療技術很能爲資本主義發揮作用，因爲它自限於完成任務而沒能更多探問問題。在一個環繞異化進行組織結構的世界中應許治癒痛苦，這是「無結構暴政」的一個例子，這就是假裝沒有權力、沒有結構，是與那些遭受資本主義、種族主義、性別歧視和其他形式的壓迫而很合理地抱怨它的人立場相違而最爲有效的意識形態辯詞。

　　令人舒服安心地斷言沒有問題，這運作成一種暴政，堵住些尋求改變世界的人的嘴使其沉默；他們被告知不要擔心，因爲它已經改變了，一切都很好，唯一的問題是他們自己。心理治療是一種虛假的、表面的「後資本主義」（'post-capitalism'），因此，儘管心理治療專業人員心存善意，它經常破壞反資本主義的鬥爭，資本主義沒有結束，心理治療如此誤導我們。

　　異化、結構和權力的其他面向，這些是精神分析處遇關注的中心，經常被預設在心理治療的技術之中且被忽視。心理治療系統性地迴避了權力的問題，或者，如果它處理權力，它假裝將其消融在它自己的臨床形式所構建的想像的溝通關係中。這些對權力有情緒感受的態度正是那些最能使其發揮作用的態度，這些情緒感受必須在臨床的移情中被重新激活，這樣它們才能被精神分析修通和克服。

　　正如同精神分析是一種批判而非一種精神醫學和心理學的形式，精神分析也是或者應該是和心理治療（包括補充、吸收和中和無效化了精神分析概念的精神分析心理療法）截然相反。精神分析不是也不可能是一種心理治療，在由資本主義建立的環境下不存在適應、修復或治癒主體，它不接受這些條件，不被它們所制約，這也是爲什麼它不是也不能與精神醫學、心理學或心理治療相混淆的原因。

　　「基進的」心理治療師和諮商師通常和我們一樣對精神醫學和心理學持批評態度，關於我們說他們也在破壞反資本主義鬥爭的說法，他們會感到不高興，他們的不滿在一定程度上是有所本的。儘管我們已經對心理治療很嚴苛，但我們必須立即地、同時辯證地限定我們的論點。這些限定條件如下：

首先，我們全然願意承認精神分析本身是被妥協了，並不是每個精神分析師都是基進的，精神分析與對婦女的壓迫、種族主義的譏諷相勾連，更不用說還直接就參與在壓迫體制的酷刑裡。

其次，更關鍵的是，我們重申，精神分析是具有療效的，許多精神分析師也認為自己是心理治療師，這不是空穴來風。我們承認，一如我們宣稱這是解放運動的「批判心理學」那樣，我們可以輕鬆地（或者帶有困難地）去聲稱精神分析是「基進的心理治療」，那麼我們基進的心理治療朋友們將會需要徹底脫離自己所屬的心理／精神相關專業，就像批判心理學家們會需要脫雜他們的專業決裂那樣。

團體

正是帶著這樣的謹慎，我們轉向*團體*（*group*）心理治療的問題。團體心理治療──會心團體（encounter groups）[3] 和精神分析工作團體的形式、以及作為一種精神分析形式的團體分析，似乎已經運作成一種較為基進的治療性實踐。因為它更直接就是「集體的」（'collective'），通常被政治運動者們視為較為基進的，即使它的集體面仍然經常侷限於臨床空間以及固定時間的次數內和被視為「病人」（'patients'）的參與者作會談。在拉丁美洲的部分地區，團體工作方法時常被基進運動者，甚至由自稱馬克思主義者的人所帶領；而**團體分析** [4]（Group Analysis）是由歐洲的精神分析學家和社會理論家以關於精神的社會理論創立的，這個理論來由非常接近「批判理論」傳統的實務工作者所發展。

對我們來說，關鍵的問題是，精神分析原則的運用是否必然會減輕、再生產或加劇一個將痛苦個體化的社會中精神分析的問題。可以說，對精神分析臨床至關重要的自由聯想可能更加基進，因為團體「自由浮動討論」（'free floating discussion'）為許多人提供了貢獻和解釋正在發生

---

[3] 會心團體（encounter groups）是一群人，以組成團體的形式，透過在情感和社交層面上的直接交流，關注此時此地的感受和互動（而不是任何理論），以促進彼此建設性的洞察力、對自己與他人的敏感性，在群體中獲得個人與集體的成長。當中帶領的人扮演催化而非指導的作用。

[4] 這是該形式團體的專有名稱，加底線作私名號並黑體加粗表示。

的事情的機會。團體中的認同形式可以轉向「共鳴」（'resonance'）的方向，因此移情不會被導向分析師一個人，移情本身在團體中以不同的方式被經驗，因爲移情的多個相互矛盾的方面同時存在，以不同的方式呈現給團體的不同成員；參與分析的團體成員與其他人處理他們的痛苦，而不是與另一個人在私人空間中工作。畢竟，團體乃是一個「集體」（'collective'），治療的一部分是學會成爲集體而不是個體。

　　無論支持團體方法的論點有多好，它們都無法說服我們這些方法比「個人」精神分析更好；我們沒被說服並不是因爲我們特別懷疑**團體分析**和其他形式的團體心理治療，而是因爲我們對基進精神分析的視野並不是聚焦於個人，而是一個與集體性一樣豐富的主體形式，它已經座落於一個特定的身體中，精神分析總是在某種程度上已經是社會性的和政治性的。

　　雖然在精神分析臨床中我們說有一個人（一個分析主體），與另一個人（分析師）交談，但如果從治療的實際圖像中結論出這只是一種兩個人的個體間實踐，這是一種錯覺。透過移情，多個主體重現於臨床，並且在無意識的層面上，在分析主體的言語中激活了許多不同的主體位置，說話的不僅是分析主體的個人「意識自我」，而是某種超越他們的、一個以過去對他們重要的人們爲模型，充滿矛盾的主體性的無意識世界，他們正在與許多在移情中出現在他們面前的不同人物交談。分析主體被驅使從他們曾經做過的許多不同類型的主體之中去重複能指，它們將爲許多其他類型的主體在未來出現在治療中開闢可能性。因此，精神分析臨床的房間裡有超過兩個以上的人，這個基進的集體取向的精神分析名符其實地是一種團體，已經是「團體分析」最基進的形式了。

　　這對我們提出了一項基進的任務，其目標是使精神分析成爲眞正解放的東西，與解放運動結盟的東西，而不是精神分析心理治療的保守形式。這個基進的任務是一個辯證性的任務，它是雙重的：我們需要採取基進的團體 - 分析的理論，並在我們的臨床實踐中使其成爲眞正精神分析的；同時，我們需要使精神分析成爲眞正具集體性的，將其開放給人類存在的群體方面，並使它超越以達集體的主體性。

　　未來是集體的，透過集體鬥爭，我們將建立一個完全的社會性替代方案的世界，以替代我們每一個人現在在此遭受異化的個別存在。我們需要

在我們的鬥爭形式中預想那個世界，因此精神分析作為一種打破個人主義心理學所有律則的「批判心理學」形式，也需要在其實踐中預想這種將成為和未來相配的一種資源和驅動力量的主體性。

確實，許多精神分析體制性的實踐與我們在此宣言中所闡述的精神分析主體的集體願景背道而馳，但是這種集體願景曾經出現過，而且可能再次出現。近年來，由精神分析學家在拉丁美洲組建的「見證診所」（'testimonial clinics'）和「免費診所」（'free clinics'）承續了二次大戰前佛洛伊德免費診所在歐洲的基進過往，再一次地，正是過去包含有通向基進的未來的答案。我們必須做的是將當前的實踐及其所有矛盾轉化為一個變遷過渡的空間，一種在理論上和實踐上都面向轉變以超越資本主義、殖民主義和父權制的世界，這另一個世界就是我們所稱的「大同主義／共產主義」（'communism'）。

轉變：在世界中與在精神分析裡

精神分析的存在並不是來為我們所生活的悲慘世界效力。這就是為什麼它根本就不是也不應該假裝是一個心理／精神相關專業，不應該為了獲得地位和權力或認可和接受而與心理治療、心理學或精神醫學勾結合謀。精神分析有一種邊緣和過渡的面向，這意味著它從來沒有真正適應得好過，就像它所治療的人類主體一樣，精神分析是「非適應的」（'disadapted'），總是無法融入，而且挑戰著使它誕生的社會。我們需要透過接合解放運動來表達它對轉變的要求，以加強這種變遷過渡的狀態，以便它超越現在的狀態，成為它真正可以成為的樣子。

訴求

我們在此提出四項*訴求*（*demands*）：

作為我們的第一個訴求，我們堅持無意識不應被視為深藏於個體內部的黑洞，而是作為鬥爭的集體資源，不只如此，還是我們作為主體存在和行動的外部場所。這意味著嚴肅地採取對個體的意識自我的批判，我們必須超越我們每一個人，找到彼此。這個理論和實踐的資源已經在無意識

中、在我們隨身攜帶的歷史中、在過去鬥爭被埋藏的記憶中。這個深沉黑洞的形象充滿了種族主義意象，它背叛了黑人與原住民族的集體鬥爭，就像它背叛了婦女一樣，順從的存在表徵不能使她們免於被視爲無意識和歇斯底里抗議的神祕所在。我們的訴求是，任何人，不因其性別、種族或文化而被視爲無意識，或是與白人、男性和西方的理性意識自我的意識形成對比下的無意識。我們還要求無意識不再被以允許性別歧視或種族主義的譏諷漫畫圖像來想像。因此，這個訴求同時是一種女性主義和反種族主義的訴求，訴求我們不要再企圖殖民**無意識**（*unconscious*），而是允許它說話。

　　我們的第二個訴求明確指向臨床，指向精神分析的臨床實踐。臨床可以是一個裝置，一台製造「好公民」（'good citizens'）的機器，一樣地，它也可以是徹底瓦解資產階級、性別歧視和種族主義主體性的空間。它可以這樣與解放運動結盟，並幫助他們改變世界；但它也可以連結權力，並使任何解放態勢在個體裡消解而無效，也就是改變個體以致於不改變世界。作爲一台機器，臨床提供了一種工具，在這種工具中，推動人類行動的驅力可以很容易地轉變成一種重複，對那種主體性最糟糕之處的重複，是對它確認而非對它挑戰。因此，我們的第二個訴求是將臨床中的**重複**（*repetition*）視爲對不同的構建機會——是不同，而不是相同。

　　第三個訴求涉及驅力本身，它在身體中的位置乃座落於言語。我們需要從黑人女性主義吸取教訓，即沉默——驅力的靜默無聲，維持了壓迫，解放的第一步來自於對權力說眞話的意願。是的，這在臨床上是關係重大的，但我們的訴求直接指向精神分析師，要求他們在權力面前——在授予他們體制性權力、聲望和特權的權力面前，別再保持沉默。向言語中的反思和轉變的**驅力**（*drive*）說「是」，對分析師必須「中立」（'neutral'）或「客觀」或者假裝他們在政治進程中必須得是一個沉默的夥伴的這種觀念說「不」予以衝擊。發聲反對權力濫用，包括精神分析師和其他心理／精神相關專業人士的權力濫用。

　　第四，回到臨床，一個批判與訴求是——臨床意義上的**移情**（*transference*）並不是被用來作爲一種模式，不是藉由精神分析把它「應用」（'applied'）到他們不理解也無法理解的社會活動領域；別假裝你能告訴我們在

解放運動中我們的鬥爭真正意味著什麼，把這假裝給丟掉，認真對待你自己的精神分析臨床實踐的關鍵功課——分析主體才是作解釋的人，不是分析師；移情在臨床中精確地作為權力的中繼而被創建，因此它可以再次被解除，並且，當精神分析師聲稱要說話而不是解放運動時，必須盡一切努力解除他們的權力。

正如我們已經明確指出的，為了服務於解放運動，精神分析必須與精神醫學、心理學和心理治療明確區分開來。「心理／精神相關專業複合體」（'psy complex'），也就是有關在資本主義和父權制下使權力正當化並加以強化的人類主體理論與實踐的密集網絡，它的這三個要素[5]，現在被一起交織進「心理學化」（'psychologisation'）的全球意識形態過程中，這是以犧牲政治、社會和文化這些我們可彼此相遇以動員和解放我們自身之地為代價的心理學擴張。心理學化，以其互異矛盾的面向，將最為多樣的文化、社會和政治現象簡化為心理機制，使我們相信我們每一個人即一個個體，應該為造成和解決這個世界普遍的痛苦負責。

只有集體才能使我們自由，我們必須保護解放運動避免它們被心理學化，我們不應該給它們更多套著精神分析外衣的心理學，我們也不應該忘記已變成了心理學的精神分析在日常生活的心理學化（包括政治性抵抗的心理學化）扮演著同謀的角色。

為了服務於解放運動，精神分析不應成為心理學化的手段。它不應該藉著將政治化約為心理、人格或主體的內在世界、他們的本能、他們的情結、他們的幻想或他們的病理，從而使政治去政治化；精神分析也不應該將社會的責任直接輸送到個人身上，或者提供一個個人化的無結構和能夠改變一切的浪漫而不切實際的圖像。

自由

我們並不承諾完全的*自由*（freedom），對精神分析作那樣的宣稱是欺騙人的，就像那些想像革命之後會有一個沒有衝突的天堂、或者地球上每件事都像是個樂園的人一樣都是欺騙人的，精神分析只能藉由幫助我們

---

[5] 指前述的重複、驅力和移情。

覺察到阻礙我們獲得自由的原因來進行解放，這種覺察是精神分析方法的直接目標；例如，它的自由聯想，其基本技術原則旨在讓分析主體清楚他們沒法說出的內容，而不是製造他們可以自由說出一切的錯覺。

我們被邀請在臨床裡遵循著自由聯想的準則也意味著政治的欲望，我們在臨床中談論欲望以使我們可以在外面談論它，不是為了讓我們在日常生活中持續隨身攜帶臨床到處傳福音，而是為了我們可以超越它、超越臨床，進入政治；政治領域是精神分析能夠成功結束的唯一領域，並且，在不假裝完全結束的情形下，它也是透過其他方法持續進行批判性分析工作的辯證方式。

精神分析的主體就是政治性的主體，不是被鎖在我們裡面孤立個體，而是我們每個人與他人一起工作，嵌入我們透過與他人接觸而發現我們自己的過程中，無意識就在這裡，它只能是政治性的，這是精神分析的地平線。

對無意識的探索將我們引向政治，這種基進的政治化歷程是心理學化的對立面，它使用精神分析治療來實現對精神分析治療的辯證「揚棄」（dialectical 'sublation'）──即真正地落實執行它而將它拋掉、用它乃為了超越它。從技術面來理解，這也是我們需要導入精神分析以使其基進化的技術含義。揚棄，乃指涉改善和超越既定的事物狀態，同時取消那些使這種狀態不可能的事物；以這同樣的方式，精神分析治療之不可能性能夠在解放運動中被克服。

這種對精神分析辯證揚棄需要在臨床內與臨床外的發生之間建立緊密的聯繫；只有這樣，我們才能彌補其他適應性心理／精神相關的治療所做的虛假承諾的缺陷。這也是精神分析治療如何能帶我們擺脫它、引導我們走入世界，從而證明它存在的合法性的方式；精神分析只有在它讓我們超越它本身時才有意義。

這種「批判心理學」最基進的目標不是將精神分析固定在原來的位置上，而是將其拋入過去，廢除使其運作的社會條件，轉化需要精神分析治療的主體形式。其倫理政治的推動力在於，另一個世界是可能的，這是一個我們自由相互聯繫的世界，在這個世界中，每個人的自由發展是所有人的自由發展的條件。我們的目標是建立一個精神分析是可能但不必要的世界。

SUBJECTIVE TRANSFORMATION: TIME FOR UNDERSTANDING AND MOMENTS FOR ACTION

We live in a world that is now structured like a gigantic globalised market-place, one that has given rise to forms of psychoanalytic theory and practice that are themselves privatized, commodified, turned into an expensive private treatment available to a limited few, only to those who can afford it. This should not surprise us in a capitalist society where every theory and practice of liberation has, at one moment or another, been turned into an academic commodity, distorted and turned against the social movements. Just as we need to rescue various currents of critical thinking from their confinement in universities and bookshops, so it is also necessary to remember what psychoanalysis was at its origins, to grasp what is true about it and not to let those with power rob us of its liberating potential as critical psychology.

We live in a world where psychoanalysis is necessary but impossible. It is usually realized in such a way that it is impoverished and disfigured to the point of being reversed. In the end it is then much less and even the opposite of what it could have been. Instead of being a revolutionary theory and practice, it is reduced to being an adaptive technique. Furthermore, it is confined to the individual and degenerates into a private practice marked by its conservatism, a relay point for reactionary ideas about sex and gender and much more.

In present-day privatised conservative forms of psychoanalysis, the four key phenomena we have described in this manifesto are distorted, turned into obstacles instead of opportunities. The unconscious, the unspoken ground of our collective being, is alienated in such a way as to turn into a threat and to privilege individual conscious instrumental reason. Our capacity to repeat action in different contexts with different results is turned from being a source of reflective freedom into the neurotic prison of the repetition compulsion. What drives us in our creative lives is turned against us in a machine-like force, subjecting us to the death drive. And transference is isolated in the clinic and, instead of showing us how social power works, is turned into a model for dependent relationships in the outside world. All of this has absolutely nothing to do with psychoanalysis. It does not display its reality, but only its impossibility.

The conditions of impossibility of psychoanalysis, in fact, are not only intrinsic; they lie not only inside it, in its disfigurements and inversions. Even disfigured and inverted, psychoanalysis is impossible for those who lack the financial resources to pay for it, for those who must work all the time and do not have even a few minutes to think about desire and for those who suffer from alienation that makes them disinterested in their existence and in their discontent in civilization.

More than that, psychoanalytic treatment is also somehow impossible for those who can easily buy it, consume it and in the end discard it just like another commodity, like any other luxury item, like a hobby among others, such as tennis, golf, yacht, yoga, Feng shui, charity, and art collections. And psychoanalysis is also made impossible, finally, for many people, particularly by those in liberation movements, whose sensitivity prevents them from accepting the commodification of the practice of someone trained and paid for listening to alienated speech and the fetish for payment elaborated as self-justification for the exercise of professional expertise, symbolic status and power.

Our task in this manifesto for psychoanalysis as the most radical possible form of 'critical psychology' is precisely to make it possible for liberation movements. More precisely, our task is to locate psychoanalytic practice in history so that we might connect it with the necessary progressive work of the liberation movements, and to combat the false futures promised by the adaptive psy professions. We need to treat psychoanalysis in the clinic as a transitional space, and turn psychoanalysis towards human liberation; instead of being an attempt to insert individuals back into this wretched society, we need to turn it into a conceptual and practical transition to communism. Part of that task is to retrieve from past struggles around subjectivity the historically progressive theory and practice of psychoanalysts who did concern themselves with misery precisely because many of them wanted to change the world.

History and revolutionary time

Psychoanalysis is at the edge of the psy professions, and often confused with psychiatry, psychology and psychotherapy by many people searching for answers, for the reasons for their distress and a way out. Psychoanalysis is actually something radically different. It is not actually a psy profession at all, but potentially a theory and practice of liberation. This means that it is crucial that we differentiate radical psychoanalysis allied with the liberation movements from psychiatric psychoanalysis, psychological psychoanalysis and psychotherapeutic psychoanalysis.

The best way of differentiating it from those false friends is through historical analysis. This analysis is, moreover, consistent with psychoanalytic radicalism. As we will see, authentic radical psychoanalysis is itself a form of historical analysis that turns to the past precisely to be able to orient us individually and collectively to the future.

We must include in our psychoanalytic work sustained focus on the repressed historical memory of our practice, on the radical history of the Freudian left, on the alliances of psychoanalysis with the socialist movement. We cannot forget the revolutionary pedagogical experiences of Marxist and Freudian inspiration in Austria and in the Soviet Union, the contribution of psychoanalysis to the Western cultural-political uprisings allied with the anti-colonial revolution in Indo-China in the second half of the twentieth century, and the commitment and persecution of psychoanalysts in Argentina and other countries. We must remember the free psychoanalytic clinics in continental Europe and acknowledge the free psychoanalysis offered now in the streets and public squares of Brazil. We must enable transference to operate again as something authentically psychoanalytic rather than as a manifestation of dependence induced by payment to one who pretends to know what we think we know what lies inside the unconscious.

These movements were, unsurprisingly, also accompanied by the so-called 'anti-psychiatry' movement. This was because many radicals recognised that psychiatry was a practice of medical mastery that turned people into patients, slaves of the mind-doctors in the old asylums, subjecting them to confinement and atrocious physical treatments. Psychiatry was attacked, quite rightly, because it was an obviously brutalising practice. Even though modern psychiatry looked to chemical cures in order to adapt people to capitalism, it actually continued a discourse and practice of feudal pre-capitalist masters. These kind of autocratic masters adapted themselves to capitalism while repeating the worst classical patriarchal sexist abuse of women and colonial racist persecution of indigenous people.

Psychiatry was a powerful tool in their arsenal. Psychiatrists were unscrupulous about putting themselves at the service of those who dominated, pathologizing people for their class, race, culture, gender or political position, torturing them and experimenting with them. When Freud, a psychiatrist, invented psychoanalysis, he had to break from psychiatry. That was a significant historical break that has to be repeated again and again to be effective today in anti-capitalist, feminist and anti-colonial struggle.

Psychiatry develops thanks to the impossibility of psychoanalysis. This impossibility is covered over and replicated in the medical psychiatric reframing of treatment in which different aspects of our distress are separated into discrete elements specified as different kinds of pathology. Medical and psychiatric diagnosis divides us by enclosing each one in their illness and by making us forget the common origin of what happens to us in this society. We are made ill by this political-economic system, by capitalism, patriarchy and colonialism. This sad world where we have no choice but to live today is now what we suffer when we become depressed or distressed, when we feel empty or persecuted, when we hear voices that others do not hear, when we are not able to work or concentrate on anything or relate in a progressive constructive way to others.

Illness

We need to treat our *illness* as a symptom of the lives we lead, not as indications of personal pathology. This kind of distress, however severe, is very different from the real physical problems that medical doctors treat. We are not the problem. Our 'illness' – and we borrow the term here as a metaphor for our distress – is only a sign and can also be a remedy against the real problem.

We need to turn this illness of the subject into a weapon, to speak of it as a weapon against power, to work through it as we speak of our desire for another world and act collectively on that desire. This is what psychoanalysis would make possible if it had not become impossible itself, if it had not degraded as much as it has, if it had not become another instrument of suggestion, ideologization, evasion of the world, seclusion in individuality, psychologization, psychopathologization, avoidance of conflict, adaptation and regulation at the service of the social reproduction of the existing world. In fact, it is psychoanalysis that, of all the psy approaches to subjectivity, is best able to appreciate the role of 'social reproduction' in the material replication of colonial and familial structures in the service of capital.

The impossibility of psychoanalysis in these conditions of pervasive racism, heterosexism and repetitive demeaning of those excluded from power is intensified by the reduction of distress to the level of individual. The individual sphere, increasingly impotent, poor and narrow, gathers force on the collective field and ends up becoming the place where all the negative effects caused in our subjectivity by the capitalist process of oppression and destruction must be resolved. Here, though, diverse forms of psychology, including forms of psychoanalytic psychology, operate alongside medical psychiatric psychoanalysis.

It is true that psychiatry is often rejected by psychologists who consider themselves to be more empathetic, sensitive, thoughtful and respectful of the human being than psychiatrists, and who are quite aware of the complicity between medicine and capitalism, as evidenced, for example, in the power of the pharmaceutical industry and in the fulfilment of the task of rehabilitation of the workforce by chemical means. Psychology then pretends to replace psychiatry which operated as a more obvious replicator of pre-capitalist relations of professional mastery and servitude in which those who suffer are treated as 'patients'. But this more modern psychology, which then arrogates to itself psychoanalytic theory the better to inform quick adaptive cognitive-behavioural treatments, thereby replicates capitalism as such by serving it with greater efficiency and speed, by adapting us to it, by making it bearable, by preventing it from being disturbed by our illness, by rehabilitating us as workers and consumers.

Work and consumption, which are the main functions of the human being for the production and realization of capital, should not necessarily be enabled by psychoanalysis, whose subject is not that of capitalism. Not everyone needs to work all the time or to shop as a form of leisure. The subject that best suits capital is that of psychology, the more or less adapted and apparently free individual, the one who controls themselves, the best worker and consumer.

This 'healthy' subject of psychology is the symmetrical and inverse ideal reflection of the 'sick' subject in psychiatry. It is from the 'disease', by denying and mystifying the truth revealed by the disease, that 'health', a kind of normality, the pathological normality of capitalism is conceived. This is why psychologists so often defer to psychiatrists as their real masters, and why psychological versions of psychoanalysis are as dangerous as psychiatric versions.

The subject of psychiatric pre-capitalist psychoanalysis, psychoanalysis harnessed to psychiatry, and capitalist psychological psychoanalysis, the adaptive version that is touted in the textbooks as a theory of mind and behaviour, is reduced to the alienated separate body or to the individual mind. In contrast, the subject of radical psychoanalysis, of psychoanalysis that is neither psychologized nor psychiatrized, is precisely the one which cannot be reduced to a mental or bodily existence. Our subject, the human subject, is not the alienated object of capitalist society, still less the slave-object treated by quasi-feudal colonial psychiatrists.

Our subject, as a *subject*, is externally related to these objects, to their alienation, to the mind and the body, to capitalism and colonialism. Our subject can be anti-capitalist and anti-colonial, and expresses its potential in the truth it speaks to power and potentially for a post-capitalist mode of being. It is that potential that is rendered almost impossible by current apparatuses of power. But history can also be made to speak, whether it is the history of the individual subject inside the clinic or the history of struggle that exposes the role of the psy professions in replicating instead of challenging power.

False futures promised by the therapeutic psy professions

Psychiatry promises to cure what it calls 'mental illness' and psychology promises to treat maladaptive thoughts and behaviour. Their practitioners who are trained in alienating practices, often struggle to find a voice for the oppressed, and some of those practitioners, such as those of the 'anti-psychiatry' movement half a century ago and of 'critical psychology' of the present-day, break from their discipline to join liberation movements.

One only has to think of the revolutionary psychiatrist Frantz Fanon who, when he joined the Algerian anti-colonial war after writing about white racism, continued working as a doctor with reactionary physical treatments of what he still thought of as 'mental illness', but then eventually put his energies full-time into liberation. Another striking case is that of Ignacio Martin-Baro, who criticized the psychological theories and practices of his time, proposing an alternative a 'liberation psychology' and fighting for the emancipation of Latin American peoples, especially the Salvadoran people, for which he was finally killed by an army death squad. It must be said that Martin-Baro sometimes used traditional psychological methods in his struggle, such as opinion polls, and he never stopped teaching and researching in the same field of psychology that he questioned.

Present-day 'critical psychologists' are caught in a similar contradiction, writing about the problems with their host discipline, but often continuing to be paid to teach in universities. The contradictions are brutally stark when these psy professionals are faced with real-world struggles for liberation.

Psychotherapy

It is here that our third false friend of the psy professions, *psychotherapy*, comes into the frame, an approach to distress with which psychoanalysis is often confused, and for good reasons because not only do many psychotherapists draw on versions of Freudian theory, but also many psychoanalysts for strategic reasons in the institutions that employ them call themselves psychotherapists, sometimes 'psychoanalytic psychotherapists' or 'psychodynamic counsellors'. The confusion is all the deeper because, in addition, it is true that the most radical forms of psychoanalysis do indeed have 'therapeutic effects'. These effects, however, are not the purpose of the psychoanalytic clinic. Its purpose, as we have seen, is a form of liberation and not simply an adaptive cure or a relief from conditions of oppression.

Psychoanalysis is not psychotherapy, but there is, nonetheless, something therapeutic about it. The difference between psychoanalysis and psychotherapy is that psychoanalysis deals with the contradictions of the subject, the world, and the subject in relation to the world. It is all the more important, then, to understand the way psychotherapy operates to smooth over the contradictory nature of this reality. Yes, it is true that there are some radical psychotherapists, just as there are some 'critical psychiatrists', but if they are really radical then they break in their practice from psychotherapy as such. The impossibility of conducting psychoanalysis today is one that psychotherapy pretends to salve, a problem it pretends to solve.

The psychotherapeutic technique can be functional for capitalism because it limits itself to fulfilling its task without asking more questions. It is an instance of the 'tyranny of structurelessness', promising a cure for distress in a world that is structurally-organised around alienation. That is, the pretence that there is no power, no structure, is the most effective ideological argument against those who suffer capitalism, racism, sexism and other forms of oppression, and quite rightly, complain about it.

The comforting reassuring insistence that there is no problem operates as a form of tyranny, silencing those who seek to change the world; they are told not to worry because it has already changed, is already all good, and the only problem is themselves. Psychotherapy is a fake, semblance of 'post-capitalism' and so, despite the best wishes of its practitioners in the psy professions, it often sabotages anti-capitalist struggle. Capitalism is not over, and so psychotherapy misleads us.

Alienation, structure and the other dimensions of power, which are at the centre of attention of psychoanalytic treatment, are usually presupposed and overlooked in psychotherapeutic techniques. Psychotherapy systematically evades the question of power, or, if it addresses power, it pretends to dissolve it in imaginary communicative relationships it constructs in its own form of clinic. These sentimental attitudes towards power are precisely those that best allow its exercise, sentiments that must be reactivated in transference in the clinic precisely so they can be worked through, overcome by psychoanalysis.

Just as psychoanalysis is a critique rather than a form of psychiatry and psychology, psychoanalysis is also, or should be, the diametric opposite of psychotherapy, including psychoanalytic psychotherapy which recuperates, absorbs and neutralises psychoanalytic notions. Psychoanalysis is not and cannot be a kind of psychotherapy. It does not exist to adapt or rehabilitate or cure the subject under the conditions established by capitalism. It cannot accept these conditions. It cannot be conditioned by them. This is also why it is not and cannot be confused with psychiatry, psychology or psychotherapy.

'Radical' psychotherapists and counsellors, who are often as critical of psychiatry and psychology as we are, will be unhappy with our claim that they too sabotage anti-capitalist struggle. And to a certain degree their discontent will be well founded. Although we have been harsh on psychotherapy, we must immediately, and dialectically, qualify our argument. The caveats are these.

First, that we readily acknowledge that psychoanalysis is itself compromised. Not every psychoanalyst is radical, and psychoanalysis has colluded with the oppression of women, with racist caricature, not to mention directly in torture for repressive regimes.

Second, more crucially, we repeat, psychoanalysis has therapeutic effects; it is not for nothing that many psychoanalysts also consider themselves to be psychotherapists. We admit that we could just as easily, or with difficulty, make the claim that psychoanalysis is 'radical psychotherapy' as we do that it is 'critical psychology' for liberation movements. Our radical psychotherapeutic friends would then need to break as thoroughly from their own host psy profession as critical psychologists will need to break from theirs.

Groups

It is with that caution that we turn to the question of *group* psychotherapy which, in the form of encounter groups and psychoanalytic work groups, and group analysis as a form of psychoanalysis, does appear to already operate as a more radical therapeutic practice. It is often viewed as more radical by political activists because it is more immediately 'collective', even if its collective aspect is still often confined to the space of the clinic and to sessions at a fixed time with participants who are treated as 'patients'. Group approaches have often been led by radicals, even by self-proclaimed Marxists, in parts of Latin America, and Group Analysis was founded by psychoanalysts and social theorists in Europe with a social theory of the psyche, by those practitioners who were very close to the 'critical theory' tradition.

The critical question for us is whether the exercise of psychoanalytic principles in groups necessarily mitigates or reproduces or exacerbates the problems of psychoanalysis in a society that individualises pain. It could be claimed that the kind of free association that is crucial to the psychoanalytic clinic is potentially more radical because group 'free floating discussion' gives the opportunity for many people to contribute and interpret what is going on. Forms of identification in groups can be turned in the direction of 'resonance' and so the transference is not channelled towards one figure, the analyst. Transference itself is experienced in a different way in groups because the multiple contradictory aspects of transference are present at the same time, present in different ways to different members of the group. Members of the analytic group work through their distress with other people rather than in a private space with one other person. After all, the group is thus a 'collective', and part of the cure is to learn to be collective rather than to be individual.

No matter how good arguments there are in favour of group approaches, they fail to convince us that these approaches are better than 'individual' psychoanalysis. We are not convinced, not because we are particularly suspicious of Group Analysis and other forms of group psychotherapy, but because our vision of radical psychoanalysis is not of it as focused on the individual, but on a form of subject that is as much collective as it is already located in one particular body. Psychoanalysis is always already in some way social and political.

We claim that although in the psychoanalytic clinic there is one person, an analysand, speaking to another, to the analyst, it is an illusion to conclude from that empirical image of the treatment that this is simply a two-body inter-individual practice. There are multiple subjects brought to life in the clinic through transference, and at an unconscious level many different subject positions activated in the speech of the analysand. It is not only the individual 'ego' of the analysand who speaks, but something beyond them, an unconscious world of contradictory subjectivities that are modelled on people who have been significant to them in their past, and they are speaking to many different figures who are present to them in the transference. The analysand is driven to repeat signifiers from the many different kinds of subject they have been, and they will open up possibilities for many other kinds of subjects to appear in the future, in the cure. There are therefore more than two people in the room in a psychoanalytic clinic; radical collectively-oriented psychoanalysis worth the name is a kind of group, already the most radical form of 'Group Analysis'.

This poses a radical task for us, which runs alongside the aim to make psychoanalysis something genuinely liberating, something allied to the liberation movements, rather than a conservative form of psychoanalytic psychotherapy. This radical task is a dialectical task. It is two-fold: we need to take group-analytic theory, which is radical, and make it genuinely psychoanalytic in our practice in the clinic; and we need to make psychoanalysis genuinely collective, opening it up to the group aspect of human existence, and taking it beyond that to collective subjectivity.

The future is collective, and it is through collective struggle that we will build a world that is a fully social alternative to the alienated individual existence that each of us suffers here now. We need to anticipate that world in our forms of struggle, and so psychoanalysis as a form of 'critical psychology' that breaks from all of the precepts of individualistic psychology also needs to anticipate in its practice the kind of subjectivity that will be a resource and driving force suited to that future.

It is true that the institutional practice of much psychoanalysis runs against the collective vision of the psychoanalytic subject that we have been elaborating in this manifesto. But there was once that collective vision, and there can be again. The 'testimonial clinics' and 'free clinics' that have been formed by psychoanalysts in recent years in Latin America redeem the radical past of Freud's free clinics in Europe before the Second World War. Again, it is the past that contains the keys to a radical future. What we must do is to turn present-day practice, with all of its contradictions into a transitional space, a practice that is geared theoretically and practically to the transition to a world beyond capitalism and colonialism and patriarchy. This other world is what we call 'communism'.

Transitions, in the world and in psychoanalysis

Psychoanalysis does not exist to serve the miserable world in which we live. That is why it is not really a psy profession at all and should not pretend to be, should not collude with psychotherapy, psychology or psychiatry in order to have status and power or recognition and acceptance. There is a marginal and transitional aspect to psychoanalysis that means that it has never really been well-adapted. Like the human subject it treats, psychoanalysis is 'dis-adapted', always failing to fit in, and challenging the society into which it was born. We need to intensify this transitional status with transitional demands of it articulated in alliance with liberation movements so that it is brought beyond what it is now, made what it truly can be.

Demands

Here we articulate four *demands*.

We insist, as our first demand, that the unconscious not be treated as a deep dark pit inside the individual, but as a collective resource for struggle and, more than that, the external place where we will have existed and acted as subjects. This means taking seriously the critique of the individual ego. We have to go beyond each one of us and find each other. The theoretical and practical resources for this are already in the unconscious, in the history that we carry with us, the buried memory of past struggles. This image of the deep dark pit is filled with racist imagery, and it betrays the collective struggle of black and indigenous people, as it does of women whose representation as obedient beings has not prevented them from being seen also as mysterious sites of unconsciousness and hysterical protest. Our demand is that no one, neither by gender nor by race nor by culture, be seen as unconscious or as the unconscious in contrast to the consciousness of the white, masculine and western ego. We also demand that the unconscious cease to be conceived in such a way as to allow sexist or racist caricatures. So this demand is simultaneously a feminist and anti-racist demand, a demand that we do not keep attempting to colonise the *uncon-*

scious, but instead to allow it to speak.

Our second demand is directed explicitly to the clinic, to the clinical practice of psychoanalysis. The clinic can be an apparatus, a machine for the production of 'good citizens', as much as it can be the space for the radical unravelling of bourgeois, sexist and racist subjectivity. In this way it can ally with liberation movements and help them change the world, but it can also ally with power and neutralize any liberating gesture in the individual, changing the individual so as not to change the world. As a machine the clinic provides an instrument in which the drive that powers human action can too-easily be turned into a repetition of what is worst about that subjectivity, confirming it rather than challenging it. So, our second demand is that *repetition* in the clinic be treated as the opportunity for the construction of difference, something different rather than the same.

The third demand concerns the drive as such, and its place in the body as location of speech. We need to learn the lessons from Black feminism that it is silence that maintains oppression, a mute silence of the drive, and that the first step to liberation comes from willingness to speak truth to power. Yes, this is relevant in the clinic, but our demand is directed to psychoanalysts that they do not remain silent in the face of the power that accords them institutional power, prestige and privilege. Yes to the *drive* in speech, reflected upon and transformed. No to collusion with the idea that the analyst must be 'neutral' or 'objective' or pretend that they must be a silent partner in the political process. Speak out against abuse of power, including the abuse of power by psychoanalysts as well as other psy professionals.

Fourth, back to the clinic, to a critique and demand that *transference* in a clinical sense is not used as a model, not 'applied' by psychoanalysis to domains of social activity that they do not and cannot understand. Drop the pretence that you can tell us in the liberation movements what our struggle really means. Take seriously the key lesson from your own clinical practice of psychoanalysis, which is that it is the analysand who interprets, not the analyst. Transference is created in the clinic as a relay of power precisely so it can be undone again, and all efforts must be made to undo the power of the psychoanalyst when they are claiming to speak instead of the liberation movements.

As we have already made clear, in order to serve the liberation movements, psychoanalysis must clearly demarcate itself from psychiatry, psychology and psychotherapy. These three elements of the 'psy complex', the dense network of theories and practices about the human subject that warrants and reinforces power under capitalism and patriarchy, are now woven together in the global ideological process of 'psychologisation', expansion of the psychological at the expense of politics, society and culture, which are the places where we can meet each other to mobilize and liberate ourselves. Psychologisation, in its different competing contradictory aspects, reduces the most diverse cultural, social and political phenomena to psychological mechanisms, making us believe that each of us, as an individual, is responsible for causing and solving the distress endemic in this world.

Only collectively can we free ourselves. We must protect liberation movements from psychologization. We should not give them more psychology concealed under a psychoanalytic veneer. Nor should we forget that psychoanalysis, turned into psychology, has played a role complicit with the psychologisation of everyday life, including the psychologisation of political resistance.

To serve the liberation movements, psychoanalysis should not be a means to psychologize. It should not depoliticize the political by reducing it to the psychological, to the personality or to the inner world of the subjects, to their instincts, their complexes, their fantasy or their pathology. Nor should psychoanalysis funnel the responsibility of society into the individual or offer the romantic unrealistic image of an individual free of structures and capable of changing everything.

Freedom

We cannot promise total *freedom*. Such a claim made for psychoanalysis would be as fraudulent as those who imagine that there is a heaven without conflict or that everything will be like paradise on earth after revolution. Psychoanalysis can only be liberating by helping us to be aware of what prevents us from being free. This awareness is an immediate objective of the psychoanalytic method. Its fundamental technical rule of free association, for instance, is designed to make evident to the analysands what they cannot speak of, rather than produce the illusion that they could ever be free to say everything.

The rule of free association we are invited to follow inside the clinic also speaks of political desire. We speak about desire in the clinic so that we may speak about it outside, not so that we continue to carry the clinic around with us in everyday life, evangelising about it, but so that we can transcend it, move beyond the clinic, into politics. The field of politics is the only one in which psychoanalysis can end successfully, and also, without pretending to ever completely end, be a dialectical way of continuing critical analytic work by other means.

The subject of psychoanalysis is the one of politics. It is not the isolated individual, locked inside us, but each one of us working with others, inserted into who we are finding out who we are through our engagement with others. Here is the unconscious that can only be politics. This is the horizon of psychoanalysis.

The exploration of the unconscious leads us to politics. This radical process of politicization is the opposite of psychologization and makes use of psychoanalytical treatment in order to achieve the dialectical 'sublation' of it, leaving it behind while actually carrying it out; with it in order to transcend it. Technically understood, and this is a technical meaning that we need to import into psychoanalysis in order to radicalise it, sublation refers to a process that improves and transcends a given state of affairs while simultaneously cancelling out what it was that made what was offered by that state of affairs impossible. It is in the same way that the impossibility of psychoanalytic treatment can be overcome in liberation movements.

Such dialectical sublation of psychoanalysis requires an intimate link between what happens inside the clinic and what happens outside it, and then, only then, can we redeem the false promises made by other adaptive psy treatments. This is also how psychoanalytic treatment can take us out of it, lead us into the world and thus justify its existence. Psychoanalysis only makes sense when it takes us beyond it as such.

The most radical aim of this 'critical psychology' is not to keep psychoanalysis in place, but to relegate it to the past, to abolish the social conditions that have made it operate, to transform forms of subjectivity that call for psychoanalytic treatment. The ethical-political impulse is that another world is possible, a world in which we freely associate with each other and in which the free development of each is the condition for the free development of all. We aim to build a world in which psychoanalysis is possible but unnecessary.

背景閱讀

我們刻意避免列參考書目，以避免使我們的宣言被分解成學術性討論的形式，但我們必須承認我們感謝對我們指導和啟發的作者們，有很多人，在此無法全部提及，謹將我們擬定本宣言引用到的一些文本列於下面作爲參考，您會發現其中的許多想法都已被納入並作了修改。

精神分析

總地來說，這份宣言談到精神分析，而我們的工作受到了一些基進傳統的影響。當然，我們談論西格蒙德・佛洛伊德，並討論他的文本像是《無意識》（*The Unconscious*）、《超越快樂原則》（*Beyond the Pleasure Principle*）、《自我與本我》（*The Ego and the Id*）以及《文明及其不滿》（*Civilization and its Discontents*）等裡面的許多思想。佛洛伊德的思想是任何保守的或基進的精神分析工作的核心。有許多精神分析的「導論」具有誤導性，某幾個實例甚至是完全錯誤，明確地值得信賴的一本導論是歐克塔夫・曼諾尼（Octave Mannoni）的《佛洛伊德：無意識理論》（*Freud: Theory of the Unconsciou*s）。

對我們很重要的基進傳統包括圍繞著佛洛伊德的第一波批判性著作的精神分析學家，他們是他的追隨者也是馬克思主義者。我們特別從威廉・賴希（Wilhelm Reich）的工作中了解到他爲共產主義和性解放而戰，這導致他被國際精神分析協會和共產黨都開除。賴希試圖用佛洛伊德的理論來理解心理的社會意識形態根源，以及資本主義社會的性壓抑，還有這種壓抑透過資產階級核心家庭傳遞到個人的方式，見諸《辯證唯物主義與精

神分析》（*Dialectical Materialism and Psychoanalysis*）和《法西斯主義的
群眾心理學》（*The Mass Psychology of Fascism*）。

　　我們也非常喜歡埃里希・弗洛姆（Erich Fromm）的著作，他是一位
深受馬克思影響的人文主義精神分析學家和社會主義者。弗洛姆強調資本
主義告訴我們應該關注「擁有」事物的方式，但這會使我們失去人性，使
我們與人性疏遠，相反地，要眞正快樂，我們應該關注「存在」；這在他
的著作《健全的社會》（*The Sane Society*）和《人類的破壞性解剖》（*The
Anatomy of Human Destructivenes*s）中都有探討。

　　我們的另一位重要作家是赫伯特・馬爾庫塞（Herbert Marcuse），他
是 1960 年代和 1970 年代解放運動的重要人物，在他的《愛欲與文明》
（*Eros and Civilization*）和《單向度的人》（*One-Dimensional Man*）一書
中，馬爾庫塞教我們意識到當代社會中某些自由形式的壓制性面向，他還
幫助我們區分了爲文化服務的壓抑和爲資本主義下的壓迫和剝削服務的剩
餘壓抑。

　　後期延續這種基進工作傳統的精神分析師包括瑪麗・蘭格（Marie
Langer）和喬爾・科維爾（Joel Kovel）。蘭格在她生命的盡頭堅持繼續
成爲一名精神分析師，而不放棄她對解放運動的參與，正如她在她的文本
《精神分析和／或社會革命》（*Psychoanalysis and/or Social Revolution*）
中所解釋的那樣。科維爾在諸如《欲望時代》（*The Age of Desire*）等書
中以受到資本主義影響的生活描述了資本主義脈絡下的臨床工作。科維爾
不再從事精神分析師的工作，而是以「生態社會主義者」的身分全職參與
馬克思主義和生態政治，而蘭格則幫助拉丁美洲精神分析的再政治化。

　　所謂的「佛洛伊德－馬克思主義」的問題在於，它有時相當化約，傾
向於視階級結構爲個人的性格結構的直接複製，並傾向於將性欲如同資產
階級社會的傳統理解視爲一種對自由的直接體驗的力量。這在賴希那兒尤
爲明顯，在弗洛姆、科維爾和蘭格那邊的程度稍小些，而這是馬爾庫塞已
經討論過的觀點和問題。斯蒂芬・弗羅什（Stephen Frosh）的《精神分析
的政治：佛洛伊德和後佛洛伊德理論導論》（*The Politics of Psychoanaly-
sis: An Introduction to Freudian and Post-Freudian Theory*）對這些不同的傳
統進行了出色的概述；另外，在伊麗莎白・丹托（Elizabeth Danto）的《佛

洛伊德的免費臨床：精神分析和社會正義，1918-1938》（*Freud's Free Clinics: Psychoanalysis and Social Justice, 1918-1938*）一書中，對在歐洲法西斯主義興起之前，精神分析作為一種為所有人而非為私人利益的福利實踐發展方式，進行了非常鼓舞人心的解說。

　　對我們影響最大但我們也有所批判的工作傳統是雅克・拉岡——一個與國際精神分析協會決裂的精神分析師，他建立了自己的學派來培訓分析師。拉岡將注意力從生物力量和性格發展的生物學關聯階段轉移到語言上，透過象徵而組織的語言不僅僅是一種溝通的媒介，一如我們在本書中所解釋的那樣，它是我們占據我們的位置的結構、是圍繞我們的外部性、它對我們來說是「大寫它／他者（'Other'）」。我們讚賞拉岡派的精神分析師們在實踐歷史中的批判性著作，例如克里斯蒂安・鄧克爾（Christian Dunker）的著作《精神分析臨床的結構和組成：當代實踐中的負面性與衝突》（*The Structure and Constitution of the Psychoanalytic Clinic: Negativity and Conflict in Contemporary Practice*）；以及在薩摩・托姆西奇（Samo Tomšič）的著作《資本主義無意識》（*The Capitalist Unconscious*）中將拉岡與馬克思主義直接聯繫起來的嘗試；我們還感謝斯拉沃伊・齊澤克（Slavoj Žižek）在《意識形態的崇高客體》（*The Sublime Object of Ideology*）中的早期理論介入，以及雅尼斯・斯塔夫拉卡基斯（Yannis Stavrakakis）的《拉岡左派：精神分析、理論、政治》（*The Lacanian Left: Psychoanalysis, Theory, Politics*）中對該作品的批判性理論評價。最後，我們覺得在進步的左翼方向上與那些試圖將拉岡精神分析再政治化的著作相當靠近，不論是像豪爾赫・阿萊曼的（Jorge Alemán）的《拉岡左派》（*LaIzquierda Lacaniana*）那樣溫和的，還是更為基進的像是埃米利亞諾・伊斯波思托（Emiliano Exposto）和加布里埃爾・羅德里格斯・瓦雷拉（Gabriel Rodriguez Varela）的《資本的享受》（*El Goce del Capital*）。

　　如果沒有來自女性主義和反殖民運動內部的批判，拉岡的批判工作將是不完整和不可行的，這些批判並不總是得到充分認可。對我們來說，精神分析家茱莉葉・米切爾（Juliet Mitchell）在《精神分析和女性主義》（*Psychoanalysis and Feminism*）中的工作對於「佛洛伊德－馬克思主義」存在侷限性、以及拉岡值得認真對待的關於連結個人變化與

社會變化的論點上至關重要。我們還受到革命家精神醫師法蘭茲‧法農（Frantz Fanon）著作中以精神分析嘗試了解種族主義嵌入白人和黑人主體的啟發，尤其是他的開創性的《黑皮膚、白面具》（*Black Skin, White Masks*）。

批判心理學

我們轉向精神分析，因為雖然我們都受過心理學訓練，我們發現該學科存在嚴重問題，包括性別歧視、恐同、種族主義、殖民運作、和資本主義共謀以及對工人階級的蔑視。心理學學科有時使用精神分析理論——通常以保守反動的方式來使用，並且通常也討厭精神分析，將其視為一種威脅。我們在本書中的論點是，精神分析是「批判心理學」的最基進的可能形式，它試圖扭轉並將心理學視為問題的一部分而不是來解決我們弊病的。

在「批判心理學」作者中對我們影響最大的，是將心理學批判與解放計劃聯繫起來的伊格納西奧‧馬丁-巴羅（Ignacio Martin-Baró）。馬丁-巴羅堅持心理學只能透過將它自身從其被異化中解放出來才能為拉丁美洲人民的解放服務。我們認為，心理學只有*從*（*from*）其自身中解放出來才能解放自身，這是我們為什麼轉向精神分析的原因。

在「批判心理學」的廣泛傳統之中，精神分析批判例如內斯特‧布勞恩斯坦（Néstor Braunstein）與馬塞洛‧帕斯捷爾納克（Marcelo Paster-nac）、格洛麗亞‧貝內托（Gloria Benedito）、弗里達‧薩爾（Frida Saal）合著的《心理學：意識形態和科學》（*Psicología: Ideología y Ciencia*）中，他們表明，心理學學科假裝是一門科學，但它不是，而是對應於為資本主義服務的意識形態和技術。當今對心理學的最基進批判之一聚焦於「心理學化」以及來自該學科的觀念作為一種全球力量運作的方式，例如，簡‧德沃斯（Jan De Vos）的著作《全球化時代的心理學化》（*Psychologisation in Times of Globalisation*）。

並非每個心理學的批判都將精神分析視為一種不同的替代選擇，這在精神醫學中肯定是這樣，所謂的「反精神醫學家」（'anti-psychiatrists'）

和「民主的精神醫學家」（'democratic psychiatrists'）往往傾向於將精神分析視爲「心理／精神相關專業複合體」（'psy complex'）的一部分，也就是一種旨在使人們適應社會的「心理／精神相關」專業（'psy' profession）。

當然，聯繫了基進政治的精神醫學內部批判是我們最感興趣的部分，這些批判包括佛朗哥・巴薩利亞（Franco Basaglia）在《徹底考察精神病學》（*Psychiatry Inside Out*）等書中的工作，以及馬里烏斯・羅姆（Marius Romme）與記者夥伴桑德拉・埃舍爾（Sandra Escher）合著《接納聲音》（*Accepting Voices*）討論關於「聽到聲音」的現象是人類經驗的一部分，而非被視爲精神分裂症的一種病理症狀，被看作是一種「精神病」（'psychosis'）。我們很認眞地取用沃爾夫岡・胡貝爾（Wolfgang Hüber）在《SPK-社會主義病人集體：將疾病變成一種武器》（*SPK: Turn Illness into a Weapon*）中爲反精神病介入的關鍵短句[1]。

我們還應該在這裡提到安妮・G・羅傑斯（Annie G Rogers）在《不可言說：創傷的隱蔽之語》（*The Unsayable: The Hidden Language of Trauma*）中關於「精神病」（psychosis）的批判性拉岡派著作，她是一位自己也接受了「精神病的」診斷而同時繼續執業實踐的精神分析師。

政治

我們來自不同的左派政治傳統，這份宣言中我們當然放進卡爾・馬克思（Karl Marx）著作中的許多想法，甚至也包括關鍵的詞彙和短句。馬克思的思想對社會運動至關重要，它使俄羅斯、中國和古巴的革命以及世界各地任何反殖民和反帝國主義運動成爲可能。馬克思主義持續啟發全世界的反資本主義和反法西斯主義的鬥爭，我們支持這些鬥爭以及先前的運動和革命的基進精神，並以反對官僚主義侵占、反對自封領導者的背叛來捍衛所取得的成果。

---

[1]　SPK 是德文 SOZIALISTISCHES PATIENTENKOLLEKTIV 的縮寫，意即社會主義病人社群。

　　在眾多影響我們的馬克思主義批判性著作中，有厄內斯特・曼德爾（Ernest Mandel）的《卡爾・馬克思經濟思想的形成》（*The Formation of the Economic Thought of Karl Marx*），它清楚地表明馬克思主義是一種歷史 - 具體的分析（historically-specific analysis），一種旨在推翻資本主義的分析；以及他的著作《權力和金錢：一種馬克思主義的官僚主義理論》（*Power and Money: A Marxist Theory of Bureaucracy*），曼德爾在其中解釋了社會主義國家的崩塌乃出於工人階級權力的政治基礎被官僚主義篡奪而瓦解。

　　我們還感謝馬克思的同事弗里德里希・恩格斯（Frederick Engels）在《家庭、私有財產和國家的起源》（*The Origin of the Family, Private Property and the State*）中的貢獻，儘管恩格斯不是一個女性主義者，但他將家庭制度與維護私有財產以及致力於保護社會當權者的國家結構聯繫在一起，是對父權制的嚴厲控訴。女性主義對父權制的批判經常有很好的理由將佛洛伊德視為敵人，例如凱特・米列（Kate Millet）的《性／別政治》（*Sexual Politics*），1960 年代和 1970 年代最基進的所謂「第二波」女性主義，隨後出現的社會主義 - 女性主義政治（socialist-feminist politics），以及「個人即政治」（'the personal is political'）的口號。

　　我們在這份宣言中主張精神分析，雖然我們已確實認真地採取了女性主義批判和反殖民批判兩者，但沒把時間用於處理對精神分析的許多批判，而關於精神分析對社會權力邏輯無意識複製的方式的批判——這是社會學家羅伯特・卡斯特（Robert Castel）在《精神分析》（*Le psychanalyse*）中所精妙闡述的議題；以及關於精神分析對其批判者予以病理化的方式的批判——這個議題在文化人類學家歐內斯特・蓋爾納（Ernest Gellner）的《精神分析運動》（*The Psychoanalytic Movement*）或《非理性的來臨》（*The Coming of Unreason*）中作了很好地處理。

　　社會主義 - 女性主義政治包括無政府主義者，包括寫了《無結構的暴政》（*The Tyranny of Structurelessness*）的作者喬・弗里曼（Jo Freeman），我們在本宣言中提到了它；辛齊亞・阿魯扎（Cinzia Arruzza）在《危險的關係：馬克思主義與女性主義的婚姻與離婚》（*Dangerous Liaisons: The Marriages and Divorces of Marxism and Feminism*）中詳細描述並討論了基

進政治傳統間交織性的不同版本；奧德麗‧洛德（Audre Lorde）作品中的黑人女性主義，例如在她的《局外人姐妹》（*Sister Outsider*）一書裡，她堅持對權力說真話的重要性，在本宣言中我們多次提及此一論點。

　　我們用西班牙語共同編輯了一卷包括不同作者們將基進政治與批判心理學和精神分析、馬克斯主義（*Marxismo*）以及心理學和精神分析（*Psicologia y Psicoanalisis*）聯繫起來的許多嘗試。此背景閱讀也可在這下面這兩個部落格頁面上找到，我們在可能的地方都放置了連結以利參閱主要的文檔，其中也包括了和我們在此涵蓋的議題相關的文章，以及在宣言上面的更新：https://sujeto.hypotheses.org/ 以及 https://fiimg.com/psychopolitics/

BACKGROUND READING

We have deliberately avoided bibliographic references so as not to dissolve our mani-festo into the form of an academic discussion, but we must recognize that we are indebted to authors who have guided and inspired us. There are too many and it would be impos-sible to mention them all now. We will refer below to just a few texts we have found useful in working on this manifesto, and you will find many ideas from them incorporated in and reworked in it.

Psychoanalysis

This manifesto speaks of psychoanalysis in general, but our work is influenced by a number of radical traditions. We speak about Sigmund Freud, of course, and discuss many of his ideas contained in texts such as *The Unconscious*, *Beyond the Pleasure Principle*, *The Ego and the Id*, and *Civilization and its Discontents*. Freud's ideas are central to any psychoanalytic work, conservative and radical. There are many 'introductions' to psycho-analysis that are misleading, in some cases quite wrong; a clear trustworthy introduction is *Freud: Theory of the Unconscious* by Octave Mannoni.

The radical traditions that are important to us include psychoanalysts in the first wave of critical work around Freud, his followers who were also Marxists. In particular, we have learned from the work of Wilhelm Reich, whose fight for communism and sexual libera-tion caused him to be expelled from both the International Psychoanalytic Association and the Communist Party. Reich tried to use Freudian theory to understand the ideological rooting of society in the psyche, as well as sexual repression in capitalist society, and the way that repression was relayed through the bourgeois nuclear family into individuals, in books such as *Dialectical Materialism and Psychoanalysis* and *The Mass Psychology of Fascism*.

We also very much like the writings of Erich Fromm, who was a humanist psycho-analyst and a socialist deeply influenced by Marx. Fromm emphasized the way in which capitalism dehumanizes us, alienating us from our humanity, and encourages us to 'have' things which we believe will bring us happiness rather than to concern ourselves with 'be-ing'. This is explored in his books such as *The Sane Society* and *The Anatomy of Human Destructiveness*.

Another key author for us has been Herbert Marcuse, who was an important figure for the liberation movements of the 1960s and 1970s. In his books *Eros and Civilization* and *One-Dimensional Man*, Marcuse taught us to appreciate the repressive aspect of cer-tain forms of freedom in contemporary society. He has also helped us distinguish between the kind of repression that serves culture and the surplus-repression that serves oppression and exploitation under capitalism.

Later psychoanalysts who continued this radical tradition of work include Marie Langer and Joel Kovel. Langer persisted at the end of her life to continue being a psycho-analyst without renouncing her participation in the liberation movements, as she explains in her text *Psychoanalysis and/or Social Revolution*. Kovel described clinical work in the capitalist context, with lives affected by capitalism, in books like *The Age of Desire*. Kovel stopped practising as a psychoanalyst and became involved full-time in Marxist and eco-logical politics as an 'ecosocialist', while Langer helped re-politicize psychoanalysis in Latin America.

The problem with so-called 'Freudo-Marxism' is that it is sometimes rather reductive; tending to see class structure as replicated directly in the character structure of individuals, and tending to make sexuality as it is conventionally understood in bourgeois society as an immediate experiential force for freedom. This is especially evident in Reich and to a lesser extent in Fromm, Kovel and Langer, but it was an idea and a problem already discussed by Marcuse. There is an excellent overview of these different traditions in Stephen Frosh's *The Politics of Psychoanalysis: An Introduction to Freudian and Post-Freudian Theory*, and a very inspiring account of the way psychoanalysis was developed before the rise of fascism in Europe as a welfare-practice for all, not for private profit, in Elizabeth Danto's *Freud's Free Clinics: Psychoanalysis and Social Justice, 1918-1938*.

The tradition of work that has most influenced us, but one we are also critical of, is that of Jacques Lacan, a psychoanalyst who broke from the International Psychoanalytical Association to set up his own school to train analysts. Lacan shifted focus from biological forces and biologically wired-in stages of character development to language. Language organised through the Symbolic is more than just a medium of communication; it is a structure in which we occupy our place, an exteriority that surrounds us; it is 'Other' to us, as we explain in this book. We appreciate the critical work of Lacanian psychoanalysts on the history of its practice, for example Christian Dunker's book *The Structure and Constitution of the Psychoanalytic Clinic: Negativity and Conflict in Contemporary Practice*, and the attempts to connect Lacan directly with Marxism in the work of Samo Tomšič in *The Capitalist Unconscious*. We also appreciate the earlier theoretical intervention made in Slavoj Žižek's *The Sublime Object of Ideology*, as well as critical-theoretical appraisals of that work in Yannis Stavrakakis' *The Lacanian Left: Psychoanalysis, Theory, Politics*. Finally, we feel close to works that try to re-politicize Lacanian psychoanalysis in progressive leftist directions, whether moderate as in Jorge Alemán's *La Izquierda Lacaniana* or more radical such as Emiliano Exposto and Gabriel Rodríguez Varela's *El Goce del Capital*.

That Lacanian critical work would be incomplete and not viable without critiques from within the feminist and anti-colonial movements, critiques that are not always fully acknowledged. For us, the work of the psychoanalyst Juliet Mitchell in *Psychoanalysis and Feminism* was crucial for the argument that there were limitations to 'Freudo-Marxism' and that Lacan was worth taking seriously for linking personal change with social change. We have also been inspired by the psychoanalytic attempts to understand the embedding of racism inside both white and black subjects in the work of the revolutionary psychiatrist Frantz Fanon, particularly in his path-breaking *Black Skin, White Masks*.

Critical psychology

We turned to psychoanalysis because although we were both trained in psychology, we came to see that there was something seriously wrong with that discipline, including its sexism, homophobia, racism, colonial functioning, complicity with capitalism and contempt for working-class people. The discipline of psychology sometimes uses psychoanalytic theory, usually in a reactionary way, and usually also abhors psychoanalysis, seeing it as a threat. Our argument in this book is that psychoanalysis is the most radical possible form of 'critical psychology', an attempt to turn around and treat psychology as part of the problem rather than as a solution to our ills.

Among the authors of 'critical psychology' who have most influenced us is Ignacio Martin-Baro, who connects the critique of psychology with a project of liberation. Martin-Baro insisted that psychology could only serve the liberation of the peoples of Latin America by liberating itself from its own alienation. We think that psychology can only free itself by freeing itself *from* itself. This is why we turn to psychoanalysis.

In the broad tradition of 'critical psychology' are psychoanalytic critiques, for example in the work of Nestor Braunstein who wrote, with Marcelo Pasternac, Gloria Benedito and Frida Saal, *Psicologia: Ideologia y Ciencia*. They show that the discipline of psychology pretends to be a science, but it is not, instead corresponding to an ideology and a technique at the service of capitalism. One of the most radical critiques of psychology today focuses on 'psychologisation' and the way that ideas from the discipline operate as a global force, in the work of Jan De Vos in, for example, *Psychologisation in Times of Globalisation*.

Not every critic of psychology looks to psychoanalysis as an alternative, and this is certainly the case inside psychiatry where the so-called 'anti-psychiatrists' and 'democratic psychiatrists' have often tended to see psychoanalysis as part of the 'psy complex', that is, as a 'psy' profession that aims to adapt people to society.

It is the internal critiques of psychiatry that have linked with radical politics that interests us most, of course, and these critiques include the work of Franco Basaglia in books like *Psychiatry Inside Out*, and Marius Romme, who wrote, with journalist partner Sandra Escher, *Accepting Voices*, which is about the phenomenon of 'hearing voices' as part of human experience instead of being seen as a pathological symptom of schizophrenia as a form of 'psychosis'. We have taken seriously the key phrase from Wolfgang Hüber's anti-psychiatric intervention *SPK: Turn Illness into a Weapon*.

We should also mention here critical Lacanian work on 'psychosis' by Annie G Rogers, a psychoanalyst who herself has lived with that diagnosis of 'psychotic' while continuing to practice, in *The Unsayable: The Hidden Language of Trauma*.

Politics

We come from different political traditions on the left. We include in this manifesto many ideas and even key terms and phrases from the work of Karl Marx, of course. Marx's ideas were crucial to the social movements that made the Russian and Chinese and Cuban revolutions possible, as well as many anti-colonial and anti-imperialist movements around the world. Marxism continues to inspire anti-capitalist and anti-fascist struggles throughout the world. We are with the radical spirit of these struggles and of the previous movements and revolutions, and with the defence of what was gained against the encroachment of bureaucracy, against the betrayal by self-appointed leaders.

Among the many critical Marxist writings that have influenced us are Ernest Mandel's *The Formation of the Economic Thought of Karl Marx*, which makes it clear that Marxism is a historically-specific analysis, an analysis of capitalism that aims to overthrow it, and his book *Power and Money: A Marxist Theory of Bureaucracy*, in which Mandel explains the collapse of the socialist countries by the disintegration of the political base of workingclass power usurped by the bureaucracy.

We also acknowledge the contribution of Marx's co-worker Frederick Engels in *The Origin of the Family, Private Property and the State*. Although Engels was not a feminist, his interlinking of the institution of the family with the maintenance of private property and the kind of state structure that is dedicated to protect those with power in society is a scathing indictment of patriarchy. Feminist critiques of patriarchy have often, for very good reason, seen Freud as an enemy, for example Kate Millet's *Sexual Politics*. The most radical of the so-called 'second wave' feminism of the 1960s and 1970s then saw the appearance of socialist-feminist politics, and the slogan 'the personal is political'.

We are arguing for psychoanalysis in this manifesto, not taking our time to deal with the many critiques of it, though we do take seriously both feminist critiques and anticolonial critiques, and critiques of the way psychoanalysis unconsciously reproduces the logic of social power, something masterfully elaborated in *Le psychanalysme* by the sociologist Robert Castel, and pathologises people who criticise it; that last issue is dealt with very well by the cultural anthropologist Ernest Gellner in *The Psychoanalytic Movement, or The Coming of Unreason*.

Socialist-feminist politics included anarchists, including Jo Freeman who wrote *The Tyranny of Structurelessness*, which we refer to in this manifesto. The different versions of intersection between radical political traditions are described and discussed in detail by Cinzia Arruzza in *Dangerous Liaisons: The Marriages and Divorces of Marxism and Feminism*. Black feminism in the work of Audre Lorde, for example in her book *Sister Outsider*, insists on the importance of speaking truth to power, an argument that we have referred to a number of times in this manifesto.

We have co-edited in Spanish a volume which includes many attempts by different writers to connect radical politics with critical psychology and psychoanalysis, *Marxismo, Psicologia y Psicoanalisis*. This background reading is also available on these two blog pages, on which we have put links, where possible, to access key texts, and which also include articles related to the issues we cover here and updates on the manifesto: https://sujeto.hypotheses.org/ and https://fiimg.com/psychopolitics/

國家圖書館出版品預行編目(CIP)資料

精神分析與革命：解放運動的批判心理學／伊
恩‧帕克(Ian Parker), 戴維．帕馮-奎亞爾
(David Pavón-Cuéllar)著；林香君譯.--初版.--
臺北市：五南圖書出版股份有限公司, 2023.12
面； 公分
譯自：Psychoanalysis and Revolution: Critical
Psychology for Liberation Movements
ISBN 978-626-366-800-3(平裝)
1.CST: 精神分析 2.CST: 政治思想
3.CST: 民權運動 4.CST: 革命
175.7   112019524

1B3L

精神分析與革命
解放運動的批判心理學

作　　者 ― 伊恩‧帕克（Ian Parker）、

戴維‧帕馮-奎亞爾（David Pavón-Cuéllar）

譯　　者 ― 林香君

發 行 人 ― 楊榮川

總 經 理 ― 楊士清

總 編 輯 ― 楊秀麗

副總編輯 ― 王俐文

責任編輯 ― 金明芬

封面設計 ― 徐碧霞

出 版 者 ― 五南圖書出版股份有限公司

地　　址：106台北市大安區和平東路二段339號4樓

電　　話：(02)2705-5066　　傳　　真：(02)2706-6100

網　　址：https://www.wunan.com.tw

電子郵件：wunan@wunan.com.tw

劃撥帳號：01068953

戶　　名：五南圖書出版股份有限公司

法律顧問　林勝安律師

出版日期　2023年12月初版一刷

定　　價　新臺幣500元

經典永恆・名著常在

五十週年的獻禮——經典名著文庫

五南，五十年了，半個世紀，人生旅程的一大半，走過來了。
思索著，邁向百年的未來歷程，能為知識界、文化學術界作些什麼？
在速食文化的生態下，有什麼值得讓人雋永品味的？

歷代經典・當今名著，經過時間的洗禮，千錘百鍊，流傳至今，光芒耀人；
不僅使我們能領悟前人的智慧，同時也增深加廣我們思考的深度與視野。
我們決心投入巨資，有計畫的系統梳選，成立「經典名著文庫」，
希望收入古今中外思想性的、充滿睿智與獨見的經典、名著。
這是一項理想性的、永續性的巨大出版工程。
不在意讀者的眾寡，只考慮它的學術價值，力求完整展現先哲思想的軌跡；
為知識界開啟一片智慧之窗，營造一座百花綻放的世界文明公園，
任君遨遊、取菁吸蜜、嘉惠學子！